methods for Teaching

Travel Literature

and writing

TRAVEL WRITING ACROSS THE DISCIPLINES

THEORY AND PEDAGOGY

Kristi E. Siegel
General Editor

Vol. 8

PETER LANG
New York • Washington, D.C./Baltimore • Bern
Frankfurt am Main • Berlin • Brussels • Vienna • Oxford

methods for Teaching Travel Literature and writing

Exploring the world and self

Eileen Groom,
EDITOR

PETER LANG
New York • Washington, D.C./Baltimore • Bern
Frankfurt am Main • Berlin • Brussels • Vienna • Oxford

Library of Congress Cataloging-in-Publication Data

Methods for teaching travel literature and writing: exploring the
world and self / edited by Eileen Groom.
p. cm. — (Travel writing across the disciplines; v. 8)
1. Travel writing—Study and teaching. 2. Travelers'
writings—History and criticism. I. Groom, Eileen. II. Series.
G151.M48   808'.06691—dc22   2003022529
ISBN 0-8204-7086-4
ISSN 1525-9722

Bibliographic information published by **Die Deutsche Bibliothek.**
Die Deutsche Bibliothek lists this publication in the "Deutsche
Nationalbibliografie"; detailed bibliographic data is available
on the Internet at http://dnb.ddb.de/.

Cover photo credit by Eileen Groom
Cover design by Lisa Barfield

The paper in this book meets the guidelines for permanence and durability
of the Committee on Production Guidelines for Book Longevity
of the Council of Library Resources.

© 2005 Peter Lang Publishing, Inc., New York
275 Seventh Avenue, 28th Floor, New York, NY 10001
www.peterlangusa.com

Printed in the United States of America

Table of Contents

Acknowledgments

The editor would like to extend appreciation for permission from the copyright holders for the use of the following:

In the "Introduction," by Eileen Groom, excerpts from class assignments by Martin Aber-Song, Kelly Blade, Erin Brown, Panduka Dasanayaka, Miriam Donkin, Aaron Glaser, Kevin Grasse, Roy Hoskins, and Oliver Le; in "Teaching Travel Writing: A Voyage of Exploration," by Ulrike Brisson, excerpt from class assignment by Matt Kavolec; in "Travel Literature, a Genre for Reluctant Readers," by Eileen Groom, excerpts from class assignments by Josh Hines, Chris Medeiros, Mark Schiller, Ric Tokoph, Matt Uhlig, Richard White, and Jake Wilkerson; in "'I wake to sleep': Traveling in the Wilderness with Writing Students," by John Bennion and Burton Olsen, excerpts from synthesis essays by Andrés Almendáriz, Collin Payne, and Melissa Haslam; in "Sweet Enchantment: Writing the Journey, Perceiving the Human Condition," by Twila Yates Papay, excerpts from English 360 Journals by Nancy Alvarez, William Harle, Kevin Miller, Amber Riley, and Alicia Stevens.

Chapter 1

Introduction

Eileen Groom

The fact that I have incorporated travel literature into my courses for the last decade led me to consider putting together a collection of articles on teaching the genre. In the spring of 2003, I had the opportunity to use a wonderful representative of travel literature, Andrew Pham's *Catfish and Mandala* in a course entitled Studies in Humanities (HU 145). For one of their writing assignments, students were asked to compose reviews of Pham's unique book, a nonfiction account of his return to Vietnam, his native country. In rereading what they wrote in their reviews, I discovered that their points very much encapsulated how travel literature, which Pham's book exemplifies, can pull students into literature in ways that other types of literature cannot. In this case, students who had never read a book in its entirety or students who were scientifically or technically oriented and did not consider literature their cup of tea (unless it was science fiction) were drawn to the literature. While the works they read in traditional literature courses are of course powerful in their own right, travel literature has the potential to "speak" to and attract readers in ways deserving of attention and often revealed in the students' reviews of Pham's book. Therefore, using my experiences teaching *Catfish and Mandala,* along with material from their reviews, seems an appropriate springboard to preface this collection of essays on teaching travel literature and writing.

Before relating the experiences with *Catfish and Mandala,* I would like to note, as can be seen in the articles in this collection, that defining the genre resembles grabbing a piece of soap in the shower—slippery and difficult to do. Sometimes, fictional accounts of travel in whatever genre are considered travel literature, the motif of the "journey" the factor determining the work's inclusion in "travel" literature. Often, however, travel literature is reserved for nonfiction accounts of travels, and for the most part and simplistically stated, that is how the contributors to the collection have defined the genre and that is one of the reasons I use Pham's nonfiction as a prism to illuminate the facets of travel literature. Travel literature is not guidebooks, is not what we would buy to find out about the food, the transportation, and so on available in a location; instead using the persona of the narrator as the needle and real people, places, and events as the threads, with spits of fiction and steady hands of contemplation to ensure the threading, the author creates a piece, some linearly constructed, some less so, as Pham's book.

Initially, the students complained about the difficulties the book presented: It was too difficult to follow with the author jumping back and forth between the times of his childhood in Vietnam, to being a boat person escaping from the Vietnam War, to his return to Vietnam; there were too many characters with funny names and too many dysfunctional people in his family. As with any genre, different works within a genre pose differing degrees of difficulty for readers. *Songlines* by Bruce Chatwin, a work similar to Pham's in its nonlinear structure, also gave students in a previous course a run for their money, so to speak. Many works in travel literature, however, are linear, chronologically developed, a structure palatable to readers who, like mine, appreciate a world presented in what they consider a logical fashion. However, when they were given the time to accustom themselves to a book with a frame different from what they were used to, they found the experience rewarding and, for the most part, understood what at first seemed bewildering. Given the opportunity to write either a positive or negative review of *Catfish and Mandala,* most students chose the former, and most students, sometimes painful in their frankness, decided that they enjoyed the book. One of the major reasons revolved around Andrew Pham's expression of his thoughts and feelings as the narrator.

Narrators of travel literature do not always reveal themselves to their readers, and when they do, they do so in varying degrees. I think of Dervla Murphy in works such as *Eight Feet in the Andes,* who spends most of the book observing and not revealing much about herself, or Bruce Chatwin whose narrator is far more reticent about his inner life than someone like Paul Theroux, who, for example, details in *The Happy Isles of Oceania* his thoughts about his divorce. Furthermore, some of the narrators who do reveal themselves sometimes may not appeal to certain students, as Mark Salzman in *Iron and Silk,* whom the students found to be culture-bound and naïve, regardless of how many times they were told that narrators of much travel literature often present themselves as less than perfect. Andrew Pham, however, they found likeable regardless of his imperfections, which he does not hesitate to share.

Travel writing at times projects itself as a treasure hunt, whether for treasures in the form of an animal as in Peter Matthiessen's *The Snow Leopard,* the "perfect memory" as Paul Theroux comments about in *The Happy Isles of Oceania* (30), or a sense of self as in *Catfish and Mandala.* This search frequently becomes more important than finding the treasure, or the treasure found is not the treasure originally envisioned. These accounts reverberate for readers, as they do in so many stories of quests, yet perhaps they resonate more deeply because the narrators are "real" people who present themselves as ordinary, not heroic or noble, in other words, not that very different from the readers and frequently bumbling and vulnerable. The persona that congeals as Pham, an individual with two worlds in his bones, writes his account is especially "human," in his confusion about where he belongs, who he is, his mixed feelings about his homeland and his adopted country.

His reflections about his relationships with others show his humanity, the positive and the negative. He loves his father yet cannot stomach his treatment, the beatings, of his children. As one student, Roy Hoskins, remarked, "Pham realized that Thong (his father) was simply trying to provide him with a better life than he himself ever had. Andrew loved his father for his intentions not his methods." Another individual, Kelly Blade, discussing Pham's relationships with others, noted how they show "that he isn't a tough guy. He shows that he is just an ordinary Joe." His relationships also often show the awkward position of wanting but not wanting to help others. Blade wrote about how Kim, a woman at a dance club, "wants him to take her to America. During a meal together Kim pleads for An [Pham] to take her. 'You can save me,' Kim tells An" (135). Pham does not know why he refuses, but in his confusion he shows Blade that he is not "a macho know-it-all. Just that he is a regular guy trying to make sense of it all." Many students in their reviews wrote not only about Kim but also about the deaf-mute boy who steals the hearts of foreigners and the cyclo driver Tin. Tin receives a huge tip from Pham because of all the misfortunes Pham hears that he has experienced— only to discover later that Tin had been giving him a sob story. "This relationship really shows me that Andrew Pham is just as susceptible to a sob story as I am or anybody else," wrote Blade.

Even so, the fact remains that Tin and others are living a life materially poorer than Pham, and while some, such as his friend Carolyn, find repulsive the thought of the lives of the Vietnamese changing, Pham notes that the beauty she sees may be "because your images are not wearing their rags" (294). Other travel writers comment similarly, such as Tim Cahill in *Hold the Enlightenment*: "Thinking of your hosts as 'natives' who can be 'spoiled' dehumanizes people and creates the kind of abyss that is impossible to bridge with friendship" (245).

Andrew Pham's response to Carolyn embodies one reaction to the question often raised in travel literature: What gives the writers the right to claim superiority? This question has to be considered when reading any work of travel literature, by any author of any nationality. Pham presents his thoughts about the question, even if they are not what some would deem politically correct. A related statement follows, written by one of my students, Oliver

Le, who referred to himself as a Vietnamese American, as does Andrew
Pham:

> Pham experienced many sympathetic feelings towards the Vietnamese people be-
> cause he feels like the lucky lottery winner. Pham often shares the thought that he
> could be the one living in poverty in Vietnam; instead he is living a life of relative
> luxury in America. Frequently, he wonders why he was lucky and wonders what in
> the universal scheme gave him the opportunity to move to America.

This thought is echoed by other travel writers, by Brad Newsham in *Take Me
with You,* for instance, who recounts his travels in search of someone to bring
to America for a visit and in a train station in New Jaipalghuri comments on
how "grossly unfair" it was for him to not be plagued by hunger as so many
around him were (105).

While some of the contributors to and readers of this collection may see
this reaction as one of western bias and sense of superiority, what other readers of travel literature often perceive is a normal reaction, not specific to
westerners, when the narrators wonder why certain individuals are born into
one culture and not another. The consequent unease may be as much a part of
human nature as it is to wonder why some develop illnesses or some acquire
great wealth or some achieve inner peace, while others may not. The unease
is felt equally when, through travel literature, readers see the shortcomings of
their own culture. I remember reading in Newsham's book about how un-
happy westerners seem to some individuals in other cultures and thinking,
yes, often that does seem the case. In short, travel writing may grant its readers a perspective through the narrators' thoughts about other cultures and the
thoughts of members of other cultures about the narrator's world—
reflections that often mirror our own contemplations, if only about differences among us. One of the benefits of reading travel literature is that it allows us to gain some comfort in knowing that we are not alone in our lack of
and desire for perspective, both frequently shown through the narrators' reflections about their wonder and their confusion, along with their restlessness, as in *Catfish and Mandala.*

Although the thought that the grass must be greener on the other side of
the hill is a cliché, that cliché nevertheless finds a home in many psyches,
keeps us on the move, and plays a significant role in travel literature. Kevin
Grasse, one of my students, wrote, "Pham's amazing personal and physical
journey from San Francisco, California, to his home country Vietnam on a
bicycle is a wonderful demonstration of human restlessness. I would highly
encourage anyone who holds a sense of adventure or love for travel to read
this book." Although the motivation for adventure and travel differs among

people, as with Pham, the impetus many times erupts from dissatisfaction with the roles we are expected to play. Aaron Glaser noted about Pham, "He didn't care for the role he was supposed to play as Vietnamese American. He grew restless. An urge to find his identity and perhaps personal fulfillment grew to the point where he decided he was going to seek out his heritage, culture, and homeland any way he could. He decided to ride to his childhood home on his bicycle." The student quoted Pham:

> I can't be this Vietnamese American. I see their groveling humility, concessions given before quarters are asked. I hate their slitty-measuring eyes. The quick gestures of humor, bobbing of heads, forever congenial, eager to please. Yet I know I am as vulnerable as they before the big-boned, fair-skinned white Americans. The cream-colored giants who make them and me look tribal, diminutive, dark, wanting. So what the hell, I have to do something unethnic. I have to go. Make my pilgrimage. (25)

The metaphor of the journey trickles through the bedrock of literature and forms the aquifers sustaining the works. To bring that metaphor to the forefront is to make overt the sometimes covert need to move and paradoxically the need to find a place where, as Isak Dinesen states in *Out of Africa*, we can say, "Here I am, where I ought to be" (4). Some travel writers clearly are searching for a sense of belonging to a culture or to a group that is not present in their "regular, present" lives. Aaron Glaser discussed returning to his own roots and stated that "searching for myself wasn't as complicated as Pham's, but I realized when I went home that places had changed in my absence as much as I had changed." Pham's reaction to his cousin, when Pham gives a young girl a gift, regardless of the cousin's opposition, surprised this same student, who was expecting Pham to find a resolution to his restlessness in his homeland. Pham states, "He [the cousin] looked slighted, but it no longer mattered to me, his feelings, his culture. Vietnamese. Honor. Obligations. Respect. I hated it all" (107). The student noted, "Pham realized that his heart and emotions were more important than culturally pressed beliefs and morals." The student also commented on Pham's visit to a prison camp where he tried to take a photograph, an act that could have resulted in him and his driver being arrested. The driver screamed at Pham, "Forget this place. Go see the world. Everything has changed. Your roots here have turned to dust. Nothing here to bind you" (161). The outburst startled Glaser, who commented that "at this point, I feel that Pham started to realize that who he is today is not at all who he was in the past. Events in our lives lead us up to who we are today, but looking at your past for the answers of today doesn't seem effective."

Another person in the class, Miriam Donkin, noted how Pham showed how individuals can lose the sense of who they are through their journeys, yet change perhaps for the better because of that loss. The student wrote about Pham riding his bicycle through his old neighborhood in Saigon accompanied by thoughts of his sister, who committed suicide, which the visit caused to erupt. However, following that loss, resulting in a sense of not knowing who he was anymore, the student noted, is a "determination to pursue life further." The student quoted Andrew Pham: "Whether my journey is a pilgrimage or a farce I am ready and anxious to see the last leg through. Tomorrow I will head north to Hanoi" (110). Other travel writers also relate the feeling of identities being eroded, sometimes comically, as with Tim Cahill in *Road Fever* describing himself and his buddy as "roto" or crazy. If one of the benefits of reading literature is how it grants us a feeling of fellowship with others, in our need for perspective, another benefit is the fellowship from becoming acquainted with a narrator who, like so many if not all of us, experience restlessness, accompanied by a need to belong and a wrinkled sense of who we are. As Louise Rosenblatt posits in *Literature as Exploration,* through reading literature, "…we seek some close contact with a mind uttering its sense of life" (6). Travel writers offer us this opportunity and the "sense of life" offered is often not neat and tidy.

Pham's search revolves around returning to his past both physically in his return to Vietnam and mentally and emotionally in his writing. Oliver Le, the Vietnamese-American student mentioned earlier, continued to explain how "Pham's external journey described a lot of negative aspects of Vietnam"—corruption in the form of bribery and scams—and wrote that

> It seems like in Vietnam, everybody is after money alone at any cost. As a Vietnamese American, I find what Pham wrote in his book is very true about the Vietnamese culture. His book describes a lot of negative aspects about the Vietnamese culture, which sounds like he is putting them down, but is the truth. He also writes about the good things about Vietnam and the Vietnamese people. I loved visiting Vietnam to discover my roots, but I would not want to live there for the reasons Pham describes in his book.

Martin Aber-Song wrote,

> Once in Vietnam, Pham hopes of finding what he thought would be the truth of his life, his past, but instead he finds it's nothing but hardship and poverty. He may have prepared himself well for traveling through Vietnam physically, but, as he states, "The bitter bile of finding a world I don't remember colors my disconsolate reconciliation between my Saigon of Old and their muddy-grubby Saigon of Now." (102)

As Paul Theroux writes in *Fresh Air Fiend*, the "unique function" of a "travel book" is to express "the dissonance as well as the melodies, the contradictions…. " (53), in short, the messiness of life.

As Erin Brown noted, in addition to seeing the lives of those in his past as being one struggle after another—as "Pham's cousin, Viet, mentions, 'they'll kill you for a bicycle'" (72)—Pham details other cultural differences that bring to life abstractions about cultures students may have heard about but not reflected upon. I am reminded of students' comments in a past semester about Joe Kane's *Savages,* to the effect that we all hear about destruction of the rainforest but Kane, through his depictions of certain Huaronani people, gave such destruction human faces. Prejudices and stereotypes and cultural norms become more than words on a page when the narrators and individuals they encounter are real people, who show varying reactions to being stereotyped or to following certain codes of behavior.

Vicariously experiencing the feeling of being a minority, as shown in the beginning of *Catfish and Mandala,* is an invaluable experience. Kevin Grasse remarked on how Tyle, a Vietnam veteran whom Pham describes meeting in the beginning of the book, asks where Pham was from: "Originally" (6). "Pham declares that he is American, but his claim bears no weight for Tyle, since he is of Vietnamese origin. Although the man does not say anything, Pham hears the words '…Chink, gook, Jap, Charlie, GO HOME, SLANT-EYES…!'" (6). Grasse noted how "this is not an easy situation to be in in my book and that Pham deals with this adversity in a very calm and controlled manner." Frequently, Pham reflects upon his sister, who, he says, he believes was tormented by these very same expressions. His sister eventually commits suicide. The student above also focused on people in a logging truck in Oregon throwing soda/urine at the author and stated that this incident "shows how hard it actually is for non-Caucasian people to live in the United States." Students further read about how Pham is badly treated by some Vietnamese at times, even in his native country, simply because he is a Vietnamese American.

Through this genre, students learn that stereotyping infects not just America but also other countries. I am reminded of my students learning through Mark Salzman's *Iron and Silk* of how some Chinese perceive Africans as subhuman, when an African studying medicine in China tells Salzman that the only way he keeps his sanity is by not thinking (189). I am reminded of how Bruce Chatwin in *Songlines* notes how the aboriginals consider the white people "meat" (56), there for the taking, so to speak.

Through Pham's book, students also view "gender issues" in the flesh, for example, people's reactions to sexuality in Pham's native country or women being treated differently. "Women are supposed to be always around the house doing all the chores and expected to clear all messes created by the men. This is clearly seen in the incident where the men spend the whole night drinking and eating and at the end all the women clean up the mess the men had created in Nguyen's house," Panduka Dasanayaka wrote. Pham's troubled thoughts about his sister who had a sex change also present a commentary about the Vietnamese culture. Erin Brown wrote, "Pham regrets that he never made an attempt to understand what had happened to Chi [his sister].... But it was the traditionalism in Pham's family that kept them from asking questions. Had they asked Minh [his sister who had a sex change] about his past it may have caused his father to lose face, and this would not have been acceptable, even within an immediate family." Another event noted by Brown and related to social norms occurs when Pham's "grandaunt" suggests that he not ride to Hanoi and "Pham nods agreement, while he notes to himself, 'Never disagree with your elders to their faces. Don't make them lose face. Whatever you must do, do it behind their backs'" (124) The student commented that this passage indicates "how Vietnamese people who follow their traditional values are constantly lying to themselves and others. Although they lie in order to uphold the respectability of the other person, this characteristic seems unnatural."

Brown also zeroed in on how the Vietnamese culture is more family oriented than American culture. "Elders' homes are not an issue as many people in the Vietnamese culture do not even know about them. This particular issue was brought out when Pham did not have a job and moved back in again with his parents. His Vietnamese relatives had wondered why he had moved out in the first place," wrote Brown, who then quoted Pham. "I did something unthinkable in America: I moved home to my parents" (23). Older children staying home and elderly parents being cared for by the children were both not unusual and not shameful.

Dasanayaka wrote in his review, "I recommend this book to the university community due to the reason that our campus is not a very diverse campus when it comes to cultures." For many of us, even those who live amidst diversity and consider themselves not culture bound, illuminations about other cultures provoke thoughts about culture in general and one's place in a culture.

Some of the assignments described in this collection ask that the student reflect on the influence of culture on the individual and in doing so, connect the personal with the abstract. Many times, such assignments reveal how this genre lends itself to what I think is a very powerful tool in writing and one that has not been acceptable until fairly recently; that is, the integration of the personal with the abstract. I think back to my own experiences working on an annotated bibliography on the subject of history as a literary art and while doing so having my eyes opened to how history once had been written, with accounts sometimes not completely true to "the facts," but nevertheless accounts that were compelling and full of life and sometimes even suspenseful. Then, when the worth of a subject depended on how scientifically it was presented, the writing of history in my mind shriveled, flesh and blood people replaced by abstractions and adherence to the "truth." Travel writing allows students to see how stories, often personal and sometimes not entirely truthful, can lead to and support abstractions, whether such abstractions take the shape of a moral or an insight. They see how the use of "I" in writing, which so many have been told not to use, does not have to drown a point but rather may allow it to surface. In *Passage to Juneau,* Jonathan Raban relates travel writing to his father's sermon writing: "…its stories, its drawing of morals and influences from everyday anecdotes. 'A few days ago, I was walking down Pound Lane'…" would be the door opening to reflection (283).

When I have had my students write about their own journeys, not necessarily to anywhere exotic (sometimes from their dorms to the class), they exhibit not only admirable powers of observation but also wonderful connections between the abstract or their ideas and the concrete, what they were actually perceiving through their senses. Given models, they quickly absorb how to balance the inner and outer journeys. When I have them imitate one of the writers in their travel account, they can do so in ways that show their analytical skills—determining the stylistic elements they want to imitate—and then showing their understanding of those elements by incorporating them into their own writing.

A variety of assignments for students can be found in this collection, many of which I would like to try in one fashion or another. Similarly, a variety of approaches to teaching travel literature also can be found. Contributors' discussion of such angles revolve around how the association of travel writing with "voluntary" travel and not with accounts of "involuntary" travel catalyze among students an analysis of their own positions in society; how students can be encouraged to come to terms with the techniques the authors of travel literature employ to convince readers to "buy into" the worlds they create; how contemplating the meaning of the words "tourist" and "traveler" can widen critical eyes; how travel literature by women grants readers glimpses into these women's inner lives and their cultures and how it can be used for assignments revolving around folklore; how actual traveling by students shapes their writing and vice versa; how the promotion of interdisciplinarity seems to be a natural offshoot of studying travel literature; how changing the readers of travel writing from the people of the home culture to those of the culture through which the writers are journeying can give the student writers insights they would not otherwise possess; how the genre promotes questioning and connection to the whole person, along with the opportunity of presenting a course itself as a journey with the instructor just another traveler, although one with more experience; how writing in this genre can allow a person to more fully experience places and people.

The approaches and activities from contributors show the value of this genre to those who have not yet discovered the wonders folded into the pages of travel literature. Obviously, I would like to see more people using works in this genre in their own courses and hope the preceding material by my students and myself sparks interest and hope the following gives ideas on how to use and appreciate travel literature.

Works Cited

Aber-Song, Martin. Essay for HU 145. Unpublished Class Assignment, 2003.

Blade, Kelly. Essay for HU 145. Unpublished Class Assignment, 2003.

Brown, Erin. Essay for HU 145. Unpublished Class Assignment, 2003.

Cahill, Tim. *Hold the Enlightenment.* New York: Villard, 2002.

———. *Road Fever.* New York: Vintage, 1991.

Chatwin, Bruce. *The Songlines.* New York: Penguin 1988.

Dasanayaka, Panduka. Essay for HU 145. Unpublished Class Assignment, 2003.

Dinesen, Isak. *Out of Africa and Shadows on the Grass.* New York: Vintage, 1985.

Donkin, Miriam. Essay for HU 145. Unpublished Class Assignment, 2003.

Glaser, Aaron. Essay for HU 145. Unpublished Class Assignment, 2003.

Grasse, Kevin. Essay for HU 145. Unpublished Class Assignment, 2003.

Hoskins, Roy. Essay for HU 145. Unpublished Class Assignment, 2003.

Kane, Joe. *Savages.* New York: Vintage Departures, 1996.

Le, Oliver. Essay for HU 145. Unpublished Class Assignment, 2003.

Matthiessen, Peter. *The Snow Leopard.* New York: Penguin Books, 1987.

Murphy, Dervla. *Eight Feet in the Andes.* Woodstock, NY: The Overlook Press, 1983.

Newsham, Brad. *Take Me with You. A Round-the-World Journey to Invite a Stranger Home.* New York: Ballantine, 2000.

Pham, Andrew X. *Catfish and Mandala.* New York: Picador, 1999.

Raban, Jonathan. *A Passage to Juneau: A Sea and Its Meanings.* New York: Random House, 1999.

Rosenblatt, Louise M. *Literature as Exploration.* 3rd ed. New York: Rosenblatt, Noble and Noble, 1976.

Salzman, Mark. *Iron and Silk.* New York: Vintage, 1990.

Theroux, Paul. *Fresh Air Fiend. Travel Writings 1985–2000.* Boston: Houghton Mifflin, 2000.

———. *The Happy Isles of Oceania.* Paddling the Pacific. New York: Ballantine, 2002.

Part I

Sample Courses

Chapter 2

Teaching Travel Writing:
A Voyage of Exploration

Ulrike Brisson

Why teach travel writing? Why teach travel writing now and how should such texts be taught? These three questions might sound rather pretentious or irrelevant as travel writing has traditionally been considered as marginal, intellectually and/or aesthetically insufficient and hence inappropriate for a literature course. Historically, travel writers always have had to contend with the reputation of dilettantism and sensationalism that made the truth of their material questionable. Steve Clark states that "the genre presents a problem for academic studies" (2). The narrated events are too empirical in nature to be considered for the "literary canon," but "too overly rhetorical for disciplines such as anthropology, geography or history" (2). Moreover, travel writing as a literary category is difficult to classify because travel writers have frequently employed multiple genres for the composition of their texts.

Such a wide scope of diverse texts seems to make the genre rather diffuse and may have been one reason for its marginalization in the classroom. Carolyn Jewett Keefe argues that in addition to its difficulty of classification, its perception in the scholarly field as a "devalued discourse form" (23) contributes to its lack of presence in academia because travel writing is associated with "narrative and the exploratory essay" (22). She demonstrates that both forms of writing are considered as "easier/less important/less intellectually challenging/of minimal academic consequence" (24) than analytical essays. In contrast, her work provides arguments that strongly support the value of travel writing in composition classes, such as an increased interest in the importance of personal writings (30) and in the learning resulting from exploratory essays (33–35). The study of travel writing also creates an increasing awareness for students of "the social construction of discourse" as well as an understanding of the "multiple subjectivities of the subject" (130).

In the wake of postcolonial studies, travel writing offers a rich field of study for scholars and students to engage in discussions on cultural encounters between western and nonwestern peoples or, in other words, to participate in cultural studies. In "Teaching Literature, Changing Cultures," Biddy Martin, addressing the question of teaching literature in general, points out that literary practices have changed over the last twenty years, including a shift toward making "literary studies more popular," partly as a result of budget cuts (7). Cultural studies are one of the offspring of these changes. The shifting of literature to cultural studies—in itself a contentious issue—opens a venue for travel writing in the course lists of literature departments.

I will ground the teaching of travel writing in courses that allow for a comparative and interdisciplinary approach instead of engaging in the wider debate of literary studies versus cultural studies. Nevertheless, I acknowledge the importance of the cultural aspects of travel writing for reasons discussed in more detail at a later point. Although this essay cannot provide the ultimate answers to all questions pertaining to the teaching of travel writing, it will open up a forum for ideas, suggestions, and caveats. It is meant to address all those who have become interested in this kind of literary genre, who have already taught such courses, and/or anticipate teaching such a subject in the future. My motivation to write about this topic stems from my scholarly interest in travel writing, women's travel writing in the nineteenth century in particular, and from one semester of teaching a course on the literature of exploration. Because the teaching of travel writing is a very recent and underrepresented phenomenon at U.S. educational institutions, the publications on the pedagogical and methodological aspects of such courses are rather scarce. This essay attempts to make one contribution.

Issues addressing the purpose, relevance, and approaches to teaching travel writing serve as the guiding points for this discussion. Within these contexts the essay will first of all delineate various terms related to travel writing, such as travel literature, travel writing, travelogues, travel accounts, and travel narratives as a point of departure for practical information to help distinguish the various terms used for this kind of genre.

Already in 1971, Joseph Strelka deplores the lack of a clear definition of travel accounts.[1] More than three decades later, not much has changed with regard to defining travel writing. The definition of this kind of genre is as complex and problematic as the genre itself, especially when considering travel writing as autobiographical texts. As with autobiographies, the limitations of memory, the selection and emphasis on specific empirical events along with the constraints of language and publishing requirements add to a newly cast creation of the lived journey and experience of travel, so that the boundaries between fact and fiction become blurred. The terms *travel literature* and *travel writing* have been used interchangeably in various sources on texts about travel.[2] For the practicality of teaching, I will classify the works about travel based on the meanings and conventions of the attributive nouns embracing this genre. *Travel writing* is most commonly understood as all texts related to writings in which empirical travels are recorded, i.e., log books, diaries, letters, travel narratives.[3] Within this essay, I use the term in a wider and more generic sense, in that it refers to all texts, fictional and non-fictional, in which travel plays a major role in the work. All of these texts are written with travel as a trope. Although the term *travel literature* is often used synonymous to *travel writing* or *travel narrative,* I prefer to use it for all fictional works in which travel is a topic because literature in its more narrow sense tends to refer to mostly fictional texts.[4] Thus travel literature includes genres such as epics, ballads, or novels of formation. The general description of *travelogue,* according to *Merriam-Webster's Online Dictionary* and the *OED* online refers to a film, lecture, or text that illustrates an actual journey. Inferring from Mary Louise Pratt's essay "Scratches on the Face of the Country," *travel accounts* are usually more scientifically oriented and tend to be addressed to a specific readership such as, for example, members of the Royal Geographical Society (125–31). *Travel narratives*, on the other hand, are usually intended for a broader and more general readership. They are written both for information and entertainment. They are very personal in nature, frequently adopt the sentimental mode, and can appear in epistolary form or as diaries (131–34).

This list of terms related to texts that address travel in many ways demonstrates the multigeneric or heterogeneous nature of this genre, which leads into the first question of why teaching a course on travel writing might be a worthwhile endeavor. Instead of perceiving travel writing as a type of texts with limited choices, its variety permits us to draw from a great number of works, both fictional and documentary. The spectrum is even broader if the term *travel* is considered in a metaphorical sense, such as "the journey of life." In addition, travel can be associated with displacement or a number of specific types of journeys, for example, journeys of discovery, explorations, pilgrimages, adventures, wanderings, a quest, exile, (im-)migration, or even tourism.

Although such a variety may seem confusing and betray a weakness of the genre at first, it also can be one of its strengths. Travel writing allows for choices and for creating a specific focus that can be explored in the class-room. Keefe suggests a number of different approaches, for example, discussing texts that are based on empirical travel events, or works that include both actual and fictional episodes. Travel writing also can be compared to the forms in which the narratives have appeared, such as letters, journals, diaries, or poems. Apart from generic questions, themes could equally be explored in a course on travel writing, such as the travelers' motivations to set out on a journey. Special topics in travel writing could be analyzed diachronically or synchronically. The development of the idea of race would ask for a historical approach, whereas the question of racism could be studied from the perspective of a specific time period. Its accounts could be based on a number of colonial encounters occurring in different countries or on various continents. Travel writing can be taught as a survey course including fictional and documentary texts. This genre also lends itself as an introductory course to literature as Carol Rhoades carried out at the University of Texas Austin.[5]

Although a course on travel writing has never really obtained the same reverence or intellectual status as a more traditional course, for example, on Shakespeare, its value is becoming increasingly recognized, especially in the wake of post-colonialism and feminism. Apart from postmodern theoretical trends, I suggest that travel writing has very concrete meaning for today's and future students in a world that is, on the one hand, growing into a global community and, on the other hand, showing tendencies of strengthening local communities at the same time. From this perspective, travel writing can serve important pedagogical missions, namely creating a critical awareness for the constructiveness of representations of other people, their identities, and cultures. The teaching of travel writing can further contribute to understanding the historical roots of past and present biases and prejudices toward groups other than one's own, and, among others, develop a sensitivity toward one's personal situation vis-à-vis other culturally constructed identities. As Rhoades argues, travel writing provides an excellent opportunity "for discovering some lesser known writings (by women)."[6]

Not all travel writing is excellently written. This fact allows students to become exposed to a greater variety of texts of different quality than they would otherwise by reading canonical works. Thus students will be able to compare well-written texts with those of less aesthetic quality and learn the differences in writing qualities. Conversely, a text that stylistically may no longer capture the (post-)modern reader may be rich in historical information or thematic explorations, such as Mary Seacole's *Wonderful Adventures of Mrs. Seacole in Many Lands* (1857), in which she confronts racial prejudices by whites or speaks about the hardships of the British soldiers during the Crimean War.[7]

A course on travel writing may also be an excellent opportunity for an interdisciplinary approach, such as extending the students' geographical, political, and cultural knowledge of other regions in the world. A world map is almost a must as a visual aid in the classroom. Pedagogically the study of travel writing thus fulfills several objectives: It sensitizes students about themselves in relation to others; it creates awareness for aesthetic differences in expression; it exposes students to lesser known authors and widens their knowledge about different geographies and cultures.

Paul Fussell renders further reasons for the value of travel writing, which I particularly estimate as important for young people on the threshold of entering the adult world. Drawing from Northrop Frye and Joseph Campbell, he describes travel writing as modern myths. The travel narrative is "a myth that has been 'displaced'"(Fussell 208). It "resembles the archetypal monomyth of heroic adventure" (Fussell 208) in which the hero's journey consists of three major phases: first, the call for adventure actualized by its separation from the familiar; second, the journey with its initial trials and adventures; third, the return of the hero rewarded with a boon and his subsequent reintegration into society (Fussell 208, Campbell 246) are therefore closely related to the adventure plot and to archetypal forms of existence, here expressed in the hero figure and his journey. Fussell adopts Campbell's argument in which "'the call to adventure' is a figure for the onset of adolescence; adult life is 'the travel'; old age, the 'return'" (Fussell 209). I suggest that travel writing therefore provides the students with points of identification through the protagonist in an adventure setting because their lives are at the beginning of the "call for adventure" or on the edge of "the travel." Furthermore, some students may relate the adventures of the protagonists in travel writing to personal adventures they had experienced on their own travels. Thus travel writing can speak to students as a myth or as a nexus to their personal travel experiences.

These are all important arguments and objectives for teaching travel writing. However, the true effectiveness of their implementation depends on multiple intrinsic and exterior factors that may affect the course. This problem takes us to the last of the three initial questions: *how* to teach travel writing. This section will address aspects regarding the paradigms of a travel writing course, i.e., departmental support, enrollment, and so on. Through a case study, it will further stress the pros and cons of certain approaches to teaching a course on travel writing, and will conclude with suggestions for further courses based on works related to travel.

The heterogeneity along with new theories allows for a great variety of approaches when teaching travel writing. Each approach will depend on the objectives of the course, the department in which it will be taught, and the personal interests of the instructors. Rhoades used nineteenth- and twentieth-century British travel literature for her course covering "literary movements from romanticism to post-modernism."[8] For another class she focused on women travel writers, because the course was cross-listed with women's studies, where it served as an introduction into women's literature.[9] My course, "The Literature of Exploration: Incredible Voyages from Antiquity to the Future," was offered by the department of Comparative Literature and was therefore open to a variety of sources worldwide. In fact, no more than 25 percent of the texts could be included from English-speaking countries. The students thus read English translations. A course on travel writing can also focus on a specific historical period and investigate texts related to European "discoveries" and early encounters in the "contact zone,"[10] or concentrate on colonial encounters from the eighteenth to the early twentieth century. Logistically challenging, but most likely very rewarding, could be an interdisciplinary approach, where instructors from different fields would speak to the class addressing questions that relate to anthropology, geography, sociology, religion, or medicine. Another interesting way to approach travel writing would be the concentration or inclusion of texts from writers "speaking back," in other words, from writers of former colonies such as Mary Seacole or V. S. Naipaul.

To what degree these approaches can be realized depends also on outside factors. As indicated above, departmental affiliation plays a role as well as coordination with courses offered in other departments, such as on postcolonialism or on Romanticism. In addition, the form of the course, such as lecture or seminar, influences the selection of sources and its approaches. In a lecture course, students may want to use an anthology such as *The Norton Book of Travel* edited by Paul Fussell,[11] rather than individual texts. Such a course would provide students primarily with a survey of the history and changes in travel writing and its represented ideas. Of course, individual sources may be equally adequate for a lecture course. An anthology is just one source among many that instructors could use. If they do not restrict themselves to "la littérature de voyage," which is travel narratives per se, but include "le voyage dans la littérature" (Cristóvão 237), the journey within a fictional work, then Internet materials can be valuable sources because many of the well-established literary works are today available in electronic form, such as *The Aeneid* or *Don Quixote.*

In this context, I should like to remark that Internet sources can be tremendously useful, not only economically, but also in terms of organizing a course. If the semester begins with literary texts from the Internet, a delayed book order no longer needs to be a disaster. The wealth of information from electronic sources has recently received much attention. Nevertheless, it is important to carefully assess the sources and to make informed choices, not only in terms of the texts themselves, but also in view of the length of the works. When I had selected Internet excerpts from *The Arabian Nights*, *The Aeneid*, and *Don Quixote,* my students made me realize that fifty pages on the Web equal more than fifty pages in a book. It amounts roughly to twice as much.[12]

Although a lecture course may be effective in familiarizing students with a variety of travel writing, more thorough investigation and more active student participation, i.e., active learning could be offered in a seminar. A smaller class would allow students to work in groups, answer questions relatively independently, engage in the texts according to their own structure of involvement, and clarify comprehension questions among themselves. Whereas in a lecture the teacher usually takes the leading role and students remain rather passive, a smaller class can be organized in a more student-centered fashion. They can engage in activities, such as student presentations on the readings, the authors' biographies, specific topics (landscape descriptions, depictions of ethnic groups), or on their own travel experiences. To lead students from the personal to the more general, I have usually asked them to link their own experiences to those represented in the texts and the concepts the works have revealed, such as representations of the self to the Other or others,[13] motivations for travel, the hero image, or to the archetypal adventure plot of departure-journey-return.

Not only did the title of the course indicate the focus of the readings, "exploration," but the class itself was conceived as an exploration into encountering numerous texts from different parts of the world. "Exploration" also referred to the students' investigation of the readings in terms of their aesthetic value, of power relations, as well as of its truth value. How far does memory fictionalize nonfictional texts? How much is fact? How much is fiction? Where do the two intersect or merge? The latter point proved to be very difficult for some of the students to handle. Jerzy Kozinski's *The Painted Bird* (1965) was challenging for the students for its graphic presentation of a boy's odyssey in Eastern Europe. It was difficult for the students to accept its fictional nature. Travel writing, therefore, is an excellent opportunity, similar to autobiographical works, to explore the differences between nonfictional and fictional readings, or rather, the overlapping between the two leading to questions such as the following: How much does the travel writer still remember? What is being blocked out, intentionally left out, and what is being enhanced, or even invented in the re-creation of actual events for certain effects?

In this respect, fictional writings on travel are often based on the authors' own travel experiences, such as Virginia Woolf's *The Voyage Out* (1915), which arose from Woolf's personal journey to Portugal a few years before the publication of her novel. Thus an author's personal experience may in some form reoccur in a fictional work. Although most scholars refrain from using biographical information about the author for a textual analysis, such an approach can be useful under certain circumstances, especially if the writers' personal experiences of journeys are reflected in the texts. Therefore I have generally provided the students with some biographical material on the authors and the time period in which they lived, usually on the overhead, occasionally through a link on my class Web page, or as an assignment for the students to find information on the Web themselves. The figure of the pilot in *The Little Prince* became more plausible after the students had learned that Antoine de Saint-Exupéry had been a pilot himself. The use of vernacular in Louise Bennett's poem "Back to Africa" made sense when the students understood it as part of maintaining Jamaican identity. The similarity to hagiography of Alvar Nuñez Cabeza De Vaca's journal describing his eight-year journey from today's Cape of Florida to California in the early sixteenth century becomes obvious in his efforts to cover up the failure of the expedition before Charles, the king of Spain. Research into the lives of the authors can explain the settings or invented time periods of the fictional narratives that thematize travel. The value of information beyond the primary texts inevitably leads to the question of how much theory should be included in the reading list.

As the course that I taught was a lower-level undergraduate survey course, my focus was mainly on primary works. However, I would have preferred to include more texts of postcolonial theory but refrained from doing so because I was concerned that the students would not want to read theory. To my surprise, they were very appreciative when I provided them with theoretical texts, such as an excerpt from George Lamming's "The Occasion for Speaking"[14] when discussing Mary Seacole's narrative of her life in Jamaica and in the Crimean War, Bessie Head's "The Woman from America."[15] Sections from Meyda Yeğenoğlu's *Colonial Fantasies* (1998) and Lisa Lowe's *Critical Terrains* (1991)[16] were helpful when analyzing travel writing to the "Orient," such as Lady Mary Wortley Montagu's *Turkish Letters* (1763) and Ida von Hahn-Hahn's *Letters of a German Countess* (1845).[17] With the help of a theoretical background, students could thus discover for themselves some of the problematic issues housed in "innocent" travel narratives, such as the author's use of sensationalism and hyperbole in order to increase the book's market value or to cover up some blunders that might have occurred in the "contact zone." In addition, the students also would be familiarized with critical writings and ideas. This experience of the students' desire to work with secondary texts along with primary readings is confirmed by Susan Lanser, who taught an undergraduate honors class entirely based on literary theory and discovered that "students are eager to engage theory at the level of evaluation" and "really don't want to be told" (40). Hence, travel writing can be a useful starting point for giving undergraduate students some grounding in literary theory as well.

Compiling a booklist and composing a syllabus for a new course can be challenging tasks because both represent the entire course in a nutshell. As travel writing has gained popularity in recent years, more and more re-editions of nineteenth-century travel narratives have come on the market, frequently in abbreviated form. This improvement thus facilitates the creation of a reading list and makes former multivolume works accessible for classroom use, such as Mary Kingsley's *Travels in West Africa* (1996) or Isabella Bird Bishop's *A Lady's Life in the Rocky Mountains.*[18] Anthologies can be helpful, such as Fussell's or specifically on travel writers who are women, Mary Morris's and Larry O'Connor's book *Maiden Voyages: Writings of Women Travelers* (1993). These are just a few examples; there are many more books on travel writing on the market.

Presumably, those instructors who are familiar with travel writing would prefer to use the sources of their field of specialty. In some instances, there already may be an existing syllabus from previous instructors of such a course. These sources could be a tremendous help for a start and for ideas. An examination of syllabi by predecessors for my comparative literature course revealed that all of them included works of their specific languages, time periods or genres—Spanish, British, Romanticism, or travel writing by women. Hence, even a survey course, as this one, can allow for a focus on one's own area of specialty. Other instructors, like Rhoades, offered writings primarily by British writers of which there exists a great wealth of sources such as Mary Wollstonecraft's *Letters Written during a Short Residence in Sweden* (1796, 1976), Emily Eden's *Up the Country: Letters from India* (1866), Robert Byron's *The Road to Oxiana* (1950), or Jason Goodwin's *On Foot to the Golden Horn* (1993).

In preparation of the course, it is important to think ahead of the types of evaluations included in the course and their score values. Established instructors probably will have worked out a system that works well, such as quizzes, examinations, reading and writing assignments, to name a few. However, suggestions can benefit others. Because this course on voyages of exploration was simultaneously conceived as a "voyage of exploration," the students were asked to keep a journal and write their responses to the readings and class discussions on a regular basis. These journals would be collected after about five sessions and returned with comments. The quality of the entries differed but improved over the course of the semester. Comments would move away from sheer descriptive class observations of the material to more intensive discussions of the readings. The students would frequently add information from other classes they were currently taking such as anthropology or other literature classes, e.g., mythology, to enrich their reading experiences. One student's response to Cabeza de Vaca's Journals reveals his discoveries in the text. Matt Kravolec wrote:

> I also found it interesting that de Vaca's desire to help the Indians seems to be inversely proportional to the strength of the expedition. When the Spaniards are strong, his benevolence and care for the Indians is weak. As they become more vulnerable, he becomes very amiable toward the Natives.

The student clearly discovered the instability and shifts in power relationship between Europeans and indigenous peoples as a result of his reflections about the text. The journals were not graded, but the regularity of the entries and submissions were made part of the overall grade. Therefore, the students felt free to comment.

Essay writing played a substantial role in this course. Even quizzes required short comments on the assigned readings. Students wrote two major essays, a mid-term, and a final examination that required writing a personal travel narrative or fictional travel account, and, as a final paper, an analytical essay on one of the readings in class. The quality of the exploratory essays was often amazingly sophisticated, whereas the quality of the analytical essays demonstrated clearly that more practice would have been necessary over the course of the semester. Plot summaries still dominated some of the papers. The title of the course was truly reflecting everyone's position, including that of the instructor—a voyage of exploration.

Students could gain extra credit by giving oral presentations about a journey they had undertaken, by providing more background information on some of the works, or by presenting on a work dealing with travel that was not part of the reading list but was one they wanted to share with the class. Some students not only used this opportunity to increase their overall grade score but also as an exercise to speak in front of a group and confront their own anxieties. Oral presentations were also part of the final grade, in which creativity, effort in presentation, such as visual aids, and clarity of presentation were evaluated. Again, I discovered that despite clear instructions on the requirements for the oral presentations, some students had difficulties stepping beyond the plots of the texts or films to present a critical perspective. Had I missed "picking up on" where the students were "coming from"? Other students, though, clearly demonstrated the ability to approach travel writing from the critical perspectives we had tried to grasp during the semester, such as speaking about power relationships between observers and observed or specific constraints affecting travel writing: the question of truth, economic factors, and the need for public recognition by the authors.

The reserve reading list, the books the students had purchased, film material, and readings from the Internet all contributed to the learning process. Students disliked being shown only excerpts of films, as happened in class with *Mountains of the Moon,* featuring Richard Burton and John Hanning Speke on their expedition to the source of the Nile. Students viewed the films individually because scheduling extra time for film viewings outside class with the entire group was very difficult due to the students' personal schedules. The videos or DVDs, such as Jules Verne's *Around the World in Eighty Days* starring David Niven and Shirley MacLaine and the *Star Wars I* episode with Mark Hamill as Luke and Alec Guiness as Obi-Wan Kenobi were available in the local video stores and could be rented by the students. They would usually have two to three weeks before the video became part of the class discussion. They also were asked to turn in a video work sheet as part of their homework. The video worksheet was to be posted on the class Web page and thus available to the students at any time.

The Internet and a class Web page proved invaluable tools for class preparation. The semester was extremely busy and left little time for research in the library. The major search machines such as Yahoo, Altavista, or Google provided access to sources with brief introductory material about the authors and their lives, maps of certain areas in the world, or data about a specific country. If time permitted, I would deepen this information with more detailed descriptions. The class Web page became a regular means to post the homework, distribute auxiliary information, such as a glossary to sections from Virgil's *Aeneid,* or post questions in preparation for the upcoming discussion in class.[19] In those cases, when the students urgently needed to receive information, I would occasionally email messages but overall tried to refrain from doing so. To have students check the class Web regularly, they needed to know that the Web was the main source of class organization and not their email. More computer savvy instructors may include student portfolios as individual student Web pages or chat rooms into their course work. As much as instructors value Internet information as time savers, students appreciate it equally. However, it is important to let students know that information from the Web is limited and does not provide in-depth knowledge on a specific subject. It can only be one of many other sources of information. Through the students' presentations I realized how much they relied on the easy availability of information from electronic sources. A critical approach to the use of Internet material as a source of knowledge will certainly become a pressing issue in the future.

Another equally challenging point of teaching travel writing resides in its surprising complexity of aspects and concepts embedded in the texts: conceptions of the geographical and social world, ideas of otherness, perceptions of dangers, or the variety of representations as expressed through multiple voices and gazes in travel writing, to name a few. Each work lends itself to a great number of aspects for discussion. Faced with time constraints for each session and each course length, selection is necessary. Sometimes the theme of the overall course helps to allow one to concentrate on specific concepts such as power relationships, questions of race, and types of imitation if the travel writing focuses primarily on the colonial period. Within a survey course, like mine, I tried to develop a cluster of readings surrounding a specific theme, such as Orientalism (*Turkish Letters* and *Letters of a German Countess*), voyages of formation (*Monkey, Siddhartha, The Little Prince, The Painted Bird*), and voyages with mythical aspects (*The Arabian Nights, The Aeneid*). "Voyages of Exploration" was therefore understood not only in terms of topographical mappings of landscapes but also in terms of the mappings of the inner topography of the protagonist. In this context, the students investigated different hero images as adopted by the protagonists or employed by the authors for their main characters, such as the adventure hero, the picaresque hero, the Promethean hero. Links to myths became obvious: Could Don Quixote be considered a trickster figure, who would make foolish mistakes and yet desire to better the world? Does Aeneas represent the archetypal foundation hero? In addition "exploration" could address racial explorations, of the black protagonist trying to be perceived as white (as in Mary Seacole's *Wonderful Adventures*) or post- or "interim" colonial explorations as described in J. Nozipo Maraire's *Zenzele: A Letter for My Daughter* (1997). Here the students learn about the transition from Rhodesia under British rule to an independent Zimbabwe in the 1960s, and about the cunning and courage of black resistance fighters at that time. These few examples provide a rough idea of the many aspects travel writing can offer for instruction and lively discovery in the classroom.

Not all aspects were received and interpreted by the students as anticipated by the instructor. In Bessie Head's "The Woman from America," a critical attitude toward one's own government and authority was perceived as self-defeating thinking: Why is she not proud of her country and village? Robyn Davidson's self-exploration, exposed to the readers in her travel narrative *Tracks*, was rejected by one student as too overtly personal. Jerzy Kozinski's *The Painted Bird* provoked reactions from utter disgust to total fascination (rejection had been the expected reaction). Saint-Exupéry's *The Little Prince* seemed to be favored by most of the students. While I had found Mary Seacole's *Wonderful Adventures* a fascinating testimony of a mixed-race Creole woman's endeavor to be "white," a number of students found her writing boring and inappropriate in tone. These differences in reactions to the texts between students and instructor allowed for stimulating discussions and wider perspectives.

While the study of travel writing should allow for pleasurable readings, it should also stimulate and strengthen the ability of critical thinking. Nineteenth-century travel narratives have been widely discussed in scholarly works, especially within the theoretical framework of colonial and postcolonial studies. Contemporary writings such as essays published in the travel sections of newspapers and magazines are still underrepresented in critical works on travel writing. Even though I had attempted to make such a study part of the students' oral presentations, they preferred to stay with more traditional texts. The increase in extreme adventures and sports such as crossing the polar regions on foot (Messner and Fuchs) or climbing without ropes and mountain biking in hazardous terrains no longer reflect a desire for finding the geographical limits of the world. Instead, these adventures often represent the search for the limits of the human mind. The multiple adventure magazines, similar to the high circulation rate of travel writing in the nineteenth century, reveal the desire of many armchair travelers and adventurers to at least vicariously search the boundaries of their own minds. This point and many other aspects could not be addressed in my class and, I suggest, would certainly be worthwhile investigating in a world that is, on the one hand, relying more and more on representations through modern media for knowledge and insight rather than on actual physical experiences. On the other hand, a handful of people go to extremes and expose their bodies and minds to the borders between life and death to emerge as modern heroes upon survival. Adventure has been capitalized on by publications, organized adventure tours, and filmmaking. To question the motivations and processes of modern adventure and travel could take up an entire course. The writings and representations of other cultures produced by tourists and by the tourist industry could offer plenty of material for investigating the politics of modern economic imperialism as well. These topics are only a few suggestions of many other possibilities that travel writing from different time periods and on different geographical locations offers.

Each text is as unique as its author and its represented journey. The great diversity of travel writing makes these works thus a very complex and rich source of material for a literature class, and, as critical studies on travel writing from other fields have demonstrated, they present a valuable treasure of information in other subjects as well, such as anthropology, history, or geography.[20] Further, travel writing offers an interesting genre in which the auto-biographical or subjective overlap with the more authoritative mode of "ob-jective" representation. Biddy Martin's critique of literary studies at universities where "extreme subjectifications in the form of authoritative rhapsodies, on the one hand, and extreme objectifications that discount the affective dimensions of the study and teaching of literature, on the other, are both misguided" (20) also could be transferred to teaching travel writing. The appeal of travel writing to students can lie exactly in the overlapping between the actual and the representational, in the idea that the protagonist really lived through the dangers or encountered fascinating cultures. They may allow for points of identification and, most of all, stir a curiosity which is generally, but often unacknowledged, the basis for travel and reading travel writing.

This chapter, of course, could not fully address all the problems and mer-its of teaching travel writing. It was rather a venture into a field still rela-tively uncharted. It is my hope that some of my experiences and suggestions will stimulate creative ideas for teaching works within this genre. It deserves wider recognition as an important genre to study, especially within the grow-ing trend of cultural studies at educational institutions. Awareness and ade-quate handling of ideas and representation of other individuals, peoples, and cultures will be important skills of a future student body and population. The world is becoming increasingly mobile—vicariously or in reality, by desire or by need—and many people will thus be exposed to difference and diver-sity. Ideally, the study of travel writing should provide students with the cu-riosity, as well as the conceptual and verbal means that will motivate and allow them to engage in an enriching exchange with peoples and cultures perceived as different from their own.

Notes

1   "Der Reisebericht gehört zu jenen literarischen Ausdrucksformen, zu deren genaueren Begriffsbestimmung bis jetzt sehr wenig getan worden ist" (The travel account belongs to those literary forms of expression that have not had much work done on specific defini-tions surrounding the form [my translation]. Joseph Strelka (1971): 63.

2   See for example: Joanne Shattock, "Travel Writing Victorian and Modern: A Review of Recent Research," *Prose Studies* 5.1 (1982): 151.

3   Jim Philip defines travel writing as "texts concerned with journeys and written by authors who are themselves frequent... travelers" (241).

4   Wulf Wülfing, however, defends the broader meaning of travel literature as inclusive of nonfictional travel writing arguing that "it need not belong to the fictional kinds of litera-ture, but that the writers' own experiences when traveling can be reported..." (1996, 289).

5   Carol Rhoades, syllabus, "Introduction to Literature: Women's Journey Literature," The University of Texas, Austin.
6   Rhoades, syllabus, "Introduction to Literature: Women's Journey Literature."
7   Mary Seacole, *Wonderful Adventures of Mrs. Seacole in Many Lands* (1857, New York: Oxford UP, 1988).
8   Carol Rhoades, syllabus, "Travel Literature: New Writing on Old Tracks," The University of Texas at Austin.
9   Rhoades, syllabus, "Introduction to Literature: Women's Journey Literature."
10   Mary Louise Pratt coined the term "contact zone" in her book *Imperial Eyes* (1992). She refers to a space in which "disparate cultures meet...often in highly asymmetrical relations of domination and subordination" (4).
11   Paul Fussell, ed., *The Norton Book of Travel* (New York: W. W. Norton, 1987).
12   The URLs to the three texts can be found on my personal Web page www.reisefrau.com.
13   "Other," capitalized, refers to a constructed and imaginary, homogeneous and essentialized idea of "other," such idea customary in nineteenth-century thinking. In contrast to such a unified concept exists a noncapitalized postcolonial perception of "other" as homogeneous and fluid. See, for example: *Post-Colonial Studies: The Key Concepts* by Bill Ashcroft, Gareth Griffiths, and Helen Tiffin (London: Routledge, 2000) and also Mary Louise Pratt, "Scratches on the Face of the Country; or, What Mr. Barrow Saw in the Land of the Bushmen," *Critical Inquiry* 12.1 (1985): 120–21.
14   From George Lamming, "The Occasion for Speaking," *The Pleasures of Exile* (London: Michael Joseph, 1960), also available in *The Post-Colonial Studies Reader,* eds. Bill Ashcroft, Gareth Griffiths, and Helen Tiffin (London: Routledge, 1995) 12–17.
15   The texts by Bessie Head and Bennett are published in *Daughters of Africa, An International Anthology of Words and Writings by Women of African Descent: From the Ancient Egyptian to the Present,* ed. Margaret Busby (New York: Pantheon Books, 1992) 277–79, 482–86.
16   Lisa Lowe, *Critical Terrains: French and British Orientalisms* (Ithaca, NY: Cornell UP, 1991) and Meyda Yeğenoğlu, *Colonial Fantasies: Towards a Feminist Reading of Orientalism* (Cambridge: Cambridge UP, 1998).
17   One problem of teaching travel writing is often the lack of re-published sources. Excerpts of Ida von Hahn-Hahn's *Letters of a German Countess: Written During her Travels in Turkey, Egypt, the Holy Land, Syria, Nubia &c. in 1843–4* (London: H. Colburn, 1845) could be made available on electronic reserve because the three volumes were part of Penn State's special collections. A new and abbreviated edition is available in German titled *Orientalische Briefe.* 1844, ed. Gabriele Habinger (Wien: Promedia, 1991).
18   The latest of Bird Bishop's re-editions by Daniel J. Boostin has appeared under the title *A Lady's Life in the Rocky Mountains* (Norman: U of Oklahoma P, 2003).
19   The syllabus, as well as all the other materials, including the reading list, used for this course are still available on http://www.reisefrau.com/AcademicCourses.htm under the link Comp. Lit. 107. There is also a link to a PowerPoint Presentation on "Why Teaching Travel Writing?" with useful links to a number of Internet sources.
20   See, for example, the publication by the geographer Cheryl McEwan, *Gender, Geography and Empire: Victorian Women Travellers in West Africa* (Burlington: Ashgate, 2000), or the discussion of Mary Kingsley in the article "Fish and Fetishes: A Victorian Woman on African Rivers" by Pat Gilmartin in the journal *Women and Environments* 12.2 (1990): 10–12.

Works Cited

Ashcroft, Bill, Gareth Griffiths, and Helen Tiffin. *Post-Colonial Studies: The Key Concepts.* London: Routledge, 2000.

Ashcroft, Bill, Gareth Griffiths, and Helen Tiffin, eds. *The Post-Colonial Studies Reader.* London: Routledge, 1995. 12–17.

Bennett, Louise. "Back to Africa." Daughters of Africa. An International Anthology of Words and Writings by Women of African Descent from the Ancient Egyptian to the Present. Ed. Margaret Busby. New York: Pantheon Books, 1992. 482–86.

Bird, Isabella Lucy. *A Lady's Life in the Rocky Mountains.* Intro. Daniel J. Boorstin. Norman: U Oklahoma P, 2003.

Byron, Robert. *The Road to Oxiana.* Intro. Paul Fussell. New York: Oxford UP, 1982.

Cabeza De Vaca, Alvar Nuñez. "Relation of Alvar Nuñez Cabeza de Vaca." *The Heath Anthology of American Literature.* Gen. Ed. Paul Lauter. Lexington, MA: D.C. Heath & Co., 1994. 130–40.

Campbell, Joseph. *The Hero with a Thousand Faces.* 1949. Princeton, NJ: Princeton UP, 1973.

Clark, Steve, ed. *Travel Writing and Empire: Postcolonial Theory in Transit.* Intro. New York: Zed Books, 1999.

Cristóvão, Fernando. "Le Voyage dans la littérature de voyage." Maria Alziro Seixo, ed. *Travel Writing and Cultural Memory. Écriture du voyage et mémoire culturelle.* Proc. of the 15th Congress of the International Comparative Literature Association "Literature as Cultural Memory." Leiden, August 1997. Amsterdam: Rodopi, 2000.

Eden, Emily. *Up the Country: Letters Written to her Sister from the Upper Provinces of India.* 1866. Intro. Edward Thomson. London: Curzon Press, 1978.

Fussell, Paul. *Abroad.* New York: Oxford UP, 1980.

———, ed. *The Norton Book of Travel.* New York: W. W. Norton, 1987.

Gilmartin, Pat. "Fish and Fetishes: A Victorian Woman on African Rivers." *Women and Environments.* 12.2 (1990): 10–12.

Hahn-Hahn, Ida. *Letters of a German Countess: Written During her Travels in Turkey, Egypt, the Holy Land, Syria, Nubia &c. in 1843–44.* London: H. Colburn, 1845.

———. *Orientalische Briefe.* 1844. Ed. Gabriele Habinger. Wien: Promedia, 1991.

Head. Bessie. "The Woman from America." *Daughters of Africa. An International Anthology of Words and Writings by Women of African Descent from the Ancient Egyptian to the Present.* Ed. Margaret Busby. New York: Pantheon Books, 1992. 277–79.

Kavolec, Matt. Journal for CMLIT 107. Unpublished Class Assignment, 2001.

Keefe, Carolyn Jewett. "On the Road: Exploring Travel and Travel Writing in Composition Studies." Diss. Bowling Green State U, 1997.

Kingsley, Mary H. *Travels in West Africa. Congo Français, Corisco and Cameroons. London: Macmillan:* 1897.

———. *Travels in West Africa.* 1976. Abr. and intro. Elspeth Huxley. London: Everyman, 1993.

Kozinski, Jerzy. *The Painted Bird.* New York: Grove Press, 1995.

Lamming, George. "The Occasion for Speaking." Ashcroft, Griffiths, and Tiffin. 12–17.

Lanser, Susan S. "The T Word: Theory as Trial and Transformation of the Undergraduate

Classroom." *Teaching Contemporary Theory to Undergraduates.* Eds. Dianne F. Sadoff and William E. Cain. New York: MLA, 1994.

Lowe, Lisa. *Critical Terrains: French and British Orientalisms.* Ithaca, NY: Cornell UP, 1991.

Lucas, George, dir. *Star Wars I.* 1983. DVD. Los Angeles: Twentieth Century Fox, 2001.

Maraire, J. Nozipo. *Zenzele: A Letter for My Daughter.* New York: Crown Publishers, 1996.

Martin, Biddy. "Teaching Literature, Changing Cultures." Introduction. *PMLA* 112.1 (1997): 7–25.

McEwan, Cheryl. *Gender, Geography and Empire: Victorian Women Travellers in West Africa.* Burlington: Ashgate, 2000.

Merriam-Webster Online Dictionary. "travelogue." May 17, 2004. www.m-w.com/cgi-bin/dictionary?book=Dictionary&va=travelogue&x=18&y=11.

Montagu, Lady Mary Wortley. *Selected Letters.* Ed. Isobel Grundy. New York: Penguin Classics, 1997.

Morris, Mary, and Larry O'Connor. *Maiden Voyages: Writings of Women Travelers.* New York: Vintage Books, 1993.

Philip, Jim. "Reading Travel Writing." *Recasting the World: Writing after Colonialism.* Ed. Jonathan White. Baltimore: Johns Hopkins UP, 1993. 241–55.

Pratt, Mary Louise. *Imperial Eyes: Travel Writing and Transculturation.* London: Routledge, 1992.

———. Scratches on the Face of the Country; or, What Mr. Barrow Saw in the Land of the Bushmen." *Critical Inquiry* 12.1 (1985): 119–43.

Rhoades, Carol. Introduction to Literature: Women's Journey Literature. Syllabus. The University of Texas, Austin.

———. Teaching Women's Travel Literature. Unpublished notes. MLA, 1998.

———. Travel Literature: New Writings on Old Tracks. Syllabus. The University of Texas, Austin.

Saint-Exupéry, Antoine de. *The Little Prince.* Orlando, FL: Harcourt, 2000.

Seacole, Mary. *Wonderful Adventures of Mrs. Seacole in Many Lands.* 1857. New York: Oxford UP, 1988.

Shattock, Joanne."Travel Writing Victorian and Modern: A Review of Recent Research." *Prose Studies* 5.1 (1982): 151.

Strelka, Joseph. "Der literarische Reisebericht." *Jahrbuch für internationale Germanistik.* Ed. Hans-Gert Roloff. Frankfurt a. M.: Athenäum, 1971. 63–75.

Verne, Jules. *Around the World in Eighty Days.* 1956. DVD. Los Angeles: Warner Brothers Home Video. DVD. 2004.

Wollstonecraft, Mary. *Letters Written during a Short Residence in Sweden, Norway and Denmark.* Ed. and intro. by Carol H. Poston. Lincoln: U of Nebraska P, 1976.

Woolf, Virginia. *The Voyage Out.* 1915. New York: Penguin Books. 1992.

Wülfing, Wulf. "On Travel Literature by Women in the Nineteenth Century: Malwida von Meysenburg." *German Women in the Eighteenth and Nineteenth Centuries. A Social and Literary History.* Ed. Ruth-Ellen B. Joeres and Mary Jo Maynes. Bloomington: Indiana UP, 1996. 289–304.

Yeğenoğlu, Meyda. *Colonial Fantasies: Towards a Feminist Reading of Orientalism.* Cambridge: Cambridge UP, 1998.

Chapter 3

American Travel Literature in the Classroom: Inward and Outward Journeys

Jacqueline S. Thursby

Travel literature is a vast, interesting, and important genre often neglected in secondary and undergraduate English classes. Academic theory and critique of travel literature includes many and various perspectives. In the following discussion, the term "travel literature" will be used both literally and metaphorically; the term suggests both literal travel and exploratory adventure but also recalls the *inward* journey of minds searching for understanding, personal insights, and even freedom. The small slice of literature presented for classroom use in this chapter has been written by American women over the past two centuries. Some of it is popular, and some little used, but it is all valuable for classroom use in the transmission of literary discourse and American cultural history. Students will gain new insights and perspectives by exploring evocative boundaries and possible meanings yielded by the discoveries afforded both by literal travel and by the inner journeying of writers seeking psychological, emotional, and spiritual growth. The very nature of travel literature, both nonfiction and fiction, both literal and metaphorical, loans itself to cross-cultural exploration, which continues to be a vital element of today's literary education.

Because cultural tourism has become a part of many Americans' experience from tasting the foods locally in "foreign" restaurants to high school and university sponsored study-abroad programs, many students have had firsthand experience with cultural boundary crossing. There was a time when few students in my high school and university classes, other than those from military families, had traveled broadly. That has changed, and it is not uncommon to have several students in class who have been to many corners of this shrinking globe. Further, as it will be explained below, there are the inner journeying metaphors that can be applied to travel literature, and these "journeying metaphors" offer unique perspectives for our perusal and examination.

American women's travel is represented repeatedly throughout American literature from the seventeenth century to the present. For instance, there are rich works available to us from the 1682 captivity narratives of Mary Rowlandson, "The Sovereignty and Goodness of God," (partial title) to Margaret Fuller's *Summer on the Lakes, in 1843*. Skipping forward through time, a small sampling might include literature representing the travels of African American Nancy Prince in the 1850s, the adventures of Isabella Bird exploring the West in *A Lady's Life in the Rocky Mountains* (1873), to naturalist Ann Zwinger's account of her journey down the Green River in *Run River Run* (1975). These few represent only a sliver of the rich store of travel literature produced by American women. In the following pages, each of the female authors named will be represented by contextualized samples of their writing, and suggestions will follow with specific ways their work can be incorporated into class discussions and assignments at the secondary and undergraduate level.

The perspective of women's travel literature focused on the metaphorical journey of inner growth, self-awareness, and female empowerment is presented in *Secret Journeys: The Trope of Women's Travel in American Literature* by Marilyn C. Wesley (1999). Wesley's accessible text presents a lucid discussion of contemporary feminist theory as applied to several feminist American authors and their work. Using the concept of self-growth and change as "journey," her central metaphor or trope (figure of speech), "is to tell the story of women's secret journeys as they have been told in literature" (Wesley ix). The opening paragraph of her preface states:

> By the 1970s the woman traveler in American literature had come of age. No longer depicted as the Victorian lady discreetly chaperoned about European monuments of high culture or the frightened immigrant come to join her husband in the new land, in influential works like *Fear of Flying* by Erica Jong and *Surfacing* by Canadian author Margaret Atwood she had embarked on extended voyages of self fulfillment; in novels of the running-away-from-home genre like *Mama Doesn't Live Here Anymore* she was being portrayed as the emergent feminist bent on escape from patriarchal domesticity, and in science fiction by such writers as Joanna Russ, Ursula Le Guin and Marge Piercy she was presented as a time traveler exploring new social options in locations where, to paraphrase another sci-fi hit of the decade, "no woman had ever gone before." (ix)

Wesley discusses a wide range of works including Mary Rowlandson, Harriet Jacobs, Sara Orne Jewett, Edith Wharton, Willa Cather, Marilyn Robinson, Eudora Welty, and Elizabeth Bishop, and others in terms of both inward, psychological journeys and outward, literal journeys. One of the comments on the back cover of Wesley's book states: "In recognizing the figure of the woman traveler, Wesley produces new readings of canonical texts that subvert social and political assumptions in texts by men and construct alternative arrangements in texts by women." In the following discussion of various texts, I will include some of Wesley's original interpretations of women's roles in a genre most associated with men. Her metaphorical interpretations are scholarly and well-informed, and they clearly apprise the reader of this important dimension in women's travel literature.

Mary Rowlandson

Reaching back to the early decades of our country, we find Mary Rowland-son's gripping narrative of her "captivity, sufferings and removes" at the hands of the Pequot Indians in 1676. In "The First Remove," as she called segments of her tortuous journeys with the Pequots, she begins to describe her plight as one of the twenty-four captives taken alive from her New England village. She wrote: "we went that night up upon a hill within sight of the town where they intended to lodge…this was the dolefulness night that ever my eyes saw…the roaring and singing and dancing and yelling of those…creatures in the night…made the place a lively resemblance of hell" (Vaughan and Clark 36). Mary Rowlandson's ability to survive depended "on her ability to conform to Indian values and practices" (Wesley 32). Wesley suggested that "Puritan practice imposed female silence, Puritan ideology enjoined female passivity" (33). The Native American expectation was obedience and silence among the captives. Rowlandson had the strength to stoically endure, yet there were times when she despaired. She gained the natives' respect and was occasionally treated with some consideration. That she and two of her children survived the ordeal speaks clearly of her understanding of her situation. Many in the group of captives taken with Mary Rowlandson either died or were brutally killed. The narrative is woven throughout with the determinism of Puritan ideology which Rowlandson believed and practiced. Her beliefs clearly sustained her through the sordid experiences she suffered.

In "The Fifth Remove," Rowlandson describes how one pregnant woman, miserable and exhausted, was punished by the natives with torture and then death by burning. Reflecting later, "cold and wet, and snowy, and hungry, and weary," Rowlandson wrote: "I opened my Bible to read… Jeremiah 31:16, 'Thus saith the Lord, "Refrain thy voice from weeping and thine eyes from tears, for thy work shall be rewarded and they shall come again from the land of the enemy,"'"and then reveals her own inward response to that scripture by writing: "This was sweet cordial to me when I was ready to faint; many and many a time have I sat down and wept sweetly over this scripture. At this place we continued about four days" (Vaughan and Clark 43). The narrative demonstrates Puritan theology and thinking in a context of forced existence in an alien society.

The website http://college.hmco.com/english.heath.syllabuild/iguide/row-lands.html on Mary White Rolandson (Contributing Editor: Paula Uruburu) includes classroom issues and strategies, major themes to be developed, connections, and questions for reading, discussion, and approaches to writing. Various themes to be developed in classroom discussion related to this piece might include separation (attack and capture), torment (ordeals of physical and mental suffering from travel and lack of food), transformation (accommodation and adaptation), and return (escape, release, or redemption). Writing assignments could be made developing any of those themes.

Folklore methodologies can be effective in combination with nature oriented texts like Rowlandson's. Folklore is the study of expressive culture; that is, things people say (verbal), things people make (material), things people do (customs), and things people believe (folk cures, folk religions). Folklore is lived experience which ranges from stories and myths, to proverbs and jokes; from making rugs and pottery to building a fire; from birth celebrations to holidays and weddings; from folk medicine to syncretized religions. Folkloric assignments related to Rowlandson's account might include collections of hiking, camping, or other outdoor travel narratives related to survival.

A student folklore project, or fieldwork collection as it is sometimes called, usually includes a title page, a table of contents, a ten to fifteen page essay discussing the items/stories collected with examples of related scholarly works, the items/stories/narratives themselves (each described on a separate page), and an appendix which includes consent forms from informants and photographs or other items considered relevant to the collection. Students enjoy conducting interviews (tape-recorded or not) and making these collections in spite of the reality that the project cannot be put together the night before it is due! My students have turned in related projects such as a collection of "fort building" experiences gleaned from childhood memories of other students to a collection of Native American (Navaho) folk cures collected on the reservation by a Navaho engineering student.

Margaret Fuller

Margaret Fuller, a transcendentalist, probably the first female foreign correspondent and the first book review editor in the United States, wrote *Summer on the Lakes, in 1843* as an account of her "summer's wanderings" (Fuller 3). Her "wanderings" took her by train, steamboat, carriage, and foot on a tour of the Great Lakes and the part of the area surrounding them. Her writings reveal life in Illinois and the Wisconsin territory as it was in 1843, but she also records a part of her *internal journey* of self-discovery and exploration. As a transcendentalist, Fuller believed in self-expression and the writing of autobiography. Though the book has been called a travelogue, it is more than that. Fuller used the text as a vehicle for her own autobiography, social criticism, sketchbook, and journal. Susan Belasco Smith wrote in her introduction to the 1991 edition, " It is, perhaps, the freedom of the form that attracted Fuller to this genre, the flexibility to explore summer wanderings both external and internal" (xii). Fuller wrote at Niagara:

> When I first came I felt nothing but a quiet satisfaction. I found that drawings, the panorama, &c. had given me a clear notion of the position and proportions of all objects here; I knew where to look for everything, and everything looked as I thought it would…. Daily these proportions widened and towered more and more upon my sight, and I got, at last, a proper foreground for these sublime distances…. The perpetual trampling of the waters seized my senses. I felt that no other sound, however near, could be heard, and would start and look behind me for a foe. (4)

As her sensitivity and awareness of the natural surroundings grew, she perceptively noted their influence on human response and behavior. Her commentary included reflections about the lives of women living on the frontier. Observing settlers in Illinois, Fuller wrote: "The great drawback upon the lives of these settlers, at present, is the unfitness of the women for their new lot. It has generally been the choice of men, and the women follow, as women will, doing their best for affection's sake, but too often in heartsickness and weariness" (38). Recognizing the value of Fuller's work, other feminist writers, including Annette Kolodny (*The Land before Her: Fantasy and Experience of the American Frontiers 1630–1860),* built upon Fuller's observations about the isolation and difficulty of life for frontier women in contrast with a more engaged and fulfilling life for the men.

The chapters in *Summer on the Lakes* provide many possibilities for classroom discussion. Suggestions might include a brief writing project that could be read and discussed in groups or in the whole class. Students could try their hand at writing careful, elaborated description, or "thick description" as opposed to less detailed "thin description" as Clifford Geertz described it (Geertz 7). They could emulate Fuller's descriptive prose: "a yellow brick, very pleasing to the eye. It seems to grow before you, and has indeed but just emerged from the thickets of oak and wild roses. A few steps will take you into the thickets…" (69). Students might reflect about and discuss human interactions or behaviors in terms of social commentary like Fuller's: "How happy the Indians must have been here! It is not long since they were driven away, and the ground, above and below, is full of their traces…. They may blacken Indian life as they will, talk of its dirt, its brutality, I will ever believe that the men who chose that dwelling-place were able to feel emotions of noble happiness as they returned to it..." (33). Another discussion topic might require reflection about one of Fuller's personal insights. Students might be given time to find and think about a passage, write down a few notes, and then compare their responses in discussion. Her reflection might help to get them started: "All around us lies what we neither understand nor use. Our capacities, our instincts for this our present sphere are but half developed" (78–79). A helpful website constructed by graduate students Trudy Mercer and Meg Roland can be found at http://courses.washington.edu/hum 523/fuller/NoFrames.html.

For a folkloristic assignment, the potpourri selection of topics could be made related to experiences with water travel. Narratives related to canoes, kayaks, boats, cruise ships, pack ships, or even barges might appeal to some students. One of the most interesting student projects I received while teaching in Toledo was a maritime project of occupational lore, including superstitions, collected from dock workers and ship hands working on Lake Erie. Other folklore collections related to water travel might include interviews with people who have taken holiday cruises. Foods, entertainment, games, and other activities on board loan themselves to a myriad of interesting anecdotes.

Nancy Prince

In *A Narrative of the Life and Travels of Mrs. Nancy Prince: Written by Herself* (1853; originally published in 1850), the students are given insight into the life of a free black woman born in Massachusetts in 1799. She and her husband were struggling to make a living in the North. Failing to earn a livable wage in Boston, the couple hired onto a ship bound for Russia and found work there as household servants. Her story tells of their adventures, including the 1824 St. Petersburg flood and the Decembrist Revolt. Her narrative shares observations and experiences from Europe, Russia (including a record of local Russian customs) and Jamaica. Returning eventually to the United States, Prince became widowed. Fearing poverty after her husband's death, she published the second edition of her narratives. In the preface she wrote:

> By divine aid, I attempt a second edition of my narrative, with the additions suggested to me by friends. My object is not a vain desire to appear before the public; but, by the sale, I hope to obtain the means to supply my necessities. There are many benevolent societies for the support of Widows, but I am desirous not to avail my-

self of them, so long as I can support myself by my own endeavors. Infirmities are coming upon me, which induce me to solicit the patronage of my friends and the public, in the sale of this work. Not wishing to throw myself on them, I take this method to help myself, as health and strength are gone. (3)

From the first story of her captured African stepfather's escape from a slave ship anchored at one of the Eastern ports of America, to her employment in Russia, the story is rich with cultural lore. Her husband served as a guard to the royal court of Princess Purtssof. She wrote that "there was no prejudice against color; there were all casts, and the people of all nations, each in their place. . . . The number of colored men that filled this station was twenty; when one dies, the number is immediately made up. Mr. Prince filled the place of one that had died" (23). Mrs. Prince was employed as a caretaker for children and as a seamstress. Describing city houses of stone and brick, and village houses of logs corked with oakum, she commented, "The rich own the poor, but they are not suffered to separate families or sell them off the soil" (38).

Because the harsh St. Petersburg cold seasons did not agree with her, Mrs. Prince returned to the United States. After her husband's death, she sailed for Jamaica to serve as a missionary for the newly emancipated blacks. In her text she recounts the Jamaican political situation and expressed the hope of establishing a school for the training of girls. She returned to the United States to raise funds, and then returned to Jamaica, but her efforts failed:

I arrived at Kingston May 6th, and found everything different from what it was when I left; the people were in a state of agitation, several were hanged, and the insurrection was so great that it was found necessary to increase the army to quell it. (57)

She returned to the United States and remained for the rest of her life.

One of the most important aspects of this work is the rare glimpse afforded of writing by a nineteenth-century African American woman. Her point of view reflects the dignity and independence of an African American woman in a consistently racist America. Traveling for a woman in her position was unique; further, her reflections provide valuable insight to her own internal struggles and her way of negotiating her survival and her position in society. Discussion and writing projects connected to this work could include historical issues: African slavery, pre-civil war New England, political turmoil in Russia, the end of slavery in Jamaica, and even Caribbean pirates.

From funeral practices (24), to holiday celebrations (28), to Lenten observances (32), to other customs in old St. Petersburg, Prince's text is abundant with descriptions of local cultural practices. Comparative folkloric studies are an option when working with a rich, culturally descriptive text. Students could compare their own cultural practices (funeral customs, holiday celebrations, Lenten observances, or other customs) with those described in the text. Alternately, focused fieldwork collections based on personal experience and/or interviews could be based on one or more of the same topics. Folklorists most often collect, classify, analyze and then discuss the possible meanings of why people sometimes do what they do. Usually customs or practices are kept because they serve a meaningful purpose in society; however, it is sometimes a guess as to what the real meanings are.

Isabella L. Bird

Isabella L. Bird, a strong-minded and ambitious English woman, threw off the restrictive bindings of middle-class Victorian Britain and traveled widely on her own. She then wrote and published informative and highly entertaining travel books. Because of her prolific publications, she was one of the most famous women in Britain in the last part of the nineteenth century. In 1876, she published *A Lady's Life in the Rocky Mountains,* after journeys to Australia, New Zealand, and the Sandwich Islands (Hawaii). After publishing the Rocky Mountain account, she continued to travel and made extended trips to Japan and Malaya, and eventually India, Tibet, Persia, Kurdistan, Turkey, and then, later, went to China and Korea and revisited Japan. Her last trip, which was to Morocco, was made in her late sixties, and though it was uneventful, it was the end of her broad explorations of the world. It is interesting to note that Isabella Bird did not enjoy good health, particularly when she was at home in Great Britain. Her physicians advised her to travel because while traveling she was strong and energetic. She was noted to be almost fearless as she faced occasional dangerous situations because of sometimes unpredictable political climates.

Several passages in *A Lady's Life in the Rocky Mountains* reflect this fearlessness; however, there were limitations to her patience:

> I killed a rattlesnake this morning close to the cabin, and have taken its rattle, which has eleven joints. My life is embittered by the abundance of these reptiles— rattlesnakes and moccasin snakes, both deadly, carpet snakes and "green racers," reputed dangerous, water snakes, tree snakes, and mouse snakes, harmless but abominable. Seven rattlesnakes have been killed just outside the cabin since I came. A snake, three feet long, was coiled under the pillow of [a] sick woman. I see snakes in all withered twigs, and am ready to flee at "the sound of a shaken leaf." And besides snakes, the earth and air are alive and noisy with forms of insect life, large and small, stinging, humming, buzzing, striking, rasping, devouring! (42, 43)

Though Isabella Bird seldom expressed many personal feelings, her sensitivity to others was steady and accepting. In the introduction to *A Lady's Life in the Rocky Mountains,* Daniel J. Boorstin wrote: "For she could live among the oddest people—pagan Chinese and uncouth Americans—without being either shocked or 'charmed' by their un-English ways" (xviii). She was a constant and keen observer of scenery and of people. Early in her exploration of the Rockies, she caught glimpses of two huge snow-capped mountains. "It was one of those glorious surprises in scenery," she wrote, "which make one feel as if one must bow down and worship" (13). She was an inveterate traveler, seasoned and wise, and she was a constant and keen observer of human behavior. Bird noted oppositions, paradoxes, and variety in the life of people in the Rocky Mountain villages. Some cabins were thick with filth; others were as carefully arranged and as clean as an English drawing room. She noted sullenness and crudity among some of the westerners, and yet she was easily charmed by frequent brushes with gentleness and chivalry. She herself was, as Boorstin noted, "an English lady wearing Hawaiian riding dress, mounted on Birdie, her borrowed pony, guided by the one-eyed desperado Mountain Jim, entertaining her with his recitations of poetry and cultivated conversation" (Boorstin xxi).

Discussion of this text in the classroom would be well served by creating a historical and cultural context of the time in which Bird visited the Rocky Mountains. It was remarkably unusual for a British woman to travel alone, and students could be encouraged to make researched presentations, or even vignettes, of Victorian life in contrast to the harsh life of early Colorado. A time line would be another helpful exercise in order to aid the students to make the contrasts between these two incongruous cultures that Bird seems to bridge so easily.

A folkloristic research project in keeping with this period would be to examine typical foods served in both of the cultures in the second half of the nineteenth century, and then write a paper discussing the findings. The same kind of research might be conducted concerning means of travel or clothing. As stated above, folklore is usually categorized under three or four general headings: *oral,* that is, things people say such as stories, jokes, riddles; *material,* that is, things people make such as baskets, recipes, rugs; and *customary,* that is, things people do such as celebrations and yearly customs, and *belief,* that is, things people believe such as folk medicines and religious belief systems. Choosing items from these categories would provide rich research topics for a period study.

Ann Zwinger

Ann Zwinger's *Run, River, Run: A Naturalist's Journey Down One of the Great Rivers of the American West* (1975), is more than a travel narrative; it is an informed reflection of love and respect for the Green River, a beautiful river, and its history. Zwinger uses quotes from earlier explorers as well as history, archeology, botany, geology, and river morphology to enrich her perspective of the river and ours. The first sentence of the first chapter begins, "Beneath the beating of the wind I can hear the river beginning. Snow rounds into water, seeps and trickles, splashes and pours and clatters, burnishing the shattered grey rock, and carols downslope, light and sound interwoven with sunlight" (3). Though her journey down the river is exciting and even dangerous, she suggests that "those who go on the river just for the rapids miss the totality of the river. Rapids are only a part, a very small part of the river" (259).

Zwinger, as she travels down the length of the river, senses the moods of the river and reflects: "I lie awake most of the night, sensitized to the river. Peace, contentment: these are programmed cultural words; what I feel is the infinity outside of culture, and although I sleep little, I awake rested…all is possible and good, a time of great expectations" (29). Traveling by foot, canoe, and raft, Zwinger describes moments with impressionistic strokes: "we push off into placid water that reiterates the low-horizoned landscape in Renoir reflections" (238). This is a book to savor, and this is a book to help students awaken to the natural beauty that is not only on a river but also nearby and often within every city. It is an impressionistic work with swirls of color:

> Raw, open sand dunes spread over the right bank, white prickly poppy and masses of yellow mustard and sand-verbena blooming across them. They undulate on the horizon, some of the dunes sandy yellow, some with a pink or salmon cast, rising to a crest, falling off steeply. (239)

In some of the notes from a former reading of this book, I have written, without a citation, "evoking for us the mood of being present in the next moment," and I believe that is what Zwinger does in many passages of this book. She pushes us through the cresting water and past the next bend, figuratively pressing us to move forward, like the river.

I would discuss this text, chapter by chapter, in the literary classroom. It is rich with allusions, analogies, metaphors, quotations, and description. The students might write two or three responses to the text as they read and bring them to class (with page numbers) to be discussed in the whole group. A variety of writing assignments connected to this text could be given and the students encouraged to write sensory essays responding to the text and reflective of their own experiences with nature. An old but still effective exercise in good weather is to give each student a four-foot long piece of twine or yarn and take them outside to a grassy area. Have them place their twine in a one-foot square and note everything they see inside of their square. Essays and poetry can be created from this simple exercise with nature.

A folkloric project for naturalist travel literature could relate again to experiences with hiking, camping, canoeing, or other outdoor explorations. One of my students interviewed rock climbers about their equipment, how they used it, superstitions attached to it, and how they began climbing. Another interviewed people (in New Zealand) about fishing lore and lures, both hobbyist and commercial. There were superstitions and good luck practices associated with both studies.

The examples of travel literature included in this paper represent a very small sample of materials easily available for use in the secondary and undergraduate classrooms. I believe that there is valid purpose in using these works with today's students. We exist in a paradox. On the one hand, we can communicate instantly through the Internet and the telephone with places on the other side of the globe. I have had e-mail conversations with students in Africa, India, South America, and New Zealand, and we know that we can travel to any place in the world within a relatively short period. On the other hand, in contrast to Isabella Bird, many of us are seldom able to interact comfortably with people in our own communities who have differing cultural, political, or religious views. Perhaps by thoughtfully examining different types of travel literature, and the positive and curious attitudes reflected there, we can be reminded that we can treat our own communities with the same interest and curiosity that we seem to have for distant lands and people. In most American cities we can visit the local Mexican or Asian market. We can attend a church service conducted in a different language. We can take part in festivals, fund raisers, and even local historical tours to broaden our perspectives about the region of America in which we live. Cultural understanding has become an imperative; perhaps the study of travel literature, and application of the knowledge and accepting attitudes gained, is more valuable than educators have realized.

We live in a shrinking world where once unfamiliar words like karma (fate) and feng shui (Chinese arrangements of space) have become known and are used in common, everyday conversation. Our classrooms have become filled with students from Mexico, India, China, Tonga, and other places far from the United States' mainland. As noted earlier, many of our students have traveled abroad and take for granted that they will travel widely again.

Travel literature, and the rich associated studies it triggers, can dissolve prejudice and stereotypes. Though customs differ, commonalities of dignity, respect, and courtesy are practiced internationally. Hospitality and curiosity are part of the shared human condition. The study of travel literature, linked to the cultural observations of the students, opens the door to improved human relationships and understanding both at home and abroad. Insights about their own inward and outward journeys await them.

Works Cited

Atwood, Margaret. *Surfacing.* New York: Anchor, 1998.

Bird, Isabella L. *A Lady's Life in the Rocky Mountains.* Norman: U of Oklahoma P, 1988.

Boorstin, Daniel J. "Introduction." *A Lady's Life in the Rocky Mountains.* Norman: U of Oklahoma P, 1998.

Fuller, Margaret. *Summer on the Lakes, in 1843.* Urbana: U of Illinois P, 1991.

Geertz, Clifford. *The Interpretation of Cultures.* New York: Basic, 1973.

Jong, Erica. *Fear of Flying.* New York: Signet, 2003.

Kolodny, Annette. *The Land before Her: Fantasy and Experience of the American Frontiers, 1630–1860.* Chapel Hill: U of North Carolina P, 1984.

Mercer, Trudy, and Meg Roland. Contributing Editors. *Margaret Fuller.* Web site: http://courses.washington.edu/hum523/fuller/NoFrames.html.

Prince, Nancy. *A Narrative of the Life and Travels of Mrs. Nancy Prince.* (1853; originally published in 1850) In *Collected Black Women's Narratives.* Henry Lewis Gates, Jr., General Editor. New York: Oxford UP, 1988.

Rowlandson, Mary. "The Sovereignty and Goodness of God." In *Puritans among the Indians: Accounts of Captivity and Redemption 1676–1724.* Cambridge and London: The Belnap Press of Harvard UP, 1981.

Uruburu, Paula, Contributing Editor. *Mary White Rowlandson (1637?–1711).* Web site: http://college.hmco.com/english/heath/syllabuild/guide/rowlands.html.

Vaughan, Alden T., and Edward W. Clark, eds. *Puritans among the Indians: Accounts of Captivity and Redemption 1676–1724.* Cambridge and London: The Belknap Press of Harvard UP, 1981.

Wesley, Marilyn C. *Secret Journeys: The Trope of Women's Travel in American Literature.* Albany: State U of New York P, 1999.

Zwinger, Ann. *Run, River, Run: A Naturalist's Journey Down One of the Great Rivers of the American West.* Tucson: The U of Arizona P, 1975.

Chapter 4

Travel Literature, a Genre
for Reluctant Readers

Eileen Groom

As Michael Kowalewski points out in *Temperamental Journeys*, the genre of travel literature has been overlooked by critics and considered "second-rate" (2) in part because it is a combination of genres, of "memoir, journalism, letters, guidebooks, confessional narrative, and…fiction" (7). However, after incorporating contemporary travel literature into three of my courses at Embry-Riddle Aeronautical University (ERAU), I have come to realize the numerous benefits of this genre for my scientifically and technically oriented students, especially those who find reading a slow and sometimes tedious chore.

What makes these books appealing not only to those who perceive themselves as "nonreaders" but also, more and more, to the population at large? By using this genre in my courses, I have identified three major reasons, which revolve around real adventures, compelling narrators, and cultural perspectives that books in this genre present to readers.

One of the more obvious appeals of this genre rests in the magnetic draw between people and adventure. Attraction to adventure, experienced or read about, has been a part of human nature throughout time but has seemed especially strong recently if one considers the craze for adventure travel instead of "couch potato" vacations, along with the prevalence of SUVs and hiking boots, symptoms of people's unrequited desire to explore the unknown. As one of my students, Ric Tokoph, wrote, in responses to surveys about the genre given at the end of the semester, people today can keep their jobs without having to have a spirit of adventure but through reading travel literature may receive that "snap, that spark" to create some "instability…to keep an individual on his/her toes" through travel. In a similar vein, Chris Medeiros, another student, commented:

> More often than not people feel they are stuck in humdrum lives, and reading these books allows them some excitement. The fact that they are nonfiction probably makes it more enticing also. Anything can happen in a work of fiction; that doesn't surprise people, but having something genuinely exciting or strange to talk about that actually happened will surprise people because it shows them that real life isn't as boring as it seems to be.

Travel writing appeals to this central human characteristic, restlessness, and according to Paul Fussell in *The Norton Book of Travel* to the desire for "escape," for "the foreign, the novel, the nonindustrial…" (277). The whole idea of taking to the road to discover oneself as a traveler instead of a tourist is central to the genre. As Fussell notes, travelers differ from tourists in that travelers direct their journeys, whereas the tourist's itinerary is one determined by the tourism business, in many respects a neatly preshrunk, comfortable trip. The traveler often experiences mental and physical discomfort whereas the tourist is made to feel as if he/she has never left home (651–52).

In *Into Thin Air,* Jon Krakauer experiences discomfort and danger while climbing Mt. Everest. In *The Happy Isles of Oceania*, Paul Theroux "roughs it" as he kayaks among the islands in the South Pacific. In *Travels,* Michael Crichton at times experiences panic, sickness, and confusion as he travels around the world. In *Road Fever,* Tim Cahill describes his condition as "roto" or deranged, as he and his friend set a driving record. In *Savages*, Joe Kane lives in the Amazonian rainforest with "the Huaorani, a small but fearsome nation of hunter-gatherers who have lived in isolation for so long that they speak a language unrelated to any other on earth" (3). In *Iron and Silk,* Mark Salzman, experiencing homesickness and confusion, immerses himself in Chinese culture. While these authors' hardships often are self-imposed, they nevertheless are real, another factor influencing the attraction, especially of the above books, to students.

The fact that these books are nonfiction or "personal stories," as one student noted, most definitely contributed to their appeal. Chris Medeiros wrote, "Reading a fiction book has a totally different mental feeling than reading nonfiction." The books' real-life tales appealed to the adventurous side of my students' personalities, as illustrated by Medeiros' comment below.

> I put myself in the shoes of the author and let him/her lead the way to a country I have never seen. Knowing that these experiences are real makes it easier for the student to identify with the writers. I believe part of the enjoyment of the books is that most of the events actually take place and are not made up.

Some of the students, who had lived abroad, realized in reading these true narratives that the culture shock they experienced was not so strange after all. Many commented on how the books provide another "world" where readers may enter and become part of the experience.

In one class, students appreciated Joe Kane's *Savages*, about living among the Huaorani tribe in the Ecuadorian Amazon whose way of life has been and is being changed because of oil drilling. About the book, students commented on how environmental problems, in this case the destruction of the rain forest, gained human faces and also about the increase in emotional involvement in such stories revolving around real people. The above sentiments are echoed by the following. "Travel literature gives the reader an opportunity to read about what they care about the most: personal experiences and events that no one wants you to know about," stated Richard White. "It's kind of like watching the History Channel, Discovery, and the Learning Channel," stated Josh Hines, and unlike reading dry history texts, remarked another.

The discomfort of the traveler, mentioned previously, is what catalyzes enlightenment about the self and the world both for the narrator and vicariously for the reader, and in the revealing of this enlightenment lies the second reason for the appeal of the genre, the magnetism of the narrator.

It should be noted first that the type of narrator very much influenced the reception of the books. Travel literature with narrators who were too contemplative, as the students described Bruce Chatwin in *The Songlines,,* or narrators who spent more time on the exterior than on the interior journey, in short, who offered little enlightenment, were not as well received as the books with narrators who achieved a balance between their presentations of the inner and outer travels, between being an observer and a participant. Also, narrators who seemed to use their travels as a means of showcasing themselves, books that "would only be interesting to the author and his/her mother," as Mark Schiller noted, were not as engaging.

Kowalewski points out, paraphrasing Fussell in *Abroad,* that one views at the heart of this literary form, a "self-revealing figure whose passion is to make sense of a new experience and whose very attempts to do so are often as compelling as the material with which the writer works" (8). The readability of these books for my students rests as much on the personalities of the narrators as on what the narrators reveal about both their own and others' cultures.

Jon Krakauer's *Into Thin Air*, Paul Theroux' *The Happy Isles of Oceania*, Michael Crichton's *Travels*, Tim Cahill's *Road Fever*, Joe Kane's *Savages*, and Marl Salzman's *Iron and Silk* all possessed narrators who were charismatic possibly because of their honesty in revealing their guilt, as with Krakauer; or because of their sometimes not politically correct judgments, as with Theroux; their mistaken perceptions, as with Crichton; their anger, as with Cahill; their confusion and frustration, as with Kane; or their ignorance, as with Salzman. For students, trying to make sense of themselves and their world, real persons as narrators, trying to make sense of their lives, prove appealing and provoke thought. In discussions and in their writing, students often commented that readers benefited from these books because of the authors' ability to reveal their inner journeys that parallel the exterior journeys they describe, a common motif of travel writing. They would note that such inner journeys involving growth and change are the most important part of traveling. Matt Uhlig commented, "What I like the most is seeing how people deal [with] and grow from the adversities placed on them by these travels." According to Gary Krist in "Ironic Journeys: Travel Writing in the Age of Tourism," the success of travel writing often rests on the persona of the author, the presence of the narrator who is on a "psychological quest" that provides "dramatic shape" to the work (599).

Jon Krakauer's *Into Thin Air* provides readers with a narrator who does not shy away from revealing and trying to come to terms with his perceived guilt about the deaths of so many people on an expedition to the summit of Mt. Everest. Students also appreciated understanding why people undertook such high-risk adventures, the spirituality in connecting with nature in an elemental way, which Krakauer relates. They appreciated the honesty of the narrators, of Theroux's pain about his divorce, and in Michael Crichton's *Travels,* his realization that he has prejudices and that frequently he is not in control over what happens to him. They appreciated the sarcasm and self-deprecating humor, as seen in Tim Cahill's *Road Fever.* Even though they found Mark Salzman's persona as a teacher in China in *Iron and Silk* naïve but clever in sidestepping cultural roadblocks, students remarked that at least he was honest. In short, the narrators who drew them into the books were not macho but somewhat ordinary people genuinely interested in learning about themselves and other cultures and unafraid of revealing their fears and mistakes. Students noted that the narrators not only were very human but also intent on experiencing new cultures, not just reporting on them. Mark Schiller wrote that by reading travel writing, people could learn about places and people they wouldn't normally know about, escape from the control of the television and other electronic media, and see the world through the eyes of someone actually interested in a particular geographic region.

Edutainment was a word coined by Josh Hines to describe these books he considered educational and entertaining. The experiences of the narrators give rise to many questions about culture and provoke discussion on key issues in cultural studies; such cultural perspectives are the third reason for the positive reception of this genre. Travel writing in the past often posited the superiority of western culture, either blatantly or subtly, and travel writing today sometimes perpetuates this idealization, only in reverse, with the romanticizing of indigenous cultures. The whole question of how a westerner approaches a third-world culture is posed: how first-world countries impose change and yet simultaneously bewail the fact that traditional peoples are disappearing. *Into Thin Air* presents this situation regarding the Sherpas, as does Joe Kane in *Savages* with the Huaorani. Students also learn from travel literature that westerners are not the only ones to possess biases. In *Iron and Silk,* Salzman relates the difficulties experienced by an African American in China, who claims, "If an African must live in China he has a clear choice; he keeps his mind, or he loses his mind. To keep his mind, he must not think. He thinks, and oh, my friend, he dies" (189). He "dies" because the Chinese do not consider his race on the same level as theirs.

The genre also highlights assumptions within western culture that students may take for granted, the desire to control, for instance. When Salzman becomes upset because he could not send a picture book to a Chinese acquaintance, his Chinese friend tells him that "foreigners get terribly sentimental about little things" (117) and relates a story often told to children. Simplified, the story highlights the lack of control human beings have and recounts a man who after every unfortunate and fortunate happening in his life, reiterates the phrase "You never know what happens" (117). Fortune often follows misfortune—the man loses a horse; the horse returns with a herd of horses; and misfortune follows fortune—the man's son is crippled while working with the horses (117). Similar to Salzman, Crichton in *Travels* also discovers how central the ability to control is in his life, how "[he] couldn't leave things alone. [He] was an urban, technological man accustomed to making things happen" (152).

As Mark Schiller stated, "Travel literature shows the culture of a land with no facade. Travel brochures are for the people who are afraid of reality and do not see beauty in everyday life." Ric Tokoph commented regarding the value of travel literature in broadening people's views of others: "Keeping your mind closed is like keeping the borders of your country closed." As students are drawn into this genre, they view both the idealization and the denigration of other cultures and thus begin to question assumptions they may hold about their own cultures. They read about Crichton expecting to see noble savages and instead seeing a squabbling family, and read about Crichton meeting two Samburu women and thinking, because of their appearance (flies creeping on their faces) that he could not see them as human, only as animals (228). Later, the tables are turned as he is being investigated by Masai children and realizes that they regard him as not being "human" enough to know he is being scrutinized (230). Regarding the importance of looking at oneself through others' eyes, Richard White wrote:

> I believe it is hard for Americans, specifically, in general to understand how they are viewed by other cultures across the world. We think that other cultures are less sufficient than we are, maybe because they don't have the benefits of technology, but refuse to believe that other cultures could possibly look down upon us. I believe it would be wise for us to learn about how other cultures view us.

That the genre can promote a perspective on culture is in part due to the way it can hold its readers. The impression the genre can have also is evidenced in the success of the following writing assignment, even among students who may find reading hard enough and then analyzing literature an added burden. The goal of the writing assignment was to mimic the style, tone, persona, or theme(s) of one of the writers when relating an account of their own travels, not necessarily to somewhere exotic, perhaps just from their dorm room to class. Some of them mimicked Mark Salzman's humor and irony in *Iron and Silk,* as one student did when he wrote about a subway ride he took in Korea, into an area with people who were known to use meat cleavers to injure foreigners. In a trip to a lake close to ERAU, another student integrated her memories, detailed description of the plant life, and questions about what she was trying to accomplish with this trip, all in the tone of Peter Matthiessen's *The Snow Leopard.* One of the students, Jake Wilkerson, pointed out that mimicking one of the authors allowed him to "fully realize the beauty behind his writing." Matt Uhlig wrote that "mimicking is great for learning and understanding because I usually learn best by doing." They also were told they could parody an element of an author's work they did not especially like and some of them did, the perceived wordiness of Jonathan Raban in *Hunting Mr. Heartbreak,* for example, with the result, according to the writer, of better understanding the author's "mindset." I often have been amazed at how well written, informative, and entertaining the students' narratives have been—like the travel accounts the students have read.

Many books in the genre of travel literature can make reading palatable for students who have not yet acquired or are only in the process of developing a taste for reading. Many books in this genre encourage an examination of the self and a world different from one's own, through the narrators own examination of themselves and the world, including the assumptions shaping it, and through the individual reader's identification with the narrator, as a real person full of cultural biases, curiosity, and a desire for adventure.

The authors' struggles on their quests, their desire to teach others about what they learned through their travels, their honesty about their ignorance, accompanied by a willingness to explore their own selves as well as different cultures, and their refusal to mythologize other cultures as either edenic or hellish characterize much of contemporary travel nonfiction. The genre should be studied in classrooms because of those attributes. The fact that students, even those who would not call themselves "readers," find the books engaging because they contain real adventures, intriguing narrators, and new worlds is all the more reason.

Works Cited

Cahill, Tim. *Road Fever*. New York: Vintage Books, 1991.

Chatwin, Bruce. *The Songlines*. New York: Penguin Books, 1988.

Crichton, Michael. *Travels*. New York: Ballantine Books, 1988.

Fussell, Paul. *Abroad: British Literary Traveling between the Wars*. New York: Oxford UP, 1980.

Fussell, Paul, ed. *The Norton Book of Travel*. New York: W.W. Norton and Company, 1987.

Hines, Josh. Essay for HU 300. Unpublished Class Assignment, 2000.

Kane, Joe. *Savages*. New York: Vintage Departures, 1996.

Kowalewski, Michael, ed. *Temperamental Journeys: Essays on the Modern Literature of Travel*. Athens: U of Georgia P, 1992.

Krakauer, Jon. *Into Thin Air*. New York: Doubleday, 1997.

Krist, Gary. "Ironic Journeys: Travel Writing in the Age of Tourism." *The Hudson Review* 45 (winter 1993): 593–601.

Matthiessen, Peter. *The Snow Leopard*. New York: Penguin Books, 1978.

Medeiros, Chris. Essay for HU 300. Unpublished Class Assignment, 2000.

Raban, Jonathan. *Hunting Mister Heartbreak. A Discovery of America*. New York: Vintage Departures, 1998.

Salzman, Mark. *Iron and Silk*. New York: Vintage Books, 1990.

Schiller, Mark. Essay for HU 300. Unpublished Class Assignment, 2000.

Theroux, Paul. *The Happy Isles of Oceania. Paddling the Pacific*. New York: Ballantine Books, 1992.

Tokoph, Ric. Essay for HU 300. Unpublished Class Assignment, 2000.

Uhlig, Matt. Essay for HU 300. Unpublished Class Assignment, 2000.

White, Richard. Essay for HU 300. Unpublished Class Assignment, 2000.

Wilkerson, Jake. Essay for HU 300. Unpublished Class Assignment, 2000.

Part II

Concerns

Chapter 5

Interrogating Houghton Mifflin's Best American Travel Writing Series

Valerie M. Smith

The best that is known and thought in the world
Matthew Arnold

This chapter focuses on a concrete approach to teaching travel literature in the undergraduate classroom. The course this essay suggests is in no way meant to be a survey; rather, it is meant to provide students with an introduction to the study of travel narratives through a useful series of questions. It focuses on a certain primary text and provides specific suggestions for useful secondary texts, which can profitably be placed on reserve for student reading and/or presented in the form of class lectures. I will begin with an overview of the rationale for such a course and then provide specific examples from class sessions to illustrate how discussions of the material might take shape.

Jason Wilson, the series editor of Houghton Mifflin's Best American Travel Writing, has a tough job. On the one hand, he is obviously aware of the critical debate that surrounds the study of travel writing—at least in general terms. On the other hand, he is not publishing a critical text; he is publishing a text designed to appeal to a general or "lay readership" (Holland and Huggan 12). Using such a text, and its apparatus in terms of a foreword and an introduction in a travel literature classroom, provides a unique opportunity to allow students to both witness and participate in this important critical moment. A markedly increased interest in travel writing and reading since the early 1990s makes the analysis of contemporary travel writing a particularly relevant project at this time. The confusion surrounding the study of travel literature (not its legitimacy, which I assume in this essay and in my class, but the direction critical approaches should take) is evident in the introduction to the *DLB 183, American Travel Writers 1776–1864,* in which James J. Schramer and Donald Ross assert that "even though most travel writing is in the first person, it is best to think of it as having a biographical rather than an autobiographical focus. The traveler is certainly the main character, but the account is supposed to display the places visited, not the traveler's personal life story" (xxi). Schramer and Ross's assertion/assumption that travel writing functions as a form of biography rather than as a form of autobiography reveals one of the most deeply imbedded contradictions inherent in current approaches to travel writing: a contradiction with which even the most sophisticated readers must grapple. The gap between what "an account is *supposed* to display"—the story of another culture—and what it in fact most usefully does display (the preconceived values and expectations of the culture out of which it is written) is a useful point of departure for both introducing students to the material of travel and to the circumference of the debate that surrounds it.

In his foreword to Houghton Mifflin's *Best American Travel Writing 2000,* Wilson provides an overview of the criteria he believes make a good travel narrative. Within this overview, he notes that the writers included in the first book of the series "are all keen observers who bring places to life by honing in on particular, human details," that "their writing also pulsates with true emotion—love, desire, humor, fear, despair," and that "they give us just a slice of the world, but in that slice they teach us a great deal" (xvi). That each of these assertions appears in the foreword to a collection entitled *Best American Travel Writing* lends them, and the text as a whole, an air of authority that undoubtedly fashions and guides lay readers' expectations concerning what constitutes "the best" as well as by what "criteria" the best travel writing is or should be read and evaluated. Texts (here I speak of the book as a whole) that carry—or claim to carry—the weight of cultural authority in this Arnoldian sense tend to discourage critical debate in less sophisticated readers, which may seem like a disadvantage for their use in the classroom. On the other hand, asking students to interrogate such texts can raise their critical consciousness because they provide what in some ways is a uniquely straightforward opportunity for reading "against the grain."[1] Encouraging students to interrogate the ideological assumptions contained in such texts from a variety of directions; to examine their formal structures along with the ways in which they "make sense" of the world for their readers is an important project that can reach far beyond the classroom experience.[2] For, if "tourism [is] just colonialism in another guise," as David Nicholson-Lord posits, then writing about touristic experiences is also implicated in the colonial or neoimperial enterprise, and teaching students how to recognize such entanglements is an important critical and cultural project.

That texts carrying the weight of cultural authority tend to discourage critical debate is complicated even more when working with material that is considered "nonfiction." Nonfiction narratives are often read as transparent texts, in just the way that Wilson's foreword encourages. For example, reviewers of travel narratives often focus on a text's "honest" or "truthful" portrayal—of both individuals with all their foibles exposed and the culture being described. Texts are often judged by and for a general readership according to their "truth-value." In *Contingencies of Value,* Barbara Herrnstein Smith defines "truth-value" as a form of evaluative judgment

> in which communication is seen as the *duplicative transmission* of a code-wrapped message from one consciousness to another, [and] 'truth-value' is seen as a measure of the extent to which such a message, when properly unwrapped, accurately and adequately reflects, represents, or corresponds with some independently determinate fact, reality, or state of affairs. (94, original emphasis)

When we believe that what we are reading is the truth or at least purports to be the truth—about a place, about a person—we read with a different sort of critical consciousness from when we believe we are reading fiction, which carries a different set of reader expectations regarding truthfulness. When we believe that what we are reading is a "duplicative transmission," we may read for information, for confirmation, or merely for recreation as arm chair travelers, but what we read may affect our perceptions of the world around us in ways that our response to fiction does not. Student readers tend to approach "nonfiction" texts as unproblematically replicating what their authors saw and experienced. In order to address this potential collapse of critical judgment, it is imperative to ask students to consider the assumptions that underlie the criteria by which the chosen works have been judged "the best" and to consider what other criteria may be in place beyond that which the editors claim.

As Smith notes in her discussion of the cultural-historical dynamics of endurance, "An object or artifact that performs certain desired/able functions particularly well at a given time for some community of subjects, being perhaps not only 'fit' but exemplary—that is, 'the best of its kind'—under those conditions, will have an immediate survival advantage" (45). Such objects/artifacts are more likely to be continually culturally reproduced—thus their influence to be felt over a considerable period of time. To ask students to explore commonalities and differences in the travel essays contained in *BATW* as they consider the following questions will help them to see beyond the criteria Wilson provides, and to understand the texts as objects that in some important way meet cultural expectations (desires) concerning the representation of other peoples and cultures. The subsequent questions offer a basic structure for a syllabus:

1. How do these writers construct their personae?
2. At what type of audience is their work directed?
3. Upon what types of sights/sites have they focused their texts?
4. What are readers meant to learn about the places being described, about the United States, and what else might they learn from reading these pieces?

5. Finally, I ask students to consider how and why this body of travel essays might be
    read as a whole.

I ask students to consider how we might read them as texts that either promote or challenge neoimperialism, both as individual works and as a whole.
How, for example, does what David Spurr calls "the rhetoric of empire"
function in these works? How, in other words, do these works "produce the
rest of the world" for an American readership as Mary Louise Pratt asks in
relation to how travel texts produce the rest of the world for a European audience?

Asking students to "tease out" the ideology that underlies the type of assumptions Wilson makes is one way to begin the important task of raising
student awareness of the persuasive function of all writing, i.e., how it
"makes sense" of the world for us. All three of Wilson's statements about the
writers he has chosen can be interrogated by bringing students' attention to
the fact that "honing in on" and recording "human details" is by no means a
neutral process. I find it useful to begin the semester by asking them to read
Horace Miner's classic work of ethnographic mockery, "Body Ritual among
the Nacerima," as a way of interrogating Wilson's first two criteria. Students
who do not realize that Nacerima is American spelled backwards feel shock,
horror, and disgust toward the people and the rituals Miner describes. Once
they are enlightened by their classmates, they often admit to feeling stupid at
having been so easily deceived. Of course, I point out to them that the deception is deliberate—on both Miner's part and mine, and that the goal of such
deception is to heighten their sensitivity toward the power of language that is
used to describe other peoples and cultures. I ask them to make note of "the
particular human details" Miner "hones" in on; on his use of certain terms
and phrases: the adjectives "exotic," "magical," "unusual," "mysterious," and
the noun "ritual" in order to produce a visceral reaction in his readers, and to
remember, should they run across such terminology again, that it might be a
signal to approach with caution. In spite of this early exposure to such concepts, students will still tend to read the majority of travel essays they encounter as transparent texts—depictions of the reality of other places—
because the majority of their writers are a great deal subtler than Miner. It is
important to continually return to the idea that authors shape meaning
through their choice of language throughout the semester.

Wilson's third assertion—concerning the pedagogical impulse of travel
writing—also deserves interrogation. The idea that travel writing has a pedagogical impulse is certainly not new; however, this impulse is markedly
complicated when we consider just exactly what and how it teaches us. That
Wilson is aware of the seriousness of the debates surrounding the pedagogi-

cal nature of travel writing is implied in his reference to Paul Theroux, in which he notes, "'The misperception is that the travel book is about a country,' Paul Theroux once told me. 'It's really about the person who's traveling'" (xvi). While I certainly agree with this statement, I find it problematic that Wilson then proceeds to sidestep the important ideological implications raised by the pedagogical nature of travel writing. Instead of considering the ideological function of much travel writing, Wilson goes on to note that "travel stories are necessarily told in the first person" and that "[t]his point of view is one of their strengths, and where the importance always lies," although he does not define what "importance" he is discussing (xvi). He appears to give a nod to the responsibility travel writers bear for creating readers' impressions of worlds by noting that "great travel writing is guided by a strong voice that is not afraid to take a stand," thus seemingly admitting that travel writing is often implicated in some sort of evaluatory process (xvi).

Instead of then following this line of reasoning to its logical conclusion—that travel writers work to convince their readers to take the same stance, he sidesteps the issue by referring to the "transparency" of travel writers' stands: "The writer's biases and misperceptions are also paraded before the reader, for they create a context for the writer's hard-won insights about a place. There's little attempt at a supposed objectivity. One of the important messages of a good travel piece is "this is my trip and no one else's" (xvi).[3] This type of claim contradicts Wilson's earlier assertion about the pedagogical nature of travel writing as well as his later assertion that "great travel writing can teach us something about the world that no other genre can" (xvi). One claim deliberately elides pedagogical responsibility; another touts it—no wonder students, critics, and general readers alike often remain confused about the importance of this genre. Asking students to consider the trap in which Wilson eventually finds himself helps to raise their awareness about the often sticky ethical issues critical travel readers and writers must always confront. Patrick Holland and Graham Huggan provide a useful discussion of what they term "artful dodgery" or the means of evading social responsibility and complicity through particular rhetorical strategies or the creation of certain types of personae in their introduction to *Tourists with Typewriters* (4–8) that works well in introducing students to a counterpoint to Wilson's claims.[4]

In his introduction to the collection, Bill Bryson, an experienced travel writer himself, and editor of the 2000 edition of the series, explains the reasoning behind his choices. Bryson explains that many of the pieces he chose "represent risky travel to challenging places" (xxvi). Because he, himself, is not adventurous he must live vicariously through others' adventures, he claims (xxvi). He admits that his central criteria came down to "liking" and that such a response was based upon finding himself "immersed and engaged, sometimes transported" by a work (xxvi). He remarks upon the works' "deftness of touch and originality of observation" (xxvi), a not unproblematic remark by any means once the class begins to recognize some of the tropes of travel writing, but one that avoids the immediate pedagogical pitfall into which Wilson fell. In what might be read as advice to future travel writers, Bryson also notes that "you don't necessarily have to go far to achieve something memorable. You just have to be able to see things in a different way" (xxvi). He describes this "way" as marked by "a penetrating curiosity, an almost compulsive desire to experience and try to understand the world at some unfamiliar level" (xxvi). Up to this point, Bryson has focused his attention upon stylistics and persona; eventually however, he finds it necessary to comment upon content, concluding his introduction by noting that "there is an amazing world out there—full of interesting, delightful, unexpected, extraordinary stuff that most of us know little about and consider much too seldom" (xxvii). Thus, Bryson's final move, in spite of his earlier avoidance, is toward the pedagogical thrust travel narratives contain—the ways in which they help their writers (and hence their readers) to understand—or make sense of—the world. Drawing students' attention to such a move helps them to consider the role genre limitations play in our understanding of the purpose of travel narratives at the present time.

The fact that, as Bryson notes, many of the narratives contained within the text are both engagingly written and contain compelling descriptions of "risky travel to challenging places" (xxvi) produces what Pratt refers to as "an intense 'effect of the real'" (220)—another important function of the effect of genre expectations to explore with students. This effect, as Pratt goes on to explain in her discussion of Paul Theroux's *Old Patagonian Express,* can undermine students' ability to read critically. Pratt explains that after reading the text her undergraduate students

> came in relieved and confident—this was it, this guy had *really* captured the way South America *really* was, you could just tell he knew what he was talking about. Theroux had fired their imaginations, empowered them to argue for his veracity by the very vividness of the writing, the richness and intensity with which their expectations, stereotypes, and prejudices had been confirmed. The students were carrying out, and being carried out by, the ideological project of third worldism and white supremacy. They were producing the metropolis's official ideologies as they had been taught to do. (220)

Asking students to keep a reading journal in which they carefully make note of particularly vivid, rich, and intense writing, and then bringing those journals into class to use as entry points for discussion, helps to remind students that travel narratives function, as does all written material, as acts of persuasion that help readers "make sense" of the world around them.

Simply asking students which essays they liked best and why they liked them best sets the stage for an examination of travel writers' narrative personae once we begin examining the actual essays. Two of the earliest questions we address in this regard follow: How do these writers construct their personae and how do they present themselves as belonging to a particular gender, class, race, ethnicity, or nationality? Do we find them likeable, trustworthy? I find it useful, in this case, to introduce students to the concept of the creation of an autobiographical persona. This can be done either through an in-class lecture or assigned readings. I then move into a specific discussion of the ways in which primary and secondary readings can work together, with examples from a specific class.

Jerome Bruner's "The Autobiographical Process" and Lynn Z. Bloom's "American Autobiography and the Politics of Genre" are both accessible and suitable for introducing students to the concept of the creation of an autobiographical persona. Bruner's discussion of the problems of representation ("there is no such thing as a 'life as lived' to be referred to" and "a life is created or constructed by the act of autobiography" 38) automatically complicates any simple understandings students might bring to class with them that equate the individual as a whole (the author) with that which appears on the page (the narrator). His discussion of the always schematized nature of memory combined with the process by which we can rewrite those memories from a number of different perspectives might provide the basis for a useful journal exercise that can help to illustrate Bruner's point more dramatically than hours of class discussion. For example, students might be asked to describe a particular experience in several ways: from their own initial perspective as accurately as they remember it, from their current perspective, from the perspective of someone else who also underwent the experience (this might include an interview), or from an imagined perspective—that of an older person, a younger person, a family member, a host rather than a guest.

I suggest moving from Bruner to Bloom, who neatly illustrates the connection between what she refers to as "personal travel narratives" and "autobiography as a genre" for students who might not otherwise understand the connection. She also lays the groundwork for a consideration of the political—rather than aesthetic—criteria that might prohibit or encourage the creation of certain types of personae:

American autobiography, what we write, read, teach, study, and critique, is insepa-
rably intertwined with political concerns. Indeed, autobiography has throughout our
national history been a conspicuously political genre. Political concerns strongly influence who writes (or tells) their stories, as well as the themes and masterplots of
these stories. Politics influence which works are published and circulated, which are
canonized, and consequently, which are read and studied in the schools. (151)

As a class we then discuss the ways in which travel writers create their personae as belonging to particular genders, classes, races, ethnicities, or nation-
alities and how such creations might influence the success or failure of their
work. We think about ways of presenting the self that might alienate certain
groups of readers. Once we have considered some general criteria, students
are then asked to think about them in relation to the texts, with a focus on
their own "gut" response to the personae of various authors.

We begin by reading William Booth's "Boat Camp," Bill Buford's "Lions and Tigers and Bears," Tim Cahill's "This Teaming Ark," Clive Irving's
"The First Drink of the Day," and David Lansing's "Confessions of a Cheese
Smuggler." Evidently, the range is fairly limited. Aside from the fact that the
collection is decidedly androcentric (a topic for another essay), I find this is a
useful way to begin—differences between the writers are not as obvious as
they might otherwise appear, and students are required to dig a bit to uncover
them successfully. The first three writers are fairly adventurous, even though
one of them (Buford) travels no further than Central Park. Students' responses to the writers' personae may range from tolerance of the middle-
aged in reference to Booth, to delight in the "crazy-funny" and completely ill
prepared Buford, to annoyance at what they perceive as crankiness on Cahill's part. Irving's essay is written in a fairly elevated tone to which several
students in one class reacted vehemently and considered it "snobbish" and
"off-putting." Irving's voice comes across clearly in the following passage,
in which he states his central argument: "It's my contention that, when traveling, the first taste of the right drink at the right moment in the right place
(and ideally with the right partner) is the highest form of serendipity" (100).
In this particular class we discussed Irving's diction, sentence structure and
tone, and students noted that the work was a success—after all, it had been
included in *The Best American Travel Writing*—yet they complained that
they found themselves feeling excluded and uncomfortable with Irving's text
because of his persona.

Lansing's "Confessions of a Cheese Smuggler" works well as a juxtaposition to Irving; they are both traveling in Europe, both texts revolve around a
discussion of consumption, yet each author has a distinctly different ap-

proach to the topic. Whereas Irving positions himself as a perhaps somewhat dissipated connoisseur, Lansing creates himself as a hapless not-quite-innocent, a bumbling neophyte. Lansing's piece, which was originally published in *National Geographic Traveler* and in which he admits "I am a dupe. A Rube. A cheese mule, as it were" (131) clearly appeals to a different type of audience from Irving's. We talk about gender (how do the authors we've read present themselves as men? What differences and similarities arise?); we talk about class (how do they present themselves as belonging to a certain class?); and we talk about alternative methods of representation—what could the authors have done differently?

As noted above, early in the semester, students are introduced to the concept that texts are constructed to appeal to and to persuade their audience. Once we have moved along a bit and have read a number of narratives, we begin to reconsider this by asking the question: At what type of audience are these works directed? If we work from the premise that audiences have certain assumptions about what it means to travel to certain places, we can begin to deduce what some of those assumptions might be from a close examination of the texts. For example, Cahill, whose work was originally published in *Outside,* seems to assume that his audience will agree that being bombarded by the feces of screaming chimps in an uninhabited forest is of course preferable to being surrounded by annoyingly idiotic human beings. A consideration of the places of publication from which Wilson and Bryson chose their essays is helpful as well. What, for example, might we say about the difference in audience appeal between *Condé Nast Traveler, Sports Illustrated, Outside, Men's Journal, The New Yorker,* and *Time* I ask. It is obviously useful to have examples on hand for this discussion to allow students to view the texts in light of surrounding material—other articles, advertisements, general lay-out. Once again we look for commonalities and differences and focus on "liking" as a criterion, with the acknowledgment that what one likes is often grounded in cultural assumptions and expectations. At this stage, the students begin to draft their first "travel" essays in which they are asked to focus on the creation of a particular persona. How they choose to present themselves will, I remind them, influence the receptiveness of their audience.

At this point in the semester I find it useful to begin to introduce students to a consideration of value judgments and the types of deeply embedded assumptions about what is or is not of value when writing about other peoples and cultures. We reflect back on the concepts of persona and audience while asking a series of questions:

1. Do these writers construct themselves as travelers or tourists and if so why?

2. How might audience expectations about the differences between travel and tourism influence these writers' choices?

3. Upon what types of sights/sites do these writers focus their texts and how do these help to "make sense" of the world for their readers?

4. What is the difference—or is there a difference—between an "authentic" experience and an "inauthentic" experience? How do we know when we are having one rather than the other? Why do we often seem to value one over the other?

5. How might the forms of evaluation we discover in our readings encourage us to "make sense" of the world in particular ways?

To this end, I introduce students to Walker Percy's "The Loss of the Creature" and Jonathan Culler's "Semiotics of Tourism." Percy's essay—replete with assumptions about what constitutes an authentic experience—raises much interesting discussion and is generally happily embraced by students. Percy's example—the Grand Canyon—is familiar to many students, at least in photographs, and his concepts are unlikely to be completely foreign to students. The idea that there is an essence or truth that can be "recovered" (514) or obscured, the idea that there is a marked difference between taking the tourist route and wandering "off the beaten track" (513) in search of the "unspoiled" (515), and the belief that "the real" (520) can be extracted from its "packaging" (519) are all fairly comfortable ideas for students. They find it easy to agree with Percy and to mourn with him the "radical loss of sovereignty" (516) and the moral outrage he feels toward the consumption of "prepared experience" (512). They can test Percy's remarks against their own experiences and against the knowledge they have thus far accrued in their reading of both the apparatus (foreword and introduction) and the travel narratives about what is believed to be of value for travelers.

In contrast, Culler's argument jolts them out of such complacency; it is useful for exploring the artificiality of the distinctions between the traveler (the good) and the tourist (the bad and the ugly), and between the authentic (that which is off the beaten track, the real, the unspoiled) and the inauthentic (the too easily accessible, the pre-packaged, the spoiled). Conversely, he in no way discounts the seriousness or power of such distinctions. His reference to Dean MacCannell's argument in *The Tourist: A New Theory of the Leisure Class* helps students understand the ways in which such dichotomies can have a powerful impact on how we perceive and judge the world in an age in which, due to the decline of other forms of moral consensus, "the touristic code is the most powerful and widespread modern consensus and a major stabilizing force in Western society. The touristic code is the sense of what one must see, what you 'ought not to miss'—a systematized knowledge of the world coupled to a widely-accepted series of moral injunctions" (139). Once students are able to recognize such distinctions along with their power to shape understanding, we turn our attention to a series of essays that either directly or indirectly engage this facet of the critical debate.

Almost any travel narrative will in some manner illustrate the distinctions Percy and Culler outline but I have found Alden Jones's "Lard Is Good For You" and Rolf Potts's "Storming *The Beach*" particularly useful at this point. Jones directly engages the debate with her references to the "polarized" voices she hears in her head. One is "the Tourist," who sits on her "left shoulder" and "encouraged [her] to ditch this dinky town and make a beeline for the beach, where I could stay in a nice hotel and sleep in a bed with fresh sheets free of that mildew smell" (110). The "Traveler," though, (ensconced on her right shoulder) is "embarrassed that it would have to share a body with someone as crude and culturally insensitive as the Tourist" (110). The Tourist complains about the food and demands special treatment, the Traveler eats what she is served without a fuss and merely wants to "fit in." Students can use Jones's distinctions to expand on what they have gleaned from Percy and Culler while at the same time witnessing what they may, until that moment, have seen as an "academic" debate played out in one of the travel essays contained in the collection. Potts's "Storming *The Beach,*" which plays with Percy's concerns with the "loss of sovereignty" (516) and the morally bankrupt consumption of "prepared experience" (512) as well as with the categories of tourist and traveler, also helps to bring the debate to life for students. After reading Alex Garland's novel *The Beach,* as well as numerous tabloids describing the film to be shot from the novel, Potts hops a plane and heads toward what is described in the novel as "an unspoiled beach utopia hidden in a national park in Thailand" (173). By storming the site on which the film (starring Leonardo DiCaprio) is being shot, Potts declares (tongue in cheek), "I hope to travel behind the curtain, to break out of the confines of the consumer experience by attempting to break into the creation of the consumer experience" (184). Whereas Percy decries the moral bankruptcy of "prepared experience," valuing the "authentic" over the "inauthentic," Potts embraces it in what Maxine Feifer would refer to as a post-touristic move.

Potts also levels references to the distinction between travelers and tourists made by fellow travelers by equating all traveling with the "hokey-pokey." He initially notes that "on the surface, it's a simple distinction: tourists leave home to escape the world, while travelers leave home to experience the world. Tourists…are merely doing the hokey-pokey: putting their right foot in and taking their right foot out; calling themselves world travelers while experiencing very little" (175), but finds this distinction ultimately inadequate. He then asks a series of questions that metaphorically break down the type of clear-cut distinctions Percy provides: "Do travelers, unlike tourists, keep their right foot in a little longer and shake it all about? Do travelers actually go so far as to do the hokey-pokey and turn themselves around—thus gaining a more authentic experience? Is that what it's all about?" (175). Thus students see yet another side of the debate memorably played out within our travel (rather than theoretical) texts as they try to "make sense" of such distinctions.

The travel texts we have been reading deal with the issue of traveler versus tourist and/or authenticity versus inauthenticity in either direct or peripheral manners. An assignment that asks students to "produce a travel essay that grows out of the travels [they] have recorded in [their] journals and that in some way, either directly or indirectly, engages the debate over authenticity versus inauthenticity/travel versus tourism in terms of [their] own travels since the beginning of the semester" is generally quite productive for helping them to think through such complex ideas. Some might choose to directly engage one or more of the essays from the collection within their own work of travel writing, speaking to/about other travel writers as they have seen the authors themselves do, while others might choose to self-consciously explore their responses to travel by examining themselves as travelers and/or tourists in search of particular types of sites (authentic or inauthentic). Trips to Caribbean islands, New Jersey boardwalks (Asbury Park), and even just "downtown" provide fruitful material for students to creatively explore a concept central to the production and study of much contemporary travel writing.

At this point, I find it useful to begin to turn the discussion in yet another direction by asking students to consider what it might be that readers are meant to learn about the places being described. A review of several of the essays that have been read thus far is helpful at this point ("why would anyone want to go there?" and "yuck!" are student responses that leap immediately to mind). Our current cultural fascination with adventure and risky travel has not necessarily filtered down to many students who seem to prefer the idea of sitting on a warm beach to being rained on by chimpanzee urine. I remind students about their responses to Miner's "Body Ritual among the Nacerima" and find it useful to have students read at least the introduction to Jamaica Kincaid's *A Small Place* (1988) as a way of focusing their attention on the variety of perspectives that can be brought to bear when considering what a particular place might mean. Kincaid's righteous anger toward neocolonialism in the form of tourists and tourism as an island-born Antiguan contrasts nicely with David Halberstam's nostalgic outrage in "Nantucket on My Mind": an outrage that cannot quite overcome the inconveniently ironic position of being himself an off-islander. Clearly Kincaid's piece is directed toward an audience of potential travelers; it is not, however, a work geared to lure travelers to Antigua. Instead it is designed to raise travelers' awareness about themselves, about the places they visit, about the ravages—economic, environmental, social—of the tourist industry.

Halberstam's "Nantucket on My Mind," originally published in *Town & Country* is also decidedly not tourist-brochure material. He is at turns resentful, angry, defensive, judgmental, and nostalgic. He resents those off-islanders whose ability and willingness to pay top dollar for a summer home have raised prices and resulted in a changing value system on the island he has been visiting for thirty summers. While some students may be uncomfortable with Kincaid's anger and the feelings of guilt it arouses ("I never really thought about it that way before" is one typical response), many are sympathetic with both Kincaid and Halberstam, coming themselves from towns dependent on the tourist dollar, but not generally having so directly experienced the ravages of colonialism. Both these works further complicate the position of traveling and travel writing as neutral activities in terms of their description of place.

Mark Hertsgaard's "The Nile at Mile One" directly engages many of the same issues we have addressed as a class thus far—problems of authenticity, tourism versus travel, the continuing effects of colonialism, and travel writing as a political activity—while describing his attempts to recreate Winston Churchill's 1908 *My African Journey* (how a re-created journey can be "authentic" is one of the questions that invariably arises). At this point we have read material from the perspective of those who host tourists, and students are generally fairly sympathetic towards host nations. Hertsgaard's piece lays further groundwork for a specific consideration of the political influence of travel writing in his discussion of Churchill's text, which, he notes,

> [a]rticulates virtually all facets of the ideology that shaped industrial man's impact on Africa in the twentieth century—the values, fears, goals, and justifications that animated European efforts to recast the human and physical environment of Africa. Churchill saw the continent through the eyes of an inveterate colonizer, an unashamed imperialist who believed that colonialism benefited colonizer and colonized alike. (60)

It is useful to follow a reading of Hertsgaard's text with a general discussion of colonialism, imperialism, and neoimperialism to clarify these terms for students and to then move on to a consideration of David Nicholson-Lord's "The Politics of Travel," Dennison Nash's "Tourism as a Form of Imperialism," and Pratt's chapter on "Narrating the Anti-Conquest." Nicholson-Lord provides a contemporary framework for a consideration of tourism as an industry that builds off Kincaid's, Halberstam's, and Hertsgaard's essays and that thus complicates our response to travel narratives that ignore the unpleasant side effects of tourism Nicholson-Lord outlines in unforgiving detail. In other words, he moves beyond Kincaid's specific discussion of a specific area and asks us to envision the problems—economic, environmental, social—that often attend tourism on a global scale. Nash's work provides an anthropological overview of host-guest relations that considers the perspective of the initially willing host to engage in what appears to be a profitable venture but who may, when the reality of the relationship as detailed by Nicholson-Lord sets in, "begin to have second thoughts about the wisdom of their calculations" (42). Students can often recall unpleasant encounters they themselves have had as either hosts or guests.

Once we ascertain that tourism is not really a "smokeless" industry from a variety of directions, the time is ripe for moving back into a discussion of the written material that grows out of the tourism industry and onto a consideration of the ethical dimension of travel writing. Pratt's chapter on "Narrating the Anti-Conquest" provides specific insight and examples into the ways in which peoples and cultures can be written in a variety of ways to support whatever political agenda might happen to be in place. Pratt's discussion of motives—"knowledge-building," "economic and political expansion" (38) — her complication of the terms "barbarians" and "civilized" (43), her references to changing discourse conventions (49), her contention that "it is the task of the advance scouts for capitalist 'improvement' to encode what they encounter as 'unimproved' and, in keeping with the terms of the anti-conquest, as *disponible*, available for improvement" (61, original emphasis), her description of the ways in which humans can be written out of the landscape (51), and her remarks about persona—"Unlike such antecedents as the conquistador and the hunter, the figure of the naturalist-hero often has a certain impotence or androgyny about him; often he portrays himself in infantile or adolescent terms" (56)—allow us to look back over everything we have read thus far as we begin to think more holistically about the ways in which the texts contained in *The Best American Travel Writing 2000*, singly and as a collection, "make sense" of tourism as a facet of the neoimperial enterprise.

I have found that Tom Clynes's "The Toughest Trucker in the World," Jessica Maxwell's "Inside the Hidden Kingdom," and Jonathan Tourtellot's "The Two Faces of Tourism" all raise interesting perspectives in terms of the above. Clynes's description of a trucker who risks life and limb to deliver beer to an exclusive fishing resort on Australia's Cape Yoke Peninsula, Maxwell's discussion of restrictions to tourism in Bhutan in order to uphold environmental integrity, and Tourtellot's exposure of the complex local, national, and international pressures faced by Mexico's Copper Canyon country allow students to think about important contemporary aspects of the debate over tourism-as-neoimperialism that reach well beyond the page and the classroom in important ways.

We can think back to narrators like Buford, and Lansing, and Wallis, and Potts—all appealing, all a little bumbling and adolescent,[5] all writing seemingly innocent tales, that now appear more weighted as we turn our attention to our final set of questions: How might this body of travel essays be read as a whole? How might we read them as texts that either promote or challenge neoimperialism both as individual works and as a whole? How does what David Spurr calls "the rhetoric of empire" function in these works? How, in other words, do the works "produce the rest of the world" for an American readership as Mary Louise Pratt asks in relation to how travel texts produce the rest of the world for a European audience? Why might the study of such texts be an important project? I find Spurr's chapter on "Affirmation" particularly useful at this stage; it provides some historical contextualization as well as insight into discursive formations. Students are provided with an invaluable framework for engaging our final set of questions through Spurr's discussion of the media's use of images of chaos and disorganization "in order that the principles of a governing ideology and the need for institutions of order may be affirmed" (109), along with his discussion of "demonstrations of moral superiority" (110), his reference to the importance of "tracing patterns of repetition and uniformity throughout the changing forms of discourse" (114) and his historical contextualization of "a characteristically American style of self-affirmation" (117) that "in more recent years has been translated into a rhetoric of commercial pragmatism and strategic benevolence in the United States' approach to the Third World" (119).

Ryszard Kapuscinski's "The Truck," P. J. O'Rourke's "Weird Karma," Tony Perrottet's "Zoned on Zanzibar," Mark Ross's "The Last Safari," Patrick Symmes's "From the Wonderful People Who Brought You the Killing Fields," and Jeffrey Taylor's "China's Wild West" and "Exiled Beyond Kilometer 101" all work well to illustrate and complicate Spurr's argument. In "The Truck," Kapuscinski early on declares that in spite of not understanding a word of the language spoken by area natives he is quite sure that the brief arrival of a truck "was vital to them: it injected variety into their lives, provided a subject for later conversation, and, above all, was both material proof of the existence of another world and a bracing confirmation that that world, since it had sent them a mechanical envoy, must know they existed" (121). His surety about the meaning of things clearly he knows little about, combined with his description of a frighteningly chaotic, near-death experience in the Sahara in which stupidity abounds (both his own and his driver's), encourages students to consider his essay in terms of its emotional and moral effect on them as readers (horrible place, needs help).

Taylor's "China's Wild West" gives us an opportunity to consider what else, besides descriptions of chaos and disorganization, he might have included in his discussion. What else might we want to learn about this area of China? How does Taylor's description aid the depiction of China as a region that needs the imposition of western-style order? How does it set China up as a site of rescue? Taylor's "Exiled Beyond Kilometer 101," with its shocked description of the juxtaposition of "favored urban areas and a neglected, poverty-stricken hinterland" (241) in the chaotic "new Russia" and its descriptions of high-levels of unemployment leading to nefarious activities on the part of youth, concludes with an outright threat:

> Ozyory was only a few hours' drive from Moscow, yet a smothering pall of futility lay on the place. I found myself thinking that if anything sends Russia hurtling into anarchy or back to totalitarian rule, it will be despair bubbling into fury over the contradiction between what 10 million Muscovites see as the fruits of the new system, shriveled though those may currently be, and what 147 million other currently voiceless Russians see. In the same way that Lenin played on widespread discontent with czarist Russia to mobilize support for a revolution whose ideology the masses could hardly understand, in the same way that Pugachev could count on a reserve of serfs' rage in the countryside to fuel his devastating peasant uprising of the eighteenth century, so might a demagogue come to power riding the crest of the legitimate grievances of those residing beyond kilometer 101, impoverished and forgotten, now more than ever, by Moscow. (250)

It does not, of course, take long for students to note that were one to travel from certain areas of Manhattan to Harlem or the Bronx, or within Los Angeles, or Chicago, or any other big city, one might find similar economic disparity, chaos, and disorganization. Although the circumstances cannot be entirely equated, there are enough similarities to make students question Taylor's politically limited perspective. Once we complete our final set of questions, I ask students to address them more formally in a written assignment that discusses individual essays in terms of the text as a whole.

This essay merely touches upon many of the works included in *The Best American Travel Writing 2000,* as well as many of the options for approaching this text critically in order to introduce students to the study of travel narratives and to more generally enhance student awareness of the constructedness of all texts. It in no way has attempted to be exhaustive, either in terms of the ways in which the essays in the collection might usefully be taught or in terms of suggestions for secondary material, but merely to provide an overview and some suggestions for one useful way of approaching travel writing in the classroom.

Notes

1   See the introduction to David Bartholomae and Anthony Petrosky's *Ways of Reading* for a full discussion of this strategy.

2   Robert Scholes's remark, although published in 1985, seems particularly relevant again today: "What students need from us—and this is true of students in our great universities, our small colleges, and our urban and community colleges—what they need from us now is the kind of knowledge and skill that will enable them to make sense of their worlds, to determine their own interests, both individual and collective, to see through the manipulations of all sorts of texts in all sorts of media, and to express their own views in some appropriate manner" (15–16).

3   Paul Theroux makes just such a claim in a decidedly cranky manner early on in *The Pillars of Hercules: A Grand Tour of the Mediterranean.*

4   Holland and Huggan provide valuable insight into the adaptation of a variety of possible personae by travel writers and the effects such personae are likely to produce in readers.

5   See note 3, above.

Works Cited

Bartholomae, David, and Anthony Petrosky, eds. *Ways of Reading*. 4th ed. Boston: Bedford Books, 1996.

The Beach. Dir. Danny Boyle. Perf. Leonardo DiCaprio, Tilda Swinton, Virginie Ledoyen and Guillaume Canet. Twentieth Century Fox, 2000.

The Best American Travel Writing 2000. Eds. Bill Bryson and Jason Wilson. Boston: Houghton Mifflin, 2000.

Bloom, Lynn Z. "American Autobiography and the Politics of Genre." *Genre and Writing: Issues, Arguments, Alternatives*. Eds. Wendy Bishop and Hans Ostrom. Portsmouth, NH: Boynton/Cook, 1997. 151–59.

Booth, William. "Boat Camp." Bryson 1–8.

Bruner, Jerome. "The Autobiographical Process." *The Culture of Autobiography: Constructions of Self-Representation*. Ed. Robert Folkenflik. Stanford, CA: Stanford UP, 1993. 38–56.

Bryson, Bill. Introduction. Bryson xix-xxvii.

Bryson, Bill, ed. *The Best American Travel Writing 2000*. Boston: Houghton Mifflin, 2000.

Buford, Bill. "Lions and Tigers and Bears." Bryson 9–18.

Cahill, Tim. "This Teaming Ark." Bryson 19–26.

Clynes, Tom. "The Toughest Trucker in the World." Bryson 27–36.

Churchill, Winston. *My African Journey*. 1908. New York: Norton, 1990.

Culler, Jonathan. "Semiotics of Tourism." *American Journal of Semiotics* 1 (1981): 127–40.

Feifer, Maxine. *Tourism in History: From Imperial Rome to the Present*. Briarcliff Manor, NY: Stein and Day, 1985.

Garland, Alex. *The Beach*. New York: Riverhead Books, 1998.

Halberstam, David. "Nantucket on My Mind." Bryson 50–58.

Hertsgaard, Mark. "The Nile at Mile One." Bryson 59–71.

Holland, Patrick, and Graham Huggan. *Tourists with Typewriters: Critical Reflections on Contemporary Travel Writing.* Ann Arbor: U Michigan P, 1998.

Irving, Clive. "The First Drink of the Day." Bryson 100–6.

Jones, Alden. "Lard is Good for You." Bryson 107–19.

Kapuscinski, Ryszard. "The Truck." Bryson 120–27.

Kincaid, Jamaica. *A Small Place.* New York: Farrar, Straus, Giroux, 1988.

Lansing, David. "Confessions of a Cheese Smuggler." Bryson 128–33.

MacCannell, Dean. *The Tourist: A New Theory of the Leisure Class.* New York: Schocken Books, 1976.

Maxwell, Jessica. "Inside the Hidden Kingdom." Bryson 134–44.

Miner, Horace. "Body Ritual among the Nacerima." *American Anthropologist* 58 (1956): 503–7.

Nash, Dennison. "Tourism as a Form of Imperialism." *Hosts and Guests: The Anthropology of Tourism.* Ed. Valene L. Smith. Philadelphia: U Penn P, 1977. 33–47.

Nicholson-Lord, David. "The Politics of Travel: Is Tourism Just Colonialism in Another Guise?" *The Nation* 6 Oct. 1997: 11–18.

O'Rourke, P. J. "Weird Karma." Bryson 145–57.

Percy, Walker. "The Loss of the Creature." *Message in the Bottle* 1975. Rpt. in *Ways of Reading.* 4th ed. Eds. David Bartholomae and Anthony Petrosky. Boston: Bedford, 1995. 510–23.

Perrottet, Tony. "Zoned on Zanzibar." Bryson 158–70.

Potts, Rolf. "Storming *The Beach.*" Bryson 171–88.

Pratt, Mary Louise. *Imperial Eyes: Travel Writing and Transculturation.* London: Routledge, 1992.

Ross, Mark. "The Last Safari." Bryson 189–204.

Schramer, James J., and Donald Ross. Introduction. *The Dictionary of Literary Biography 183: American Travel Writers, 1776–1864.* Detroit, MI: Gale Research, 1997. xv-xxv.

Scholes, Robert. *Textual Power.* New Haven: Yale UP, 1985.

Smith, Barbara Herrnstein. *Contingencies of Value.* Cambridge, MA: Harvard UP, 1988.

Spurr, David. *The Rhetoric of Empire: Colonial Discourse in Journalism, Travel Writing, and Imperial Administration.* Durham: Duke UP, 1993.

Symmes, Patrick. "From the Wonderful People Who Brought You the Killing Fields." Bryson 216–28.

Taylor, Jeffrey. "China's Wild West." Bryson 229–40.

———. "Exiled Beyond Kilometer 101." Bryson 241–50.

Theroux, Paul. *The Pillars of Hercules: A Grand Tour of the Mediterranean.* New York: G.P. Putnam's Sons, 1995.

Tourtellot, Jonathan. "The Two Faces of Tourism." Bryson 251–59.

Wallis, David. "One Man and His Donkey." Bryson 277–82.

Wilson, Jason. "Why Travel Stories Matter." Foreword. Bryson xi-xvii.

Chapter 6

Negotiating Privilege in the Teaching of Travel Literature

Denise Comer

> Travel writing these days seems to be many things; but in my opinion it is not what usually passes for travel writing. It is not a first-class seat on an airplane, not a week of wine tasting on the Rhine, not a weekend in a luxury hotel. It is not a survey of expensive brunch menus, a search for the perfect margarita, or a roundup of the best health spas in the Southwest. In short, it is not about vacations or holidays, not an adjunct to the public relations industry.
>
> —Paul Theroux, *The Best American Travel Writing, 2001* (xix).

> Q: What interested you in the course?
> A: "I took the class because I like to travel."
> A: "I took the class because I'm planning on traveling this summer."
> A: "I took the class because I've traveled a lot."
> A: "I took the class because I hope to travel a lot."
> — Conversation with students in Duke University's Writing 20 class, 2003.

However much we might want to agree with Paul Theroux's argument that travel writing can no longer be characterized as "about vacations and holidays," a brief dialogue with our students indicates that Theroux might be overly optimistic when it comes to student perceptions of what travel writing is or is not. When asked what motivates their interest in taking a course that addresses travel literature, students almost invariably equate travel in their responses to desirable, privileged journeys that, if not always pleasurable, nevertheless presume significant quantities of autonomy and leisure. I have encountered this assumptive predilection on the part of students over the past eight years and across a wide spectrum of institutions and classrooms: in courses ranging from first-year writing and lower-division literature to advanced writing and upper-division British literature and in academic environments as varied as community colleges, low-to-mid-level state institutions and private, top-tier universities. This tendency is all the more troubling because travel narratives are inherently and inextricably bound within rich contexts of geography, colonialism, imperialism, race, class, and gender and, as such, offer an unparalleled opportunity for achieving what is for me a paramount pedagogical aim in literature and writing classrooms—encouraging students to critically interrogate their own and others' positions in the world and the concomitant relationships therein. A number of factors, however, including the student privilege, assumptions, and expectations gestured to in the student responses above, trouble the realization of this aim.

Effective inclusion of travel writing in the writing and literature class-rooms demands a deliberate awareness of these potential stumbling blocks and a precise foregrounding of and navigation through the complex class and social structures inherent in travel texts. Fortunately, over the past few decades this proposition has enjoyed significant support within the academy; most teachers of travel literature would now prompt students to acknowledge issues of power as they interrogate various travel texts. This pedagogical philosophy has prompted an expansion of that which is read in the travel writing classroom, with female travel writers and travelers of color gaining increasing recognition, as well as the more frequent inclusion of travel narratives depicting travel to places that do not exemplify conventional first-class vacation sites. There is, however, room for improvement. Even the travel texts written by so-called marginalized writers about so-called marginalized places are often authored by comparatively privileged individuals and, more often than not, narrate journeys initiated on a voluntary basis or on a leisured or professional pretense. Pre-empting any genuine, sustained consideration of alternative notions of travel—such as literatures of migration, exile, escape, captivity, diasporas, or military movements, for example—the most frequently adopted pedagogical strategies for unraveling the tightly woven threads of privilege typically entail dissecting complex layers of power undergirding comparatively privileged travel texts and privileged occasions for travel. While these efforts showcase in important ways the inequities that often enable and permeate travel experiences, unless they are augmented by a range of types of travel texts, authored in a myriad of formats by diverse travelers, they ultimately do little to reconstitute what travel is and who travelers are and instead merely reaffirm the notion that travel exists primarily under the purview of a relatively elite group of people.

While privileged versions of travel can and should be legitimately situated within the genre of travel literature, the exclusivity accompanying assumptions that travel writing emerges predominantly from leisure pursuits deserves reconsideration. Attempting to reconfigure a more inclusive concept of "travel," Caren Kaplan sets forth in *Questions of Travel* to call "attention to the continuities and discontinuities between terms such as 'travel,' 'displacement,' and 'location,' as well as between the particularized practices and identities of 'exile,' 'tourist,' and 'nomad'" (2). Where Kaplan takes up this endeavor from a theoretical stance, teachers of travel literature must also question what is at stake in these pervasive conceptions of travel as being almost unilaterally synonymous with privileged journeys. What are the possible pitfalls accompanying such critical myopia? How might teachers of travel literature compensate for student assumptions and expectations? What modes of and occasions for travel remain commonly overlooked and at what expense? What services and disservices are teachers of travel literature providing to students when syllabi consist primarily of privileged versions of travel? In the interest of exploring the possibilities of a more expansive pedagogy of travel literature, I will in the following pages discuss the ways in which travel literature is often framed as an overly narrow genre in the classroom and I will consider strategies for and implications of expanding notions of what constitutes travel literature.

The linkage between travel and privilege frequently found in students' initial approach to travel (as indicated by the opening dialogue of this paper) reflects widespread, popular assumptions about what constitutes travel and travel writing (despite Theroux's hopeful commentary otherwise). One need only venture into the travel section of Barnes & Noble or Borders to glean how students might develop their expectations. A brief perusal of the "travel" shelves in these stores reveals a plethora of *Fodor's*, *Frommer*'s and *Lonely Planet* guides, intended for use by the tourist, and a sprinkling of what Bill Bryson labels "literary travel titles" (xx), such as Bryson's *The Lost Continent* and Jan Morris's *Hong Kong,* intended perhaps to serve as inspiration for their readers' own subsequent wanderings or as fodder for daydreaming about what one might be able to go and see or do one day. The travel area of the magazine section consists of similarly focused publications, catering to the image of travel as an enterprising or leisured glory; here one can find *Islands*, with an April/May 2003 feature on Micronesian ghost stories (*Islands*); *Condé Nast Traveler,* which promotes itself to readers who would "dash in a flash to a spa. A ski slope. A château. A chalet. A pretty Portuguese Posada. Or a quaint New England inn" (*Condé Nast Traveler*); and *National Geographic Traveler,* which offers in the October 2002 edition an article by P. F. Kluge on Bali (written before the explosion of the Sari Club, a nightclub) entitled "Return to Paradise." A recent article in *National Geographic Traveler,* "Around the World in 80+ Books," by George Stone, demonstrates the pervasiveness of the assumption that travel literature constitutes primarily texts narrating privileged journeys. The article identifies the top travel narratives by region; its selections are dominated by such titles as John Steinbeck's *Travels with Charley,* M. F. K. Fisher's *Two Towns in Provence,* and Pico Iyer's *Video Night in Kathmandu.* Even the more financially conservative magazine *Budget Travel* still appeals to travelers who may be generally characterized as leisured vacationers: One recent cover shouts to readers, "This Autumn Europe is yours for $399!" (*Budget Travel*). The travel sections of newspapers follow suit with the construction of travel as an exciting or relaxing journey, offering great vacation deals and highlighting great vacation destinations for subscribers. The Travel Channel on television hardly even deserves mention for how much it promotes travel for the privileged.

Remarkably and regrettably, academic circles are no less guilty of promoting the pervasive conception that travel is often privileged in essence. Many of the anthologies and collections available for use in the travel-literature classroom sponsor conceptions of travel as an advantaged activity. Paul Fussell's *Norton Book of Travel,* for example, remains one of the most widely known texts of its kind. Excluding the possibility of identifying accounts of exile or writings of the diaspora as "real travel," Fussell declares in his introduction that "to constitute real travel, movement from one place to another should manifest some impulse of non-utilitarian pleasure" (21). Similarly, delimiting notions of travel, I have used such publications as *The Best American Travel Writing* to introduce students to travel literature in my Academic-Writing course at Duke University. This annual anthology features accounts of travel authored primarily by professional travel writers who have submitted their writing to popular American periodicals. The 2002 edition includes such narratives as Devin Friedman's "Forty Years in Acapulco," where Friedman learns life's "rules" from his grandfather Mort, who spends "one full month in Acapulco, Mexico, every February for the last forty years" (97). One narrative in the collection, "Roman Hours," edited by André Aciman, seems initially capable of expanding the notion of travel since Aciman "first arrived in Rome as a refugee in 1965" (6). However, this potential is quickly subsumed under Aciman's current life, which consists of returning to Rome from a privileged vantage to reminisce about his former days of destitution and to enjoy unhurried strolls, endless afternoons at a *caffé,* and dinner "with old friends" (9).

Only three of the narratives, all of which address New York's Ground Zero—Scott Anderson's "Below Canal Street," Adam Gopnik's "The City and the Pillars," and Thomas Swick's "Stolen Blessings"—offer a departure from the formula of a professional writer venturing to what is often an out-of-the-way, exotic place to avoid typical tourist spots (á la Fussell's "anti-tourist" from *Abroad).* Even these two narratives, however, ultimately do little to challenge student assumptions about travel; as one student succinctly put it during a recent class discussion of why these three narratives might have been included in a travel writing anthology: "The [editors] were bound to include something about New York. How could they not?" Even if the student could eventually be encouraged to think of other reasons for the narratives' inclusion, he does have a point. Perhaps these narratives were finally included because the editors felt obligated to acknowledge the year 2001 in its entirety.

Collections such as *The Encyclopedia of Women's Travel and Exploration* are similarly inclined—despite their emphasis on historically subjugated groups of people—to position travel as generally privileged and elitist. Explaining the selection process for her encyclopedia, for instance, Patricia Netzley writes in her preface: "Throughout *The Encyclopedia ...,* which has 315 entries in all, the emphasis is on women who have been the first to accomplish a travel- or exploration-related feat or whose exploits have been extensive enough to warrant fame" (x). Among the 315 entries, one can learn about comparatively privileged women such as Jane Goodall, "one of the best-known women to travel for the sake of science" (94), or Elizabeth Fry, "representative of women who traveled for social reform" (88), or Elizabeth Marshall Thomas, who "made new discoveries regarding the Bushman people during her travels to Africa in the 1950s" (207). Similarly forwarding these narrow ideas of what travel involves, Jennifer Speake's *The Literature of Travel and Exploration: An Encyclopedia* may include in its 630 entries references to such terms as *exile,* but nevertheless primarily emphasizes places and routes of travel ("Afghanistan, Black Sea, Egypt, Gobi Desert...") and relatively privileged travel writers ("Isabella Bird, Gustave Flaubert, Walter Raleigh..."). The synopsis that advertises Speake's compilation on amazon.co.uk, reveals not only the text's heavy emphasis on privileged versions of travel, but also the assumption that potential buyers will be more inclined to purchase the $250 item if it subsumes travel within its familiar, advantaged cocoon. Note in the following description the tacit assumption that typical travelers seek out and enjoy adventure and excitement: "There are entries on...methods of transport and types of journey (balloon, camel, grand tour, hunting, and big game expeditions, pilgrimage, space travel and exploration), genres (buccaneer narratives, guidebooks, New World chronicles, postcards), [and] companies and societies (East India Company, Royal Geographical Society, Society of Dilettanti)" (*The Literature of Travel...*).

This commonplace of travel being a leisured, often voluntary journey, which is found in so many collections of travel narratives, (predictably) infiltrates the pedagogy of travel-literature classrooms. A search of the term *travel* in the online catalog of Blackboard.com results in course titles such as "Hospitality & Tourism 1" (Secrest), "Early American Explorers" (Cubelli), and "Travel Orientation for the Yellowstone Region" (Eickstedt). One listed course, "e-travel," describes itself as "intended for magnet high school students, grades 11–12" (Jennings). The teacher outlines the course structure as follows: "On the first of the month several locations from around the world will be posted and marketing teams will have until the end of the month to research the location and teenage tourist sites and do a presentation in PowerPoint or create and present a travel brochure" (Jennings). An examination of travel texts found on syllabi dovetails many students' tendency to associate travel with a privileged leisure pursuit. Rather than working to destabilize these exclusive notions of travel literature, many syllabi that self-avowedly incorporate travel literature (my own at times included) instead exacerbate this narrow notion of travel by featuring relatively canonical travel texts authored primarily by elite travelers. This trend emerges in historical contexts, such as in the plethora of Victorian literature courses that include travel narratives such as Queen Victoria's journal accounts of Switzerland and Scotland, Mary Kingsley's *Travels in West Africa,* or Charles Darwin's *The Voyage of the Beagle.* The trend also appears in courses that address broader, less historically grounded categories of travel writing. A literature course at the University of Essex, for example, "Contemporary Travel Writing," asks students to read such texts as Peter Matthiessen's *The Snow Leopard* and Peter Robb's *Midnight in Sicily* (Hulme). An English course at the University of Hong Kong, "Travel Writing," introduces students to comparatively well-to-do travel writers such as Herodotus, Lady Mary Wortley Montagu, Mark Twain, and D. H. Lawrence (Smethurst).

This over-reliance on travel texts of privilege also permeates courses intended to train students in the actual craft of travel writing, such as a University of Denver course, "Advanced Creative Writing: Travel Writing," in which students discuss travel writing exemplars that include George Orwell's *Homage to Catalonia,* James Clifford's *Routes,* and Amitav Ghosh's *In an Antique Land* (Kiteley). A similar course at George Mason University, "Advanced Writing in the Humanities," highlights Gerald Brenan's *South from Granada,* Robert Byron's *Road to Oxiana,* Eleanor Clark's *Rome and a Villa,* and Robert Louis Stevenson's *Travels on a Donkey in the Cevennes* (Moody). I too am prone to an overdependence on privileged travel; in my upper-division "Advanced Composition" course at the University of South Carolina, I asked students to read Lynn Bloom's *Fact and Artifact*; in the chapter entitled "Writing about Places," Bloom insists on defining travel as that which involves a "wish" or a comparable form of "satisfaction": "Travel literature is, for most readers, an agreeable form of escape from wherever they are, whether or not a trip to Katmandu, Kenya, or the Grand Canyon is more a wish than a reality. For some, reading about a trip is an inspiration to make it happen. For others, reading about a trip is just as satisfying as actually taking the trip" (139).

Perpetuating this conflation of leisure and privilege onto travel, the standard histories of travel almost always turn to the elite European Grand Tour as a beginning point for the contemporary culture of travel. John Urry maintains in *The Tourist Gaze* that the elite history of travel extends even farther back in history: "This is not to suggest that there was no organized travel in premodern societies, but it was very much the preserve of elites.... In Imperial Rome, for example, a fairly extensive pattern of travel for pleasure and culture existed for the elite.... The Grand Tour had become firmly established by the end of the seventeenth century for the sons of the aristocracy and the gentry, and by the late eighteenth century for the sons of the professional middle class" (4).

This all-too steadfast marriage between travel and privilege is compounded by the tendency of courses focusing on less advantageous occasions for travel—such as exile, nomadism, and diaspora—to often avoid (deliberately?) identifying themselves as travel-literature courses. A University of California, Davis, course, entitled "Literatures of Migration," for example, includes texts that could legitimately constitute travel writing—Salmon Rushdie's *The Satanic Verses*, Zadie Smith's *White Teeth*, and Sebastião Salgado's *Migrations*, but avoids promoting *travel* as a lead term in the course title (Ghosh). Similarly, a course posted on blackboard.com, "History of Immigration and Ethnicity in America," asks students to read Roger Daniels's *Coming to America* but does not directly mention "travel" anywhere in the course description (Ezzo).

Attempting to challenge the narrowness accompanying conventional approaches to travel, a number of scholars have worked to theorize broader visions of what constitutes travel. Regrettably, though, many of these efforts have ultimately only reinforced the privilege too often synonymous with travel and further marginalized literatures of immigration, migration, exile, and diaspora away from the concept of travel. One such attempt to broaden what travel includes and excludes involves differentiating between "travel" and "tourism." A well-known example of this is Fussell's effort to do so in *Abroad,* which results in his making headway in unpacking the semantic distinctions between the terms, but almost no progress at dissociating the intimate connections between leisure and travel. Astoundingly, Fussell instills travel with an even heightened sense of privilege as he reminds readers of the bourgeois nature of mass tourism: "From the outset mass tourism attracted the class-contempt of kill-joys who conceived themselves independent travelers and thus superior by reason of intellect, education, curiosity, and spirit"

(40). Neglecting to distance himself from this group of "kill-joys," Fussell laments, "One by-product of real travel was something that has virtually disappeared, the travel book as a record of an inquiry and a report of the effect of the inquiry on the mind and imagination of the traveler" (39). Lambasting the elitism that undergirds Fussell's assumptions about "real travel," Kaplan maintains in a biting critique of Fussell that "the absence of any Euro-American women writers from Fussell's canon suggests that 'real' travel books (and 'history' and 'truth') are the creation of an elite group of British, male writers between the two World Wars" (54).

Just as Fussell's attempt to differentiate between tourism and travel awards travel an even more profound aura of privilege and falls short of facilitating any real inquiry into travel literature that exists outside of conventional elitist structures, so too do other similar attempts to challenge conventional notions of what constitutes "real" or "worthwhile" travel. Alain de Botton, for instance, in his *The Art of Travel,* takes issue with the notion that travel must involve a departure from home. In his concluding essay, "On Habit," de Botton contrasts Alexander von Humboldt, who narrated his 1799–1804 journey of exploration around South America in *Journey to the Equinoctial Regions of the New Continent,* with Xavier de Maistre, who narrated his 1790 and 1798 treks around his bedroom as, respectively, *Journey around My Bedroom* and *Nocturnal Expedition around My Bedroom.*

While de Botton goes far in discounting notions that travel must involve substantive movement—and thereby expands traditional notions of travel— he nevertheless uses as a counterpoint the relatively well-to-do de Maistre, who enjoys enough comfort and privilege that he can evidently name a room "my bedroom," which implies single proprietorship, autonomous rather than shared space, and additional rooms that presumably make up the rest of his residence. Further delimiting the potentially inclusive idea that travel does not need to involve long, far-away journeys, de Botton's main purpose for showcasing de Maistre is to assert that "the pleasure we derive from the journey may be dependent more on the mind-set we travel with than on the destination we travel *to"* (242, original emphasis). De Botton goes on to suggest that receptivity is the "chief characteristic" of this "mind-set" and that de Maistre's gift to us as readers is that he tries to "shake us from our passivity" (242–43). Such insinuations that travelers should be "receptive" and non-"passive" produce, at heart, the same effect as Fussell's dictum about real travel—they cast the traveler as a privileged observer rather than accommodating the possibility of a real traveler being an unwilling or underprivileged observer.

One popular pedagogical strategy for offsetting the hegemony of elite notions of travel is to foreground grids of power as part of the approach for reading privileged travel texts. This work interrogates the layers of (often subtle) elitism embedded within much travel literature and has been emerging with increasing prominence in the past two decades. However, while inquiries into the power structures supporting travel writing do foreground class issues, upon closer scrutiny they actually emerge as unlikely and unwitting accomplices to the promotion of notions that link travel and privilege. For, as this scholarship showcases the privileges buoying up the authors who write travel texts or the tourists who visit various sites, it simultaneously reifies the impression that travelers and tourists are privileged. This well intentioned work (though inadequate unless subsidized by other types of scholarship) is often most clearly articulated in historical contexts. In *Imperial Eyes,* for example, Mary Louise Pratt positions eighteenth-century travel writing (both scientific and sentimental) as a glorification of the "imperial *I"* (self), who subordinates the Other under perpetual surveillance with the "imperial *eye.*" Similarly, David Spurr reinforces notions that travelers are the elite in *The Rhetoric of Empire,* where he enumerates twelve different strategies of colonial discourse—such as negation, debasement, and idealization— that permeate journalistic accounts, travel writing, and other official documents pertaining to imperial administration.

Offering similar work on a more contemporary basis, Jane Desmond, in *Staging Tourism,* counters the assumption that all Hawaiian visitors are wealthy; she highlights the military personnel stationed there at varying times over the twentieth century and presents research on class codifications of Hawaiian tourists. As she allows for the possibility that many Hawaiian tourists are working or middle class, she also suggests that, despite this range of class status, "the one thing that all four clusters of tourists ['Salt of the Earth,' 'Nest Builders,' 'Achievers,' and 'Attainers'] have in common is their 'whiteness'" (139). She also emphasizes that Hawaiian tourism caters overwhelmingly to heterosexuals: "Complicit with and implicit within this notion of American whiteness is a presumption of heterosexuality" (141). Thus, while Desmond hints at the possibility of a wider range of travelers, she ultimately perpetuates assumptions that travelers are primarily white and relatively privileged.

This is not to say that work by such scholars as Pratt, Spurr, and Desmond is not crucial to understanding, interrogating, and exploring travel literature. Rather, this scholarship merits a vital and well-deserved space in the travel-literature classroom. Offered alone, however, without corresponding insights into unprivileged travelers and travel texts, this scholarship only reinforces assumptions that travel is, in essence, elitist. Instead, such theory should be accompanied by scholarship that interrogates diasporas through a contrapuntal postcolonialism, such as Edward Said's "Reflections on Exile," which promotes "exile not as a privilege, but as an *alternative* to the mass institutions that dominate modern life" (184, original emphasis), Paul Gilroy's *The Black Atlantic,* which traces the movement of (counter)culture throughout the black diaspora, or Homi Bhabha's "Signs taken for wonders," which argues that the "discovery of the book is, at once, a moment of originality and authority. It is, as well, a process of displacement that, paradoxically makes the presence of the book wondrous to the extent to which it is repeated, translated, misread, displaced" (102). It is no coincidence that the latter two of these suggested texts trace the travels of not only people, but also inanimate objects and concepts (i.e., books and music). Re-theorizing travel literature should, as in these examples, allow for the incorporation of inanimate travel.

Another potentially promising approach to generating a more expansive notion of what constitutes travel—one that, as with scholarship such as Pratt's, Spurr's, and Desmond's, similarly requires careful, supplemented application—involves questioning and reconfiguring the genre of travel literature. To a certain degree, such endeavors run the risk of aligning travel literature too closely with fiction and thereby divesting it of many of its real-world implications. Percy Adams's work in *Travel Literature and the Evolution of the Novel* proceeds in this direction, as does Brigid Brophy, who remarks in *In Transit* that travel writing involves "those vertical take-off flights directly out of the present into the never-never tense: fictions" (qtd. in Lawrence 23). Casey Blanton likewise suggests in *Travel Writing* that travel writing borrows extensively from fiction: "A more consciously crafted work of travel literature, while usually existing within a chronological framework, often borrows from the world of fiction to establish motivation, rising and falling action, conflict, resolution, and character" (4). Elton Glaser highlights in "Hydra and Hybrid: Travel Writing as a Genre" the intersections between novelists and travel writers: "Many travel writers today are also novelists, and some of them have obviously drawn on their travel experiences to create their fictions. Most prominent among these writers are V. S. Naipaul and Paul Theroux" (50). Exemplifying the rapid movement from aligning travel with fiction to aligning travel with privilege, Bill Bryson constructs an elite historical trajectory of privileged travel writers: "In Britain, travel writing has long been a mainstay of publishing. Since at least *Smollett's Travels Through France and Italy* (sic), published in 1766, scarcely a writer of note in British literature has not at some time turned his hand to travel writing. Johnson and

Boswell, Lawrence Sterne, Charles Dickens, Charles Darwin, Anthony and Frances Trollope, Robert Louis Stevenson, D. H. Lawrence, E. M. Forster, Evelyn Waugh, George Orwell, Graham Green, Winston Churchill, and others well beyond enumerating all produced travel books, often very good ones" (xxi). As is evident from Bryson's litany of canonical, privileged authors, which grounds travel even more firmly within a western elitist context, the pitfalls that attend linkages between travel and fiction must be negotiated carefully.

A more successful effort at reconfiguring the genre of travel writing beyond privilege involves expanding the genre to include not only fiction, but other genres as well. Bill Buford argues in a 1981 editorial for *Granta* that travel writing "borrows from the memoir, reportage, and most important, the novel" (7). Even Fussell contributes to this dialogue in *Abroad* by positing, "Travel books are a sub-species of memoir" (203). Other theorists have worked to unite travel literature with such genres as history, anthropology, and ethnography. As Bryson maintains, "Write a book or essay that might otherwise be catalogued under memoir, humor, anthropology, or natural history, and as long as you leave the property at some point, you can call it travel writing" (xix). Opening the genre of travel writing often leads to a slightly more expansive and inclusive version of what constitutes travel. Bonnie Frederick and Susan McLeod, for example, include in their anthology *Women and the Journey* the nonfictional fourteenth-century travels of Ibn Battuta alongside Margaret Atwood's *The Handmaid's Tale*. Karen Lawrence unites in *Penelope Voyages* such voyages as Margaret Cavendish's "Assaulted and Pursued Chastity" with Mary Wollstonecraft's *Letters Written during a Short Residence in Sweden, Norway, and Denmark*.

While these examples do not completely wrench travel writing away from modes of privilege, they do pave the way for increasingly inclusive conceptions of what might constitute travel. Expanding the notion of the genre of travel writing might allow a teacher of travel literature to include in her course war and captivity narratives such as Michael Herr's experience of the Vietnam War in *Dispatches*, Bill Daughtery's narrative of his Iranian captivity, *In the Shadow of the Ayatollah*, Michael P. E. Hoyt's trying post as U.S. Consul in Kisangani, *Captive in the Congo*, Mary Rowlandson's "A Narrative of the Captivity and Restoration of Mrs. Mary Rowlandson," or Harriet Jacobs's *Incidents in the Life of a Slave Girl*. Broadening the genre of travel literature might also prompt a travel literature class to focus on exile and nomadism, using such texts as Aciman's *Letters of Transit*, which features "five voices, five tales, five worlds, five lives" (11) of exile, Jane Helleiner's *Irish Travellers*, which documents her experiences in Traveller

camps, Anatoly M. Khazanov and André Wink's collection of articles entitled *Nomads in the Sedentary World,* and Charlotte Kahn's "Emigration
without Leaving Home," which argues that East Germans after the unifica-
tion in 1990 "expressed feelings integrally related to experiences of immigration…emotionally they were immigrants" (255).

Removing the long-standing dissociation that divides privileged and underprivileged modes of travel carries with it some challenges. One such challenge is the obscurity of voices available to tell their own stories. As some of
the above examples testify, many narratives of exile and displacement are
collected by editors who then filter the text through their own lenses. Even
the noble intentions of someone like Zohreh T. Sullivan, who collects stories
of the Iranian disapora for *Exiled Memories,* are still troubled by the fact that
Sullivan must ultimately collect, translate, and edit the stories. Despite this
potential pitfall, however, there are significant benefits to exposing students
in travel-literature classrooms to such narratives. It not only challenges their
assumptions about who travels, but it also raises questions about accessibility
and silence, about vocalization and censorship.

Underscoring another possible sticking point that might attend a more
inclusive conception of travel, bell hooks maintains in *Black Looks* that
"travel is not a word that can be easily evoked to talk about the Middle Passage, the Trail of Tears, the landing of Chinese immigrants, the forced relo-
cation of Japanese-Americans, or the plight of the homeless" (173). Echoing
a similar sentiment, Dean MacCannell insists in his 1989 introduction to *The
Tourist* that "it would be theoretically and morally wrong to equate the
forced nomadism and homelessness of the refugee and the impoverished with
the supercilious voluntaristic Abercrombie and Fitch tourist or other soldiers
of fortune" (xxiii). The concerns expressed by bell hooks and MacCannell
deserve sustained attention. Is it possible to reconstitute travel as more inclusive without diminishing the import and difference that defines less advantageous occasions for and modes of travel?

Offering a beginning point to addressing this question, MacCannell reveals that "if [*The Tourist*] were being written now…several changes *would*
be necessary" (xxii). Among these, MacCannell writes, would be to unpack
the intersections between the tourist he traces throughout his original text and
more contemporary travelers now circulating around the globe: "Today, the
dominant force—if not numerically at least in terms of its potential to re-
shape culture—is the movement of refugees, 'boat people,' agricultural la-
borers, displaced peasants, and others from the periphery to the centers of
power and affluence…. The rapid implosion of the 'Third World' into the
First constitutes a reversal and transformation of the structure of tourism"

(xxii). MacCannell stresses to readers that "the test of the integrity of current research on tourism and modernity will be its contribution to our understanding of these new historical cases" (xxiii). Although his commentary reinforces the privileged position of the conventional "First-World" tourist, MacCannell does acknowledge the power of displaced people to exert and enact change. In so doing, MacCannell's vision simultaneously unifies various types of travelers (tourists and refugees, for example), yet underscores the differences that so importantly fracture monolithic constructs such as "tourist" and "traveler." Thus, MacCannell provides a means of embracing a more expansive notion of travel that carefully avoids obfuscating the very real and important differences that exist among varying travelers and diverse moments of travel.

Unfortunately, however, MacCannell's vision has not yet been realized in the travel-literature classroom. *The Tourist,* in its original form, continues to find implementation as one of the cornerstone texts for travel-literature courses. While much progress has been made in terms of considering who travels, where they travel, and why they travel, the stereotypical image of the traveler remains, regrettably, conflated with a privileged, often leisure-driven tourist or adventurer. Such assumptions about who constitutes travelers and, by extension, what constitutes travel literature, have particular ramifications for the teaching of travel literature. I use travel literature to teach academic writing to first-year students at Duke University. Generally—though not exclusively—students at Duke enjoy relatively privileged positions in comparison to students at many other postsecondary and secondary institutions around the United States. Many students in my classroom have access to multiple family homes across the globe; they have traveled to and/or lived in all five continents; their parents take extended national and international vacations yearly; and they plan to take advantage of Duke's Study Abroad Program so they can live in Europe or Asia for a semester during their junior year. Other students in my classroom, though, have never traveled outside of the country; they may have never been away from home; and their families do not regularly regale them with stories of vacation adventures. Because it is predominantly white and wealthy, the context of the academic-writing classroom at Duke University offers an unparalleled opportunity for using travel literature as a means of encouraging students to critically interrogate their own and others' positions in the world and their relationships to other peoples and places. However, this opportunity would also be immeasurable in a different setting, where students might be less likely to enjoy privilege and status, where students might experience travel literature as also occupying territory familiar to their lived experiences.

Teaching travel literature always presents a potential trap, where I might inadvertently perpetuate and reaffirm long-standing circuitries of privilege and elitism. I find I am continually wondering what is at stake for us as teachers, readers, and students of travel literature. Developing a more inclusive and expansive notion of what constitutes travel facilitates student (and teacher) acknowledgment of difference. Addressing less conventional forms of travel encourages students to foster a broader and keener world view. Although these (understandably) might not be the pedagogical goals of all teachers, working toward a more inclusive notion of travel will, at the very least, challenge errant assumptions that travel exists predominately as a privileged leisure holiday.

Works Cited

Aciman, André, ed. *Letters of Transit. Reflections on Exile, Identity, Language, and Loss.* New York: New York Public Library, 1990.

Aciman, André. "Roman Hours." *The Best American Travel Writing.* Ed. Frances Mayes. Boston: Houghton Mifflin, 2002.1–10.

Adams, Percy G. *Travel Literature and the Evolution of the Novel.* Lexington: UP of Kentucky, 1983.

Anderson, Scott. "Below Canal Street." *The Best American Travel Writing.* Ed. Frances Mayes. Boston: Houghton Mifflin, 2002.11–19.

Atwood, Margaret. *The Handmaid's Tale.* Boston: Houghton Mifflin, 1986.

Battuta, Ibn. *The Travels of Ibn Battuta A.D. 1324–1354.* 3 vols. Ed. H. A. R. Gibb. Cambridge: Hakluyt Society, 1958–1971.

Bhabha, Homi. "Signs Taken for Wonders. Questions of ambivalence and authority under a tree outside Delhi, May 1817." *The Location of Culture.* London: Routledge, 1994. 102–22.

Blanton, Casey. *Travel Writing. The Self and the World.* New York: Twayne, 1997.

Bloom, Lynn Z. *Fact and Artifact. Writing Nonfiction.* 2nd ed. Englewood Cliffs: Prentice Hall, 1994.

Botton, Alain de. *The Art of Travel.* New York: Pantheon, 2002.

Brenan, Gerald. *South from Granada.* London: H. Hamilton, 1957.

Brophy, Brigid. *In Transit: An Heroi-Cyclic Novel.* New York: Putnam, 1969.

Bryson, Bill. Introduction. *The Best American Travel Writing.* Ed. Bill Bryson. Boston: Houghton Mifflin, 2000.

———. *The Lost Continent: Travels in Small-Town America.* New York: Perennial, 1989.

Budget Travel. Advertisement. 20 April 2004 <http://www.magazines-risk-free.com/cover_view.cfm?id=63067&cov=20031001&CFID=15360282&CFTO KEN=26519343&sid=2>.

Buford, Bill. Editorial. *Granta* 10 (winter 1981): 5–7.

Byron, Robert. *The Road to Oxiana.* London: J. Lehmann, 1950.

Cavendish, Margaret [Duchess of Newcastle]. "Assaulted and Pursued Chastity." *Nature's Pictures Drawn by Fancies Pencil to the Life. Book II: Feigned Stories in Prose.* 2nd ed. London: A. Maxwell, 1671.

Clark, Eleanor. *Rome and a Villa.* New York: Pantheon, 1975.

Clifford, James. *Routes. Travel and Translation in the Late Twentieth Century.* Cambridge: Harvard UP, 1997.

Condé Nast Traveler. Advertisement. *The New Yorker.* 3 Feb 2003: 43.

Cubelli, Rose. Early American Explorers. Course home page. 19 Jan 2003 <http://coursesites.blackboard.com/bin/common/search.pl>.

Daniels, Roger. *Coming to America. A History of Immigration and Ethnicity in American Life.* New York: HarperCollins, 1990.

Darwin, Charles. *The Voyage of the Beagle.* New York: Bantam Books, 1972.

Daughterty, William J. *In the Shadow of the Ayatollah. A CIA Hostage in Iran.* Annapolis: Naval Institute P, 2001.

Desmond, Jane. *Staging Tourism. Bodies on Display from Waikiki to Sea World.* Chicago: U of Chicago P, 1999.

Eickstedt, Ingrid. "Travel Orientation for the Yellowstone Region." Course home page. 19 Jan 2003. http://coursesites.blackboard.com/bin/common/search.pl.

Ezzo, Joseph. "History of Immigration and Ethnicity in America." Course home page. 19 Jan 2003 <http://coursesites.blackboard.com/bin/common/content.pl?action =LIST&course_id=_4906>.

Fisher, M.F.K. *Two Towns in Provence.* New York: Vintage, 1964.

Frederick, Bonnie, and Susan McLeod, eds. *Women and the Journey: The Female Travel Experience.* Pullman: Washington State UP, 1993.

Friedman, Devin. "Forty Years in Acapulco." *The Best American Travel Writing.* Ed. Frances Mayes. Boston: Houghton Mifflin, 2002. 97–106.

Fussell, Paul. *Abroad. British Literary Traveling between the Wars.* New York: Oxford UP, 1980.

Fussell, Paul, ed. *The Norton Book of Travel.* New York: Norton, 1987.

Ghosh, Amitav. *In an Antique Land.* New York: Knopf, 1993.

Ghosh, Bishnupriya. "ENL 264 Literatures of Migration." Course home page. Dept. of English, U of California, Davis. 19 Jan 2003 <http://wwwenglish.ucdavis.edu/English/ graduate/spring2003.htm>.

Gilroy, Paul. *The Black Atlantic. Modernity and Double Consciousness.* Cambridge: Harvard UP, 1999.

Glaser, Elton. "Hydra and Hybrid: Travel Writing as a Genre." *North Dakota Quarterly* 59.3 (1991): 348–53.

Gopnik, Adam. "The City and the Pillars." *The Best American Travel Writing.* Ed. Frances Mayes. Boston: Houghton Mifflin, 2002.124–30.

Helleiner, Jane. *Irish Travellers. Racism and the Politics of Culture.* Toronto: U of Toronto P, 2000.

Herr, Michael. *Dispatches.* New York: Knopf, 1978.

hooks, bell. *Black Looks: Race and Representation.* Boston: South End Press, 1992.

Hoyt, Michael P. E. *Captive in the Congo. A Consul's Return to the Heart of Darkness.* Annapolis: Naval Institute P, 2000.

Hulme, Peter. "LT351: Contemporary Travel Writing." Course home page. Dept. of Literature, Film, and Theatre Studies, U of Essex. 19 Jan 2003 <http://www. essex.ac.uk/literature/Current/Teaching/Undergraduate/Undergraduate/lt351. htm>.

Islands. Advertisement. 20 Apr. 2004 <http://www.magazines-risk-free.com/ cover_view.cfm?tid=10099&CFID=15360282&CFTOKEN=26519343&sid=2>.

Iyer, Pico. *Video Night in Kathmandu. And Other Reports from the Not-So-Far East.* New York: Knopf, 1988.

Jacobs, Harriet. *Incidents in the Life of a Slave Girl.* New York: Modern Library, 2000.

Jennings, Jennifer. "e-travel." Course home page. Hallandale High School. 1 Jan 2003 <http://coursesites.blackboard.com/bin/common/content.pl?action=LIST&course_id=_70 98...>.

Kahn, Charlotte. "Emigration without Leaving Home." *Immigrant Experiences.* Ed. Paul H. Elovitz and Charlotte Kahn. Madison, NJ: Fairleigh Dickinson UP, 1997. 255–73.

Kaplan, Caren. *Questions of Travel. Postmodern Discourses of Displacement.* Durham: Duke UP, 1996.

Khazanov, Anatoly M., and André Wink, eds. *Nomads in the Sedentary World.* Richmond: Curzon, 2001.

Kingsley, Mary. *Travels in West Africa, Congo Francais, Corsico, and Cameroons.* London: Cass, 1965.

Kiteley, Brian. "Travel Writing. English 4017: Advanced Creative Writing: Travel Writing." Internet. 19 Jan. 2003. Available http://ww.du.edu/~bkiteley/3017.html.

Kluge, P. F. "Return to Paradise." *National Geographic Traveler.* October 2002: 40–52.

Lawrence, Karen. *Penelope Voyages. Women and Travel in the British Literary Tradition.* Ithaca: Cornell UP, 1994.

The Literature of Travel and Exploration: An Encyclopedia. Advertisement. 19 Jan. 2003 <http://www.amazon.co.uk/exec/obidos/.ASIN/1579582478/202-2930556-5739029>.

MacCannell, Dean. *The Tourist. A New Theory of the Leisure Class.* Berkeley: U of California P, 1999.

Matthiessen, Peter. *The Snow Leopard.* New York: Viking Press, 1978.

Mayes, Frances, ed. *The Best American Travel Writing.* Boston: Houghton Mifflin, 2002.

Moody, Ellen. "English 302: Advanced Writing in the Humanities." Course home page. Dept. of English, George Mason U. 19 Jan 2003 <http://mason.gmu.edu/~emoody/travel.htm>.

Morris, Jan. *Hong Kong.* New York: Random House, 1988.

Netzley, Patricia. *The Encyclopedia of Women's Travel and Exploration.* Westport, CT: Oryx Press, 2001.

Orwell, George. *Homage to Catalonia.* London: Secker & Warburg, 1997.

Pratt, Mary Louise. *Imperial Eyes. Travel Writing and Transculturation.* London: Routledge, 1992.

Robb, Peter. *Midnight in Sicily: On Art, Food, History, Travel & Cosa Nostra.* Boston: Faber and Faber, 1998.

Rowlandson, Mary. *The Narrative of the Captivity and Restoration of Mrs. Mary Rowlandson.* 1682. Boston: Houghton Mifflin, 1930.

Rushdie, Salmon. *The Satanic Verses.* Dover, DE: The Consortium, 1992.

Said, Edward. "Reflections on Exile." *Reflections on Exile and Other Essays.* Cambridge: Harvard UP, 2000. 73–186.

Salgado, Sebastião. *Migrations. Humanity in Transition.* New York: Aperture, 2000.

Secrest, Joseph. "Hospitality & Tourism." Course home page. 19 Jan 2003 <http://coursesites.blackboard.com/bin/common/search.pl>.

Smethurst, Paul. "ENGL2045 Travel Writing." Course home page. Dept. of English, U of Hong Kong. 19 Jan 2003 <http://www.hku.hk/english/courses 2000/2045.htm>.

Smith, Zadie. *White Teeth. A Novel.* New York: Random House, 2000.

Smollett, Tobias George. *Travels through France and Italy.* New York: Oxford UP, 1979.

Speake, Jennifer, ed. *Literature of Travel and Exploration: An Encyclopedia*. New York: Fitzroy Dearborn, 2003.

Spurr, David. *The Rhetoric of Empire. Colonial Discourse in Journalism, Travel Writing, and Imperial Administration*. Durham: Duke UP, 1993.

Steinbeck, John. *Travels with Charley: in Search of America*. New York: Penguin Books, 2002.

Stevenson, Robert Louis. *Travels on a Donkey in the Cevennes. And Selected Travel Writings*. New York: Oxford UP, 1992.

Stone, George W. "Around the World in 80+ Books." *National Geographic Traveler*. April 2002: 63–69.

Sullivan, Zohreh T. *Exiled Memories. Stories of Iranian Diaspora*. Philadelphia: Temple UP, 2001.

Swick, Thomas. "Stolen Blessings." *The Best American Travel Writing*. Ed. Frances Mayes. Boston: Houghton Mifflin, 2002. 316–20.

Theroux, Paul. Introduction. *The Best American Travel Writing*. Ed. Paul Theroux. Boston: Houghton Mifflin, 2001. xvii–xxii.

Urry, John. *The Tourist Gaze. Leisure and Travel in Contemporary Societies*. London: Sage, 1990.

Wollstonecraft, Mary. *Letters Written during a Short Residence in Sweden, Norway, and Denmark*. 1796. Ed. Carol H. Poston. Lincoln: U of Nebraska P, 1976.

Chapter 7

Teaching Travel Literature in the Tourist Age

Jeffrey Alan Melton

[Tourism] spoils all rational travel; it disgusts all intelligent curiosity; it repels the student, the philosopher, and the manly investigator, from subjects which have been thus trampled into mire by the hoofs of a whole tribe of traveling bipeds, who might rejoice to exchange brains with the animals which they ride.

— "Modern Tourism," *Blackwood's Magazine* (1848)

People here in Western Civilization say that tourists are no different from apes, but on the Rock of Gibraltar,... I saw both tourists and apes together, and I learned to tell them apart.

— Paul Theroux, *The Pillars of Hercules* (1995)

The epigraphs above typify a pervasive and often passionate disdain for tourists long held in western culture, and such attitudes show no sign of abating. Although the comments are separated by almost a hundred and fifty years, the sentiments are the same: Tourists are a particularly low form of animal.[1]

For the editors of *Blackwood's Magazine,* tourists represent an all-out assault upon higher civilization itself. Emphasizing their position by using strong verbs such as "spoils," "disgusts," and "repels," the editors assert that tourists stand in opposition to any "rational" traveler, who is a "student," "philosopher," and "manly investigator." (Let's leave aside the problems with "manly investigator" for another time.) Tourists, "traveling bipeds," would benefit, it would seem, from trading gray matter with the donkeys they ride. Paul Theroux, a well-known crank who is also a first-rate travel writer, grants tourists a raise in the evolutionary chain by comparing them to apes rather than mules. Late-twentieth-century tourists, indeed, can be distinguished from lower primates—but only with a practiced pair of eyes. I call that an improvement.

The issues raised by these two quotations are crucial to any student of travel literature. Tourism and travel writing share a vital and undeniable co-existence that is symbiotic in nature. This intertwining, however, is an uneasy interdependency. Travel writers over the generations, as well as scholars and teachers, have chosen most often to ignore the connection. They do so for compelling and understandable reasons, but their positions, nonetheless, remain illegitimate and unnecessarily reductive. Examining the cultural and theoretical relationship between tourism and travel writing not only helps broaden our understanding of both, but it also serves as a natural and fruitful starting point for discussing travel writing in the classroom.

Few avenues of inquiry intrigue students of travel writing more consistently than tourism. For me, it has become the essential first step rather than an appendix to reading travel. Its primary advantage is that students come into the class well aware of the popular perceptions of stereotypical tourist behavior. Even for those who have traveled little, tourism conjures clear, powerful images. They have learned also to denigrate tourist behavior. That context is useful and helps set up an automatically energetic class discussion based on one simple factual assertion: we are all tourists. Few people readily accept being called tourists, and I suspect that some readers here embrace it only with reservations. Similarly, few literary travel writers appreciate it either. This resistance provides a helpful starting point for talking about tourism and its uneasy but inevitable relationship with travel writing, and, furthermore, its intrinsic place within all travel narratives. First, however, I would like to scrutinize the history of the trouble with tourists.

Tourists or Travelers?

"Don't be a tourist," advised a high-rotation commercial in the mid-to-late 1990s for *The Travel Channel,* a popular cable television network that offers travel documentaries, promotions, and information. These words convey two messages simultaneously: the direct one encourages viewers to tune into *The Travel Channel* to learn about foreign cultures and thereby avoid mistakes and embarrassing situations while traveling; the indirect one encourages viewers to stay at home and watch the rest of the world from the comfort of their armchairs. "Don't be a tourist," indeed. We need also to consider a third implication, a message that has been intertwined with the tourist mentality since the beginning of the boom in the mid-nineteenth century. The subtext of the direct message reads: by learning of foreign cultures—by watching television in this case—one can transcend being a "tourist" (a lowly creature) to become a "traveler" (an altogether impressive creature). The promotion taps into one of the most pervasive sentiments of this touristic era: Everybody wants to travel, but nobody wants to be a tourist. As Dean MacCannell, in his seminal study *The Tourist* (1976), wryly states, "tourists dislike tourists" (10).

Our cultural ambivalence toward tourism has engendered an ongoing battle between "travelers" and "tourists," a struggle for self-identification that ultimately exists only semantically. The word *tourist* has been around for quite awhile (*The Oxford English Dictionary* cites the earliest reference in 1780), yet it did not begin to take on widespread negative connotations until the mid to late nineteenth century, coinciding with the astounding increase in the numbers of tourists moving energetically around the globe.

As the tourist movement became firmly rooted in the United States, cultural critics echoed *Blackwood's* disgust. Henry James, in his "Americans Abroad," regrets the tourist boom and laments how, in his view, it reflects poorly on the nation as a whole. He writes, "a very large proportion of the Americans who annually scatter themselves over Europe are by no means flattering to the national vanity. Their merits, whatever they are, are not of a sort that strikes the eye—still less the ear. They are ill-made, ill-mannered, ill-dressed" (209). Thus begins the notion of the "ugly American." Interestingly, James goes on to note that the American tourist travels to Europe as "a provincial who is terribly bent upon taking, in the fulness of ages, his revenge" (209). Perhaps, James is correct; if so, the American "revenge" upon Europe in the tourist age continues well over a hundred years later, best evidenced by Euro-Disney.

The great movement itself created its own self-loathing. Critics have long recognized this struggle and illustrate the deep, abiding desire to distinguish between desirable travelers and undesirable tourists. Among twentieth-century cultural critics, Daniel Boorstin provides the most energetic and aggressive defense of the separation between traveler and tourist identity.[2] By emphasizing the historical connections between *travel* and *travail,* he reminds us that in effect to travel is to work, thus making a crucial distinction: The traveler is active, and, by contrast, the tourist is forever passive. Travelers seek and earn experience, while tourists sign up for a program and sit back to wait for experiences to come to them. For travelers, there is work to be done; it will not be easy, but it promises rewards worth the discomfort. This image is powerful and attractive; it is also romantic—the lone traveler enduring trials and tribulations because he or she has to— "because it's there." Many of us are up for the ideal, but few, really, are up to the actual physical and emotional challenge such a self-image requires in practice. For tourists, there is little work to be done; it will be easy, and it promises comfort. Though this image may attract our more hedonistic urges, it does, nonetheless, suffer aesthetically in comparison to the romantic traveler.

Students see themselves as travelers, even if they have done very little of it. As I cover the history of the tourist-versus-traveler culture war, I ask students to define tourists, first in groups then to the class as a whole. They quickly fill up the chalkboard with characteristic habits of tourists and the countering behaviors of travelers. They also bring in pictures of their own travels or images from newspapers, magazines, and comic strips. They quickly realize the pervasiveness of popular culture images of tourists. These images have made differentiating between "traveler" and "tourist" easy for students, and this ease helps me set up the first difficult assertion: The words are synonyms. Before they are willing to consider this point, however, I ask for more indulgence as I try to move beyond touristic behavior to touristic experience.

Tourist Experience and Authenticity

Although tourists have earned derision for generations, they may deserve some sympathy. Walker Percy, in his essay "The Loss of the Creature," offers an interesting appraisal of the dilemma facing modern tourists. In referring to the Grand Canyon, he questions whether any of us can approach the same sense of wonder—the authentic sense of discovery—that the first Spanish explorer, Garcia Lopez de Cardenas, felt upon his encounter. Using "P" to denote the value of the authentic discovery, Percy asserts, "if the place is seen by a million sightseers, a single sightseer does not receive value P but a millionth part of value P" (46). The primary reason for this devaluation is not only the numbers of tourists but also the amount of information that we unavoidably carry with us as we go to the canyon. We store a complex, deeply rooted collection of data that creates in us expectations of "The Grand Canyon" —an image in addition to a geological phenomenon. Cut by the churning of the Colorado River, this remarkable canyon itself changed in human perception when it became "grand." We can see the canyon, therefore, not for what it is but for what we have been told it is (by travel writers among others). The "symbolic machinery" (49), as Percy phrases it, that creates our expectations and informs us also causes a "loss of sovereignty" (54). We are, as a result, no longer in charge of our experience, and the more we travel (and the more we read travel writing), the more we risk losing the horizon.

I do not mean to denigrate travel writing; rather, I am trying to urge students of it to embrace its implicit imaginative power. Breaking down the self-imposed separation with the essential realities of tourism, to my mind, helps move readers toward this goal. Percy's lament introduces an important point. Though we should probably apply the value "P" not to a Spanish explorer but to an unknown Native American, Percy's example still illustrates intuitively that the trouble with tourism, in this sense, is the trouble with travel writing. The pervasiveness of both undermines the value of the seen. This paradox affects anyone who follows another, and, with very few exceptions, we are followers. Even Neil Armstrong in taking his first small step on the moon did so with expectations derived from extensive training and based on copious advance research. This frustration, of course, is not a new one. Mark Twain, in *The Innocents Abroad* (1869), confronts the issue as he tours Rome:

> What is it that confers the noblest delight? What is that which swells a man's breast with pride above that which any other experience can bring him? Discovery! To know that you are walking where none others have walked; that you are beholding what human eye has not seen before; that you are breathing a virgin atmosphere.... To be the *first*—that is the idea. (266, original emphasis)

Mark Twain, arguably the finest American travel writer of the nineteenth century, in celebrating the thrill of discovery, also recognizes that for the tourist—even at the beginning of the tourist age—such a feeling is unavailable. He continues, "what is there in Rome for me to see that others have not seen before me? What is there for me to touch that others have not touched? What is there for me to feel, to learn, to hear, to know, that shall thrill me before it pass to others? What can I discover? —Nothing. Nothing whatsoever" (267).

After discussing Percy's assertion that no fully authentic sense of discovery is available to any of us, whether we define ourselves as travelers or tourists, students are generally ready to investigate their own experiences when they travel. I continue with the Grand Canyon as a primary example because students know it so well. I say that, though I rarely encounter a student who has been there. They know "The Grand Canyon"; that is, they know the remarkable postcard image (it's called "grand," after all). I cannot say the phrase without an image popping in their minds (as it pops in your mind as you read and mine as I write). If students are heretofore hesitant to accept Percy's observation, they begin to understand a difference in experience. Indeed, they easily recognize that they cannot have the same experience of seeing the canyon for the first time; they already know that it is "grand," and they already know that they should be impressed. If they ever stand on the rim of the canyon, will they be disappointed that their view is not quite as "grand" as the postcard image?

At this point, I ask students if they have ever been disappointed by a tourist sight?[3] The answer is always "yes," but the key is for students to explore why they were disappointed. I also ask them to look for moments of disappointment in the travel narratives we are reading; such passages are omnipresent. In exploring this staple of travel writing, students may begin both to accept that tourism is an intrinsic part of the genre and to recognize a connection with travel writers themselves. Assessing the causes of such disenchantment is more difficult, however. The most common impression (beyond complaints about inconvenience and discomfort) is that the sight is a sham, somehow inauthentic. To address this problem, we first need to consider what motivates tourists.

No matter what term we choose to describe ourselves as we travel, all tourists in one form or another seek to escape from their daily lives, but it remains unclear precisely what it is they escape to. How do the back-packing tourists, the automobile tourists, the bus tourists, and even the vicarious tourists at home respond to their travels? The seminal study of the behaviors and assumptions implicit in mass tourism is Dean MacCannell's *The Tourist,* which remains invaluable in examining how we define tourist experience. Rejecting any reductive dismissal of touristic behavior, MacCannell argues that tourists deserve critical attention rather than condescension. Moreover, their search is definitive of modernist western culture, and as such offers opportunity for deeper understanding of that culture's values. He notes, as well, that, despite the protestations from the good-old-days-of-travel camp (represented here by Boorstin and Percy), all tourists seek "deeper involvement" with the cultures they visit "to some degree" (10). The phrase "to some degree" is a crucial one. For those who insist on an absolute distinction between traveler and tourist, MacCannell allows for some solace. Yes, everyone is a tourist, but there are variations of behavior within that realm.[4] One tourist's desire for "deeper involvement" with the Grand Canyon, for example, may be satisfied by a cursory glance over the edge before a return to the gift shop; another's degree of interest may only be met by a ten-day hike down into the canyon itself.

As beautiful as much of the Grand Canyon landscape is, it remains, after all, a desert. It is hot and dry. Conveniently, though, the gift shops have air conditioning and ice cream. The tourist at the Grand Canyon who has little interest in moving beyond the ready-made, programmed sights from the rim prefers to remain always near comfort that closely resembles home. The tourist who chooses to hike deeply into the canyon itself prefers to forego his or her normal amenities and escape from the solace of home, momentarily. They are both tourists, but the question remains: how should we define their disparate experiences? Is one more "authentic" —real—than the other?

Henry David Thoreau can help us with this query. According to *Walden* (1854), one of the most provocative and challenging travel books ever written, Thoreau went to the woods to "live deliberately" and thus avoid coming to the end of his life only to realize, too late, that he "had not lived," that he had remained too passive, too comfortable (90–91). By expressing his desire "to suck out all the marrow of life," Thoreau perfectly encapsulates the ideal of the romantic traveler. Still, it is important to remember that he had plenty of help, being only a few miles from Concord, and that his stay was temporary. In any case, is such an experience truly still available? We may appreciate Thoreau's rather local traveling and his two-year-two-month experiment on Walden Pond, but few modern readers opt for his brand of travel even if they embrace his desire "to live deliberately." Moreover, there are few ponds like his Walden around (Walden itself perennially faces the prospect of development), and few of us, for that matter, have a friend like Ralph Waldo Emerson who owns lakefront property. (Students are always ready to point out these problems with Thoreau's narrative arguments.) The impulse to argue for authentic experience remains, and students, despite their willing disdain for Thoreau (mainly because he is so challenging), they wish, still, to argue for some touristic authenticity that can be achieved through specific behavior. I offer the following points for their consideration.

Some tourists may alter the form and diverge from the masses (and boldly call themselves "travelers"), but they are part of the ritual nonetheless. If a few tourists seek to reject the cultural production, they are put in a difficult position because few sights remain off the beaten path. What are their options? Should they avoid the Grand Canyon, the Statue of Liberty, the Sphinx, the Great Wall, all highly ritualized sights? Even if these tourists eschew such well-marked sights, the question remains: why? Are they rebelling against programmed travel? If so, the program, nonetheless, shapes their itinerary as they consciously (desperately) try to avoid it.

There may be another way to get around the program, though. For example, a tourist may live with a family in the Yucatan—eat, sleep, and work with them. She may be like a chameleon and change from tourist, to guest, to friend and come much closer in the process to an authentic experience. However, one day—in a week, a month, or a year—she will return home. She knows this all along, and so do her hosts. This knowledge alone alters the experience, differentiates between her and everyone else. Therefore, if she writes a travel narrative expounding on her authentic knowledge of real life in Yucatan, readers should pause. Because tourists, by definition, are outsiders, they can never know pure authenticity. The essence of any touristic experience, that it is a temporary condition, will inevitably re-enter her consciousness, and the illusion of authenticity, however strengthened by extended personal—even intimate—contact, will be shattered. There is no escaping this reality of the tourist age, even for travel writers and readers. This assertion does not dismiss her narrative, but it demands recognition that the genre has limitations that can be negotiated but never erased.

Nonetheless, we share Thoreau's basic desire to touch "essential facts of life," and this craving manifests itself most often in the tourist age as a search for authenticity. If we cannot match the ideal (and delusory) image of romantic traveling, we can at least tour places that promise genuine experiences vicariously. MacCannell argues that this quest is definitive of modernity and belies an intuitive belief that life in western civilization itself is devoid of authentic experience due, ironically, to our political, technological, and social successes. Tourists, then, seek it elsewhere, in more primitive cultures or in the past. Herein is the key to the ultimate and inescapable failure of tourism: no matter how often it promises authenticity, it can never deliver, and, moreover, it never did, even when tourists called themselves travelers, even when the trees grew dense and undisturbed on the shores of Walden Pond.

At this point, I encourage students (in groups) to produce three lists of popular tourist sights: one each for the state, the nation, and the world. They should not edit their list to fit any personal preferences; rather, they should aim for consensus. I generally discourage sights like ski resorts or beach resorts, places where the draw is dominated by recreational appeal, sights that, likewise, draw few literary travel writers. Also, I ask that they be somewhat specific and write "the Eiffel Tower" rather than "Paris." The goal behind this exercise is to set up a discussion about reasons behind the popularity of certain sights. One point becomes evident almost immediately: the lists are dominated by sights with historical significance. Moreover, the world list contains many sights that are defined by a cultural curiosity for distinctive native populations. Students enjoy this exercise and quickly embrace a discussion about how they made their choices. The next step is for them to make a wish list for personal travel. They write down five places that they would like to visit and why. This process begs the question: Are their individual choices truly their own?

At this point, students may be wondering if there is any point to traveling or even reading about it. They may even wonder if I really enjoy travel literature. I do, and for many reasons. The primary attraction for me, though, is the feature of travel writing that comes directly from the realities of tourism. Because tourists are always outsiders, because they are always shut out of the authentic experiences of native cultures, because they know so little, they must delve into their imaginations. When those tourists choose to write narratives to share their experiences with readers, their imaginations bring us along, and that opens up the world.

The Play's the Thing: Imagination and Tourism

So what is the tourist to do? To try answering this question, we can begin by using one of Shakespeare's most memorable lines: "All the world's a stage, and we are merely players." The bard's analogy for life applies as well to tourism in that it requires staging and play-acting. The search for the impression of authenticity relies on careful staging and meticulous production design. Tour promoters and sight marketers, among others, have long recognized the drawing power of "authenticity," and they have touted it accordingly— "see live killer whales!" (in a concrete pool) or "watch a real Hawaiian luau" (in the hotel courtyard).[5] Authenticity is a commodity of the tourist age, and its presentation is a cultural production wherein tourists are willing and necessary participants.

Consider, for a moment, a re-enactment of the 19 April 1775 battle between colonial minutemen and British regulars, a popular tourist production in Concord, Massachusetts. If this "play" is "real" enough, then the onlookers have gained a typical tourist experience, and the cultural production is complete. Of course, different tourists may have different standards of authenticity (as in the example of the Grand Canyon), and their reactions could easily range from "I could feel the tension of the battle" to "I really doubt that the real minutemen wore digital watches." In either case, the show must go on, and so must the tourists. The next "battle" will be in a few hours, and the next sight is just down the road at a pond called Walden.

At this juncture in the class discussion, I urge students to expound upon their own disappointments and characterize their own responses to particular sights. It may also be productive to have students go to a local sight. If available, it should be one that is well known, one for which they already have established expectations. If no such sight exists locally, pick one and provide them with exhaustive information before they see it. After they make their trips, they should write their own short narrative focusing on their responses as they visit the sight. I try to focus the class discussions on failures in the trip and how the actual place differed from their expectations. This activity will help students recognize the importance of imagination to any touristic experience.

The Concord battle re-enactment may garner another reaction from the tourist, one that is more directly fundamental to the nature of tourist experience, especially as it relates to travel writing: "It is just as I had imagined the battle to be." The expectations with which we visit a sight cannot help but influence our reaction to it. However, it is difficult to separate our imagination from our concept of the real, especially when it comes to historical re-enactments, wherein tourists are not only separated from a place but also from a time. Until someone invents real time-travel, we simply cannot touch the original experience of the battle in Concord, and we can never hear the "shot heard around the world." In addition, even if someone perfects actual time travel, we could only witness the event distanced by our knowledge of how the day turns out. So we are stuck, and we can only try to gather as much information as we choose to, and then, as spectators, imagine the experiences of others.

This battle re-enactment, what Boorstin would call a "pseudo-event," is central to tourism, and although it is a staged production, a "play," it becomes associated nevertheless with the authentic, not because of its accuracy so much as because many people see it.[6] The authenticity of any sight, then, increases with each tourist moving through the turnstiles. Sticking with the battle example, we can see that tourists do not simply travel to Concord to see the re-enactment and experience the actual day of 19 April 1775. More significantly, they go because of all that has followed that original event—the starting of the Revolutionary War, the founding of a nation, and the founding of a tourist sight and the building of an elaborate tourist apparatus, roads, guide-maps, hotels, historical markers, and so on—and the re-enactment is but a part of it.

Any touristic production, in addition to asking for imaginative leaps from the audience, also implicitly asks for what I call touristic faith, a phrase adapted from Coleridge's "poetic faith," wherein readers experience a "willing suspension of disbelief." Touristic faith, likewise, implies that tourists ignore that they are watching a production, that they willingly dismiss their skepticism and pretend to believe, at least for the moment, that they are gaining an authentic experience.

We have forever enjoyed travel as a metaphor for life, one in which we move through an often strange landscape and in the process see, hear, smell, and touch new experiences. We learn and grow wiser. Ostensibly, that is why we want to travel, whether we move across oceans or ponds. We all want, at least aesthetically, to suck the marrow from life. Implicit in this desire, however, is the assumption that such experiences are innately authentic simply because they stand in seeming opposition to the modernity of our everyday lives. They are not. No intellectual meditation or wordplay between "traveler" and "tourist" can change this definitive fact of the tourist age. This assertion, however, does not remove the potential value of touring; it simply updates Shakespeare's line and casts travel writers and readers alike in a remarkably varied play called tourism. The play's the thing.

Reading with the Eyes of a Tourist

This context offers readers of travel narratives much room to explore the play itself and their roles in it, influencing their interaction with any travel narrative. It adds a provocative component to their reading no matter which travel narratives are on the syllabus. Once students have worked through the theoretical context and have investigated their own attitudes about tourists and their experiences as tourists, they are ready to examine travel texts. As they read, they will be surprised (pleasantly, I hope) at the wealth of material within any travel narrative that is influenced by a touristic context. I generally ask for them to search for three major types of passages.

First, I ask them to look for tourists. The students should be especially sensitive to remarks by narrators concerning tourist behavior, whether the writers denigrate others or mock themselves (Mark Twain, for example, is masterful at both). Students also are wary of the points of view the narrators adopt in any given situation and their tone. Are they within a group? Are they separated physically from the objects or peoples they describe? Second, I ask students to cull out points of disappointment confessed by narrators and consider the causes and implications. Is the narrator fatigued or frustrated? How does the narrator assign blame for the disappointment? Is he or she fair and accurate? Third, and most importantly, I ask students to search for imaginative passages wherein narrators capture a place by freeing themselves of the disappointments of concrete details and wherein they challenge the imaginations of readers.

The first two groups of passages are quite fun to discuss, and students enjoy it. The third group, however, is the one that hooks them on travel writing. As we discuss them, students may have a harder time explaining why they chose a particular passage, but as they talk, for the most part, I see that they understand what I discovered long ago. If I am lucky, I see that they are curious about the world and their place in it in a romantic way after all. Tourism did not take that away; it simply made it necessary.

The Trouble with Tourists

At some point in a section considering the role of tourism in travel writing, students typically question why I love travel literature and, more importantly to them, why they must read it. I have to acknowledge that, given how hard we work undermining the reality of tourist experience, their skepticism is valid. Once a particularly bright student caught me off guard after I had taken the class through the theoretical material. He asked, "If travelers are really tourists, why do you still call it 'travel writing' rather than 'tourist writing'?"

(Insert uncomfortable pause here.) It was a good question, and I muttered an answer emphasizing that my point was not to remove "travel" or "traveler" from our lexicon but to remove false distinctions that ignore the intrinsic role tourism plays in travel writing (or tourist writing). Using "traveler" is only a problem if one believes that doing so removes the respective traveler from a touristic context.

That was the right answer, but I hesitated because I honestly did not want to call it tourist writing (I did not admit that to the class). I was convinced intellectually that the terms were interchangeable and that any difference was arbitrary and misleading, but I still felt a difference. I am at peace with the inconsistency now and continue to use "travel" writing because doing so does not ignore the touristic context, and moreover, to insist on "tourist" writing would inevitably cause confusion between narratives and advertising copy. Still, I should warn anyone who puts tourists in the classroom; they can be trouble.

Notes

1   The first epigraph appears in "Modern Tourism," *Blackwood's Magazine*, 64.394 (1848): 185. This passage comes from an essay bemoaning not simply the pervasiveness of tourists but also of travel narratives. The essay is particularly critical of women travel writers and focuses on Harriet Martineau at length. The second epigraph is from Paul Theroux, *The Pillars of Hercules* (New York: Putnam, 1995) 1. The passage is in the opening paragraph of a narrative chronicling a trip around the Mediterranean Sea.

2   See Daniel Boorstin, *The Image: A Guide to Pseudo-Events in America* (New York: Atheneum, 1985). Boorstin's comments are in the chapter "From Traveler to Tourist," which argues that tourism threatens to undermine our ability to distinguish between reality and image; as a result, we increasingly crave shallow experiences. See also, Maxine Feifer, *Tourism in History* (New York: Stein & Day, 1986).

3   Throughout this essay, I use "sight" rather than "site" to indicate the place of a touristic experience. Although "site" may indicate a physical location, it cannot cover the broader implications of touristic behavior discussed in this essay. Tourists are, after all, sightseers. This use of "sight" is well established. In addition to the *Oxford English Dictionary*, see, for examples, Paul Fussell, "From Exploration to Travel to Tourism," *Abroad: British Literary Traveling between the Wars* (New York: Oxford UP, 1980) 37–50; and Jonathan Culler, "The Semiotics of Tourism," *Framing the Sign: Criticism and Its Institutions* (Norman: Oklahoma UP, 1988) 153–67.

4   Erik Cohen, "A Phenomenology of Tourist Experiences," *Sociology* 13 (1979): 179–201. Cohen builds on MacCannell and argues for a broader definition of tourists, identifying five modes of tourist behavior: recreational, diversionary, experiential, experimental, and existential. The first two modes revolve around a partial escape from the daily life of the tourist, and the remaining modes represent varying degrees of the tourist's need to alter identity.

5   MacCannell, *The Tourist: A New Theory of the Leisure Class* (1976, Berkeley: U of California P, 1999) offers an extended discussion of authenticity, especially p. 105.

6   For helpful discussions of authenticity, see MacCannell, *The Tourist,* especially 14–15; Boorstin, *The Image,* especially 252; Cohen, "A Phenomenology of Tourist Experiences" and "Authenticity and Commoditization in Tourism," *Annals of Tourism Research* 15.3 (1988): 371–86; and Chris Ryan, "The Tourist Experience," *Recreational Tourism* (London: Routledge, 1991) 35–49.

Works Cited

Boorstin, Daniel. *The Image: A Guide to Pseudo-Events in America.* New York: Atheneum, 1985.

Cohen, E[rik]. "A Phenomenology of Tourist Experiences." *Sociology* 13.2 (1979): 179–201.

Culler, Jonathan."The Semiotics of Tourism." *Framing the Sign: Criticism and Its Institutions.* Norman: Oklahoma UP, 1988. 153–67.

Feifer, Maxine. *Tourism in History.* New York: Stein & Day, 1986.

Fussell, Paul. "From Exploration to Travel to Tourism." *Abroad: British Literary Traveling between the Wars.* New York: Oxford UP, 1980. 37–50.

James, Henry. "Americans Abroad." *The Nation* 27.692 (3 October 1878): 208–9.

MacCannell, Dean. *The Tourist: A New Theory of the Leisure Class.* 1976. Berkeley: U of California P, 1999.

"Modern Tourism." *Blackwood's Magazine* 64.394 (August 1848): 185–89.

Percy, Walker. "The Loss of the Creature." *The Message in the Bottle.* New York: Farrar, Straus, and Giroux/Noonday Press, 1975, 1997. 46–63.

Ryan, Chris. "The Tourist Experience." *Recreational Tourism.* London: Routledge, 1991. 35–49.

Theroux, Paul. *The Pillars of Hercules.* New York: Putnam, 1995.

Thoreau, Henry David. *Walden.* Ed. J. Lyndon Shanley. Princeton: Princeton UP, 1971.

Twain Mark. *The Innocents Abroad.* 1869. The Oxford Mark Twain. Ed. Shelley Fisher Fishkin. New York: Oxford UP, 1996.

Part III

Outside the Traditional Classroom

Chapter 8

"I Wake to Sleep": Traveling in the Wilderness with Writing Students

John Bennion and Burton Olsen

In *Walden,* Thoreau writes, "I have traveled a good deal in Concord" (4), proving with his essays and his life the importance of local travel. More recent natural history writers have emphasized that essential discoveries come from close observation of the home region. Edward Abbey made the nation conscious of the beauty of the red rock arches and canyons in the West. In similar manner Annie Dillard pioneered on Tinker Creek in Virginia; Wendell Berry helped readers explore the Red River Valley in Kentucky; Gary Snyder through his writing reveals the Rockies of Northern California; and Terry Tempest Williams has claimed as her literary territory the Bear River Bird Refuge on the edge of the Great Salt Lake. As Dillard states, "Like the bear who went over the mountain, I went out to see what I could see. . . . I am no scientist. I explore the neighborhood" (11). Through Wilderness Writing—a program formed out of a partnership between the Youth Leadership and Recreation Management Department, the English Department, and the Honors Program at Brigham Young University—we have discovered that a combination of traveling locally, reading natural history essays, and writing meditative narratives transforms students in unpredictable ways: a woman with agoraphobia finds the inner strength to walk down a steep, slick rock canyon; a man ready to summit turns back to help some behind him who are becoming wet and cold, in danger of hypothermia; a woman from the East with a prejudice against the Utah desert learns solace in the pine forest on Mt. Nebo.

The program consists of two classes: an honors writing class and an introductory recreation management class. In the recreation class we take the students into the wilderness; in the writing class the students read natural history essays and write about their experiences. Utah is exceptionally rich with red rock, Alpine, and desert areas. We have hiked in Zions National Park (the Narrows and the Subway), Grand-Staircase National Park (Coyote Gulch and Calf Creek Falls), and the San Rafael Swell Wilderness Study Area (Virgin Springs Canyon, Devil's Canyon, Eagle Canyon, the Lower Black Box, Cow and Calf Canyons, Wildhorse and Bell Canyon, and Goblin Valley). We have day-hiked in canyons close to our campus, explored Nutty Putty Cave, kay-aked through the rushes at the edge of Utah Lake, built snow caves high in Utah and Sanpete counties, and snowshoed and skied in the Uintah and Wa-satch mountains. We have backpacked to some of the highest peaks in Utah: Timpanogas, Nebo, Deseret, and Ibapah. We have watched a biologist tag bears in the Book Cliffs of Ashley National Forest.

How do we open students' eyes to what is there? How do we introduce them to wild environments and return safely? These are the questions we propose to explore in this essay, primarily through an examination of two student narratives. Both were written after a backpacking trip in October of 1999 to Deep Creek Canyon, close to the border between Utah and Nevada. One essayist describes an epiphany experienced after leaving the group and walking at night alone; the other describes a situation that felt emotionally edgy to her. From these two we can begin to discover the effect on students of an unfamiliar natural environment.

Student Journals
Case #1, Andres

In the following extract a young man, Andres Almendariz, climbs up to the top of a massive chunk of granite where he has a transcendent experience. We encourage students to walk in pairs, and we would ardently discourage climbing unprotected in the dark. However, he attributes part of his exhilaration to stepping outside the rules and being in some degree of danger. Early in his essay, Andres describes his desire to leave the campfire where the other students are talking and telling stories. He wants to have some alone time, so he heads off into the night.

I wanted to turn my flashlight on, not knowing exactly what the bleak darkness promised to present, but I kept it off. Somehow the thought of navigating my way in the dark intrigued me. The adrenalin associated with the thrill of the dangerous terrain was driving me forward. Relying on past experiences of overcoming physical challenges such as this one, I rationalized away any real possibility of personal injury. I had somehow broken the bounds of normal human experience, and the thought endowed me with a power to traverse the slope.... I imagined that I was in a professional rock-climbing contest and found the courage to keep climbing. I began scrambling up a crack that ran up the face of the rock.... Although the rock's surface was rough and covered in barnacles I kept a good pace. After about twenty feet up, the crack shrunk (sic) *until it measured no more than two feet wide....*

Finally, through some frightening gymnastics, he pulls himself to the top of the huge granite boulder. He continues:

The display of celestial splendor that played out above my weary body was spectacular. I don't believe that what I felt can be effectively put into words.... My body felt like a balloon being filled with helium, and for a moment I was afraid that I would burst and splatter myself all over the universe. The stars pulled at my desire to stay within myself. I felt my will to stay on this planet slowly being consumed. I desired to live a lifetime as bright and memorable as the stars I was gazing upon....

I nearly lost my balance trying to gaze up towards Ibapah Peak, shrouded in a gray haze as it towered over me in the silence of the night. I salvaged my equilibrium, with the help of a sustaining boulder, and realized that I had come within inches of falling from the top of the granite temple. This reality rushed over me like nausea, and I dropped to my knees.

Lying back on the incline of the boulder I felt a need to chant.... The magical beauty of the high pitches I achieved with my voice transcended me (sic) to another realm of spirituality. I was a part of the human family, in a mystical place where ethnicity and the color line did not exist. Speaking words that I did not know vocally, but understand intrinsically with my heart, I became enthralled in the chorus of shouts and lulls that accompanied my praise.

Spiritual fatigue, combined with mental and physical exhaustion of limb and cranium, made me feel as if I had just completed a championship-wrestling match.... But with this fatigue came a power of sound, of environment, and of memory that synergized enough to propel me into another reality. So focused in its aim of discovery, whatever I wished to be true and applicable existed in this realm, and everything else became irrelevant. My re-creation of this consumed me with spiritual illumination....

While Andres's heightened awareness depended on being outside convention and the rules of safe outdoor behavior, it also grew out of what he'd observed before and out of his view of the stars, undimmed by any close city lights. He had this experience because he stepped away from the other students and made himself available to the shower of beauty. Gary Snyder in *A Place in Space* describes the pleasure of living open to the influences of the natural world. He writes, "permeability, porousness, works both ways. You are allowed to move through the woods with new eyes and ears when you let go of your little annoyances and anxieties. Maybe this is what the great Buddhist philosophy of interconnectedness means when it talks of 'things moving about in the midst of each other without bumping'" (198). Openness to the environment may be instinctive but so are mistrust and fear. The reading done by Andres in the class made him open to a positive interpretation of his adrenaline rush and the expanse of the stars. Other students, reluctant to be alone in the strange place, had different, perhaps less ecstatic experiences. Still their perceptual faculties were aroused by the foreign environment, and this alertness helped most of them to produce strong essays, essays which generally become meditative.

In "The Journey's End," Wendell Berry describes how he felt upon first entering the drainage of the Red River Gorge. "The strangeness, as I recognized after a while, for I went in flying no flag and riding no machine, was all in me. It was my own strangeness that I felt, for I was a man out of place. . . . It became possible for me to leave the place as it is, to want it to be as it is, to be quiet in it, to learn about it and from it" (227). Later as the place becomes familiar to him, he writes,

> Our fear has ceased to be the sort that accompanies hate and contempt and the ignorance that preserves pride; it has begun to be the fear that accompanies awe, that comes with the understanding of our smallness in the presence of wonder, that teaches us to be respectful and careful. And it is a fear that is accompanied by love. We have lost our lives as in our pride we wanted them to be, and have found them as they are—much smaller than we hoped, much shorter, much less important, much less certain, but also more abundant and joyful. We have ceased to think of the world as a piece of merchandise, and have begun to know it as an endless adventure and a blessing. (232)

To produce good writing, the surroundings must be familiar and foreign at once.

It is this, not so much the danger, that enabled Andres to garner insights about his relationship to the world. In any unfamiliar environment, the students are open to making new connections and seeing new patterns. In his introduction to *Words from the Land,* Stephen Trimble quotes Barry Lopez, who comments on the interrelatedness of things. He states, "When you pick up something in the woods, it is not only connected to everything else by virtue of its being a set piece in an ecosystem, but it's connected to everything else by virtue of the fact that you have an imagination" (13). Standing on his rock, Andres made connections between the stars and Native American poetry. Because he was wandering without an overt or practical purpose, he opened himself to the possibility of these new insights.

Perhaps any change of surroundings or deviation from habit can serve as a catalyst for self-discovery. In "Street Haunting" Virginia Woolf extols the virtue of wandering the streets of London without specific purpose. She writes that when the door to her apartment shuts behind her: "the shell-like covering which our souls have excreted to house themselves, to make for themselves a shape distinct from others, is broken and there is left of all these wrinkles and roughnesses a central oyster of perceptiveness, an enormous eye" (256). As teachers, we can enable students to see that wandering can be productive. Many students believe that outdoor experience is just another kind of physical exercise. These students have a propensity to turn hikes into races to the top of the mountain. While no teacher can force students to change their minds, we can give them the opportunity to see time differently by talking about cultural values such as efficiency, speed, and hunger for thrills. We can also provide time for them to be alone and time to write and meditate. None of these behaviors can be forced. Both the active and passive mind sets are legitimate ways of experiencing the wilderness. The best alternative is to open to ourselves and our students the range of ways we can apprehend wilderness and then discuss the inherent virtues in each mode.

Case # 2, Melissa

While Andres was dancing on top of the granite boulder, Melissa Haslam allowed a male student, Josh, to braid her long hair. Despite the fact that Josh was a sensitive and courteous man, Melissa felt uncomfortable because he was invading women's territory. The event enabled her to focus on the different ways males and females view the act of touching a woman's hair. As with Andres, her epiphany came as a result of allowing something new to happen in an unusual environment. She meditated through writing on her experience at the fire. In her own words:

There is an innocent bond between women and girls [who] braid each other's hair. The act of braiding is among the purest acts of service they exchange. It is more relaxing than a massage, it is more intimate than an "I'm thinking about you" note. It is a skill that is passed down from mother to daughter to granddaughter to great-granddaughter.

She then describes her mother braiding her hair, making clear how this ritual felt. Then she continues:

This bond built between women when they braid each other's hair is one reason why it felt so awkward to have Josh's fingers weaving my hair at a campfire. He did a great job. The braids were tight and stayed in. But it was almost like he was an outsider when he braided my hair. The initial awkwardness came when I rested my back on his legs and he picked up my hair with his fingers. Where were the fingernails that usually scratched against my scalp? Why were his knees so tall? Victoria coached Josh through his braid, and Heather, a veteran braider looked on from the side overseeing the process. But there was that female wisdom that they could not pass on to him. There is almost no way to convey that wisdom through words, and it is very difficult to convey it through actions. But the fact that Josh was unfamiliar with the art of braiding made him try more earnestly to get it right.

Josh was a little thrown by my request for two French braids instead of one. He tried the first one three times before he listened to Victoria and did a few practice runs with one single braid. When he got back to two braids, Josh got down to business. Doing the braid became an attempt at perfection.... His long fingers moved through my hair like a novice weaver that has no confidence in his ability to work with a new medium. I can picture him staring at my hair in his hands, a little puzzled, trying to figure out where the pieces fit. He tied the hair into place very tightly to make up for his lack of experience. I was surprised when one clump of hair was flung over my forehead in front of my eyes. The slight shock almost made me laugh. It felt like Josh was making a boondoggle for a key chain instead of weaving a braid. However, this simplistic activity has left my head and his hands connected in some minor story of creation.

The next day, our group drove away from camp, back to civilization. When our group stopped for lunch at the bird reserve at Fish Springs, Josh came over to check on my braids. His braids stayed in well, but did not last through my tossing and turning during the night. I had redone them a few hours earlier in the van. He came over to inspect the new braids, to see if he could improve on what he had done before. There was a moment when we exchanged understanding: [H]e was the braider, and I had displayed his braid.

If Josh had braided my hair in the middle of a crowded subway station I am sure we would have some pretty interesting looks thrown at us. Most people do not stop to braid hair in the middle of commuter traffic. They do not take the time to stop and soak in the richness of communing spirits. Nor do they take time to give in to the urges of their simple child-like desires. Both are essential to braiding.

I think at some time in every boy's life he wonders about the bond that women exhibit through braiding. They [boys] may look at two girls and wonder why the one can show such confidence and security with her own hair in the hands of the other. Maybe they even think that they would someday like to stroke her hair, to seduce her to give in to her girlhood vulnerabilities and become his playmate for life. Some try to braid and some just stand on the side, amazed by the skill of the braider. That skill lies in the braider's ability to produce something beautiful while the skill of the braidee is to communicate a complete sense of trust and confidence in the braider. The act is not seductive, but innocent and caring.

A boy or a man could be an expert braider, although, I have never met one. As fun and pure as the act of braiding is, I have not resolved why it feels awkward for a male to braid my hair. Have I placed men and women in gender roles so tightly that I cannot fully accept the braid of another sex? Maybe I hold the act of braiding to be a sacred communion among women. In that case, my awkwardness would be fully justified.

As Melissa notes, her experience would not have happened in many social settings. The isolation in the wilderness and the closeness of the group of students allowed a relaxing of convention. While her experience was not as physically dangerous as her classmate's, the strangeness of the environment helped produce an epiphany about the importance of this woman's ritual in her life. At first she did not understand why Josh's braiding made her nervous. The foreign, complex terrain is an inner one in this case. As with Andres dancing on the rock, no teacher could plan the wonder of what happened. The context—a group of students sitting inside the circle of light with dark wilderness surrounding—aided the approach to intimacy, but other students sat at the same campfire and did not discover something that they felt like writing about. Even though there are no guarantees, teachers can through careful reading and talking urge students to open themselves to the universe, to process that experience through writing, and to avoid narrow interpretation of what happened.

"I learn by going"

Through experience with these two students and hundreds of others, we have discovered that a heightened awareness occurs when the surface occupations of the rational mind are distracted by an unusual and partially foreign environment. This edge of unfamiliarity enables students to see newly, and then to make further discoveries through writing about what they see. This is an essential kind of recreation—placing ourselves and our students in unfamiliar locations, breaking down some of the traditional barriers between us as individuals, and getting outside the tradition-laden walls of the classroom, where every act is governed by expectation. As can be seen from the two examples, many of their epiphanies are connected to ritual and performance, actions such as singing, gaming, and storytelling. In most cases, students begin a conscious exploration of something their subconscious already knew.

In "The Waking," Theodore Roethke describes the paradoxical relationship between the conscious and subconscious aspects of our being. New bridges between the two, his poem implies, can result from walking in unfa-

miliar paths instead of planning each act and thinking in abstractions. The
two lines he repeats throughout the stanzas of his villanelle are:

> I wake to sleep and take my waking slow.
> I learn by going where I need to go.

The waking that we experience while hiking or camping and then talking and
writing about that outdoor activity is like sleeping because thought and image
are bound into one entity; the conscious and subconscious aspects of our
minds become more open to each other.

In "Seeing," one of the essays in *Pilgrim at Tinker Creek*, Dillard describes this paradoxical act of unconscious looking. It requires one to release
the conscious occupations of the mind and to forget usual modes of seeing.
She writes, "But there is another kind of seeing that involves a letting go.
When I see this way I sway transfixed and emptied" (33). After describing an
evening spent on Tinker Creek when she was transported by what she saw,
she writes,

> When I see this way I see truly. As Thoreau says, I return to my senses.... But I
> can't go out and try to see this way. I'll fail, I'll go mad. All I can do is try to gag the
> commentator, to hush the noise of useless interior babble that keeps me from seeing
> just as surely as a newspaper dangled before my eyes. (34)

She writes that seeing this way requires tremendous discipline, developed
through long practice.

> The world's spiritual geniuses seem to discover universally that the mind's muddy
> river, this ceaseless flow of trivia and trash, cannot be dammed, and that trying to
> dam it is a waste of effort that might lead to madness. Instead you must allow the
> muddy river to flow unheeded in the dim channels of consciousness; you raise your
> sights; you look along it, mildly, acknowledging its presence without interest and
> gazing beyond it into the realm of the real where subjects and objects act and rest
> purely, without utterance. (34)

But sometimes a film of familiarity blinds us to the world.

To prepare themselves for the happy accident of seeing with new eyes,
students first read writers, like those mentioned above, who have spent much
of their lives learning to observe closely. We've used several anthologies of
natural history writing: *Words from the Land*, edited by Stephen Trimble;
"This Incomperable Lande": *A Book of American Nature Writing*, edited by
Tom Lyon; *Being in the World*, edited by Scott Slovic and Terrell Dixon, and
A Place in Space, a collection of essays by Gary Snyder. Reading these an-

thologies, students create images of the natural world from words, replicating the writer's original act of describing a place. The students learn to see geologically through reading "Basin and Range" by John McPhee. They begin to sense the romance in the language used by geologists and begin to imagine the dance of the great geologic plates under the skin of the earth. From Anne Zwinger in "Cabeza Prieta," they learn the patience to focus for hours at a time. From Gretel Ehrlich, they learn the preciousness of water. From Edward Abbey in "Down the River with Henry Thoreau," they find out how to mingle someone else's text with their own observations. From David Quammen in "Chambers of Memory," they recognize the power of metaphorical vision. From Wendell Berry in "The Journey's End," they discover the importance of seeing oneself as the stranger rather than constantly thinking the environment is foreign and uninviting. From Peter Matthiessen in "At Crystal Mountain," they learn to imagine what they might have missed while they looked elsewhere.

Focused by what they have read and strengthened by the community of the class, students then experience the mountains, canyons, plateaus, forests, and desert flats of Utah. They carry journals to help them think about what they are observing. In their self-evaluations, students describe how knowing they would have to write affects their habits of observation. One student writes, "Generally speaking it made me more observant of my surroundings. In fact, last night as I was walking during the snowfall, I began thinking about how I would describe my experience and the effect the snowfall has on my senses. I loved the thoughts that came to my mind. I am much more aware of my surroundings when I write about them. It makes all my senses more acute." Another student writes that she found herself actually composing as she hiked: "As I participated in each activity my mind would formulate phrases and descriptions that I planned to use later in my writing." A final example is from a student who focuses on the fact that writing amplified the experience for her: "I seem to think and sort things out a lot more clearly when it's done in writing, rather than my head. I don't consider anything that has occurred in my life real until I have written it down." Whether or not they are conscious of the links between observation and language, the act of carrying a journal makes them focus on the landscape, trees, and streams before their eyes. Talking is one way of re-imaging, seeing again; journal writing and essay writing also help. When students sit in front of their computers and visualize again what they described in their notes, they push this matter of seeing to a new level.

To write his introduction to *Words from the Land,* Stephen Trimble traveled across the country, interviewing many writers about their composing habits. He discovered that they think of two overlapping arenas of explora-tion—research in the field and research in their study. Both parts of their writing lives had to do with seeing newly. Anne Zwinger has said that being a "writer of natural history is a visual discipline. It requires a great deal of observation, a lot of research. Every question you ask—why is that flower blue? why is a sunset red? why is the grass green? every time you get an an-swer you get ten more questions. And somehow you have to put it in a form that somebody can read, and in sentences that have some life of their own" (Trimble 5). Gary Nabhan writes that "writing is the major vehicle through which I sort out the universe" (qtd. in Trimble 5).

The act of writing about their experiences in the wilderness becomes an exploration of a second undiscovered country, one which requires students to turn inward to explore. Annie Dillard: "When you write, you lay out a line of words. The line of words is a miner's pick, a woodcarver's gouge, a sur-geon's probe. You wield it, and it digs a path you follow. Soon you find yourself deep in new territory" (3).

In summary, we have discovered that reading, observing, and writing are various aspects of one thing—the sharpening of vision. The precursors of the students' transitional experiences are reading carefully the observations of professional natural history writers, carrying their journals, and wandering without overt purpose. Their writing is made stronger by an edge of fear at unfamiliar surroundings and the sensory overload resulting from the complex and uncontrolled wilderness.

A Word on Safety

Any teacher, who leads students away from the relative safety of the campus environment, needs to be aware of potential dangers. Because many of the students may be foreigners to the desert, we encounter some risks on our ad-ventures. Hiking narrow desert canyons involves danger of flash floods. Hik-ing on slick rock involves the chance of falling. Winter camping exposes students to the risk of hypothermia. Wherever we go, students who are not in shape are subjected to fatigue and the emotional stress of an unfamiliar envi-ronment. Any hiker in Utah risks exposure to hantavirus pulmonary syn-drome, which is a serious, often deadly, respiratory disease passed to humans through infected rodent urine, saliva, or droppings. We travel to these wil-derness areas on highways where there is the chance of accident.

Despite these dangers we have a remarkably low accident record. Ours is not a program that emphasizes adventure at the expense of safety. It is the strangeness of the natural world, not its danger that opens students' eyes to beauty. Specifically, we begin class with a formal session on safety in the out-of-doors; then we continue to stress safety throughout our program. We teach students to work together as a team, all realizing the importance of watching out for each other. We obey all local, federal, university, and Parks Service laws and rules, and we have two or more qualified instructors on each major event. When we have activities that require specialized training we use qualified and certified instructors. Good writing is produced when an edge of strangeness accompanies an assurance of safety.

Conclusion

Much of Roethke's poem "I Wake to Sleep" talks about the revelatory beauty in the natural world. When we go over, under, or around the mountain with students, they can make remarkable discoveries about their relationship to the natural world. In *Pilgrim at Tinker Creek* Annie Dillard discusses this same idea:

> If the landscape reveals one certainty, it is that the extravagant gesture is the very stuff of creation. After the one extravagant gesture of creation in the first place, the universe has continued to deal exclusively in extravagances, flinging intricacies and colossi down aeons of emptiness, heaping profusions on profligacies with ever-fresh vigor. The whole show has been on fire from the word go. I come down to the water to cool my eyes. But everywhere I look I see fire; that which isn't flint is tinder, and the whole world sparks and flames. (9–10)

Although any foreign environment would enable students to explore themselves in new ways, the local wilderness is an ideal environment for this kind of travel. Another student from the same class as Andres and Melissa, Colyn Payne, writes in his final essay:

... Using the environment as the context for creative writing would have to be the most inspirational way to motivate students to write. I appreciate the context as well in being the background to cultivating friendships with amazing and artistic classmates and professors. The "other" activities that were performed without classmates (in many cases classmates participated together) helped me to realize how much fun it is to be alive.... I felt alive every time I was outdoors with our class.... I can say that this is my only class...that taught me to explore my heart."

Through teaching them to link outdoor experience and meditative writing, teachers can help students like Andres, Melissa, and Colyn develop lifetime habits of exploring themselves and their environments, of learning by going where they need to go.

Works Cited

Abbey, Edward. "Down the River with Henry Thoreau." *Words from the Land.* Ed. Steven Trimble. Las Vegas: U of Nevada P, 1995. 50–76.

Berry, Wendell. "The Journey's End." *Words from the Land.* Ed. Steven Trimble. Las Vegas: U of Nevada P, 1995. 226–38.

Dillard, Annie. *Pilgrim at Tinker Creek.* 1974. New York: Bantam Books, 1982.

———. *The Writing Life.* New York: Harper and Row, 1989.

Ehrlich, Gretel. "On Water." *Words from the Land.* Ed. Steven Trimble. Las Vegas: U of Nevada P, 1995. 200–10.

Lyon, Thomas J. *This Incomperable Lande: A Book of American Nature Writing.* New York: Penguin Books, 1989.

Matthiessen, Peter. "At Crystal Mountain." *Words from the Land.* Ed. Steven Trimble. Las Vegas: U of Nevada P, 1995. 244–63.

Melville, Herman. *Moby-Dick.* 1851. New York: Houghton Mifflin Company, 1956.

Roethke, Theodore. *Selected Poems.* London: Faber and Faber, 1969.

Slovic, Scott H., and Terrell F. Dixon. *Being in the World.* New York: Macmillan Publishing Company, 1993.

Snyder, Gary. *A Place in Space.* Washington, DC: Counterpoint, 1995.

Thoreau, Henry David. *Walden.* 1854. New York: Alfred A. Knopf, 1922.

Trimble, Steven. "Introduction." *Words from the Land.* Las Vegas: U of Nevada P, 1995. 2–29.

Woolf, Virginia. "Street Haunting." 1942. *The Art of the Personal Essay.* Ed. Phillip Lopate. New York: Doubleday, 1994. 256–65.

Zwinger, Ann. "Cabeza Prieta." *Words from the Land.* Ed. Steven Trimble. Las Vegas: U of Nevada P, 1995. 80–91.

Chapter 9

Writing to Host Nationals as Cross-Cultural Collaborative Learning in Study Abroad

Leeann Chen

In contrast to education in the home country, where academic life generally separates itself from other aspects of students' lives, study abroad opens up the classroom to the whole society. Students' learning about cultural differences occurs, to a large extent, in their leisure time and in serendipity: with host families, in dorms shared with host-country students, in restaurants, parks, on the streets, and so on. All these out-of-classroom aspects are where ambiguity starts. Many students find study abroad appealing exactly because these aspects resemble vacationing (Altschuler).

Thus, in the context of study abroad, traditional classroom education, independent of students' experiences, falls short of guiding students to reach their learning potential. Experiential education, by contrast, rests on drawing students' daily experiences into a "process" of "collective" learning (Carver 8–9). Such pedagogy answers the unique challenges of teaching study-abroad courses.

What specific methods have study-abroad instructors been using to carry out experiential education? One of the most common seems to be writing, defined in this article as nonprivate journals and essays, in order to provide students with a process of discovery and learning. To name a few, Mildred Sikkema and Agnes Niyekawa's *Design for Cross-Cultural Learning* centers on journal writing. "Spanish Culture and Civilization," a course taught in Spain by an American instructor, requires students to write about their "cultural observations" and turn in the writing weekly for class discussion (Talburt and Stewart 4–5). So do Professor Ghislaine Geloin's French culture course in Nantes (Geloin), and Professor Donald Vanouse's course "Contemporary British Writers" in London (Vanouse). Indeed, with a relatively informal format, journals, as well as essays, invite students to reflect frequently on and make sense of their serendipitous experience. Furthermore, writing functions as a tangible record of students' learning outcomes. This essay is thus written for study-abroad instructors and directors who have been or who are interested in using writing as an effective structure of experiential education in study-abroad programs.

Who is the intended audience for students' writing? Should we be concerned with audience-awareness? Whereas audience-awareness has been recognized as a determining factor of the purpose of all writing (Lee 353) and is taught in all college writing courses, it has rarely been addressed in literature about students' overseas writing. None of the sources mentioned above discuss the issue of audience. By audience-awareness, I refer to one's means of shaping a piece of writing by anticipating responses from intended readers—readers with assumptions, attitudes, expectations, knowledge, and habits that may differ from one's own. As such, audience-awareness can be an effective way of communicating differences. If a writer is unaware of audience, as Douglas Park points out in "The Meaning of Audience," the writer's words, images, tone, and other linguistic features still imply the writer's subconscious assumption of audience (236). In study abroad, without audience-awareness, students' writing seems to imply a collective "us" as audience—students themselves or those who share the same home cultural habits and values—versus a collective "them," people in the host country. The actual readers of study-abroad writing have been home instructors and classmates from home (Geloin 31; Vanouse 75). Such an audience raises the question of how effectively study-abroad writing serves as a means for students to learn about cultural differences and how to adjust to living in other cultures. To what extent does a culturally homogeneous audience encourage students to realize the relativity of their home culture and to understand the perspectives of host nationals? To what extent does such an audience encourage quality communication between our students and natives?

Born and educated in China and then in the United States, I am an experienced study-abroad learner and instructor. Examining the issue of audience in students' overseas writing from a cross-cultural perspective of both students and natives, I argue that overseas courses taught by home instructors do not have to be limited to students from home. We can design study-abroad writing to be intended for a native audience, and train students to explain feelings and thoughts in such ways that local readers can be empathetic about them. We can also create opportunities for students to discuss their writing with local people. Our students will thus increase their learning about cultural differences in ongoing, dialogic communication with natives, who, in turn, can learn about our students as individual Americans. If the goal of study abroad is to make students believe that knowledge is culturally bound (Kline 4), writing to a host audience is an effective way of putting students in the shoes of the host, by making students reflect on the culture of the host country and their own.

My own experiences as well as those of other instructors indicate that people in other countries truly appreciate opportunities to participate in collaborative learning with our students. I will also address how to prepare both host nationals and our students for using writing addressed to the former as a structure of cross-cultural collaborative learning in study abroad.

An Analysis of Implied Home-Cultural Audience in Students' Writing

In *Writing Across Culture,* Kenneth Wagner and Tony Magistrale recommend that overseas students use a journal to express and analyze their thoughts and feelings in their cross-cultural encounters (ix–xiv). Evidently, journal writing has helped many of their students to develop empathy and tolerance, such as the well-documented case of the observant and comparative reflection of American and Swedish culture in the journals of one of their students, Sarah (Wagner and Magistrale 59–106). However, an implied home-cultural audience seems to have fostered students' perceptions centered on their home culture. Even the best journals, like Sarah's, occasionally reflect such perceptions. Moreover, such an implied audience does not encourage students to exchange feelings and thoughts with local people.

Many of our students stay with host nationals in close quarters, such as with a host family. Students' writing about their cross-cultural experience, however, implies a pull back from the local community to a community of home-cultural readers, where local people are referred to in the third person: "they," "them," "my host brother," and so on. This third person is not just a matter of pronoun reference. It facilitates a forum to comment about local people and culture behind the locals' backs. For instance, Andrea, a student in Sweden, writes, "Why don't they have normal salads, why don't they have chocolate chips?" (Wagner and Magistrale 9). "Can't this country afford to make better produce available?" asks Denise (10). Another student, Bill, writes two entries about social introductions. In the first one, he is surprised that he needs to introduce himself at a party: "Had I been to a party in the States, the host would have introduced me to everyone...not so in Sweden!" (10). The second entry reads: "I am getting madder and madder at my host brother. He never introduces me to his friends. Last week, we met a friend of his on the subway and they talked as if I was not there. How rude!" (15). While Sarah reflects upon her frustration with such "little things" as "ethnocentricity," after her second arrival in Sweden (9), more than two months into the study-abroad program, she writes, "I simply cannot ignore those damn toilets" (85). Sikkema and Niyekawa's study includes similar complaints about daily matters from water to mailboxes (78–79).

Studying cultural differences on a home campus and abroad is dramatically different. In the latter situation, students' lives are directly affected and challenged. All the above students are disoriented in daily matters from food to social etiquette, and there is nothing wrong in expressing their feelings. Disorientation is a necessary component in overseas learning. However, does venting lead to learning? Must students "bash" natives to express themselves? Unfortunately, students do whine frequently about the foreign cultures because they know that their writing is not intended for local people.

Their writing implies an assumption that when it is read, without an explanation of "normal" salads and "better produce," readers will understand what the students mean. Students' home culture thus becomes the standard against which other cultural habits are measured. Bill, for example, is aware that the United States and Sweden do not have the same social customs, but he resents the fact that his host family follows a different custom, reacting as if his home-cultural custom were universal and preferred. Study abroad offers an opportunity for students to learn about cultural differences via experience and how to communicate with people of different cultures. Current students' writing, however, records only fragmentary cultural dialogues between students and locals. I would like to turn to Sarah's writing, because it is composed over a period of several months. Sarah has learned from a conversation with a Swedish woman named Catarina that many Swedes may vote for common good rather than for individual interests, contrary to what many Americans do. This conversation leads Sarah to speculate why Swedes like Catarina think so (Wagner and Magistrale 68). However, Sarah does not seem to have pursued the issue by asking any natives why. The same lack of continued dialogue is true of her confusion about the Swedish society. Why would someone be class conscious in a society that seems to strive for social equality (75–76)? Why is there a noticeable absence of Swedish middle-aged or old people on the street (77)? Why do some Swedes value the environment (73)? Why do some Swedes wonder about the advantages of cable TV (86)? What do many Swedish women consider a beautiful hairstyle (88)? All these questions remain unaddressed and are mere questions of reflection. Similarly, in Bill's case, there is no communication of his feelings with his host family; his continuous writing only serves to increase his self-righteous anger.

The issue of home-cultural audience in study-abroad writing is not isolated. It seems as if, when we apply the concept of writing as a process of learning in study abroad, we have nonetheless followed perpetual patterns from the Anglo-European tradition of nonfiction travel writing: letters, diaries, logs, and memoirs. Despite differences in historical and literary conventions as well as individuality of travelers, one convention remains the same: that all travel writing has been intended for a home audience. As Steve Clark observes in a recent study on travel writing:

> Something very strange has always happened in every travel narrative: the decision to be there, rather than here, and yet still wish to be heard here. The telling must be done on home ground, or at least a voice articulated within the home culture. Conversely, the native can thus never fully know the intruder, whose testimony becomes a kind of secret withheld, a ritual of communal bonding achieved through this very act of exclusion. (17)

Let me give a few brief illustrations of Clark's point. In the late fourth century, a Roman pilgrim, Egeria, traveled to the holy land and wrote about the biblical sites and church services. Her *Travels* is "the earliest surviving" record of personal traveling experience (Campbell 16). Addressed to her fellow nuns at home, who are familiar with the sites described in the Bible, Egeria only needs to refer to these sites as a witness. To quote, "a mile away on the river bank is the village where Holy Mary stayed with the Lord when she went to Egypt" (in Wilkinson 94). "In Galilee is Shunem, the village of Abishag the Shunammite and of the woman in whose house Elisha stayed" (in Wilkinson 95). What about secular matters such as the population, housing, the food of the village, and the clothing the villagers wear? These matters are not of interest to Egeria the pilgrim nor her readers. In other words, although being in the Holy Land for three years offered Egeria an opportunity to learn about these other aspects of the local culture, Egeria's purpose and audience, as well as the fact that secular curiosity was regarded as a sin at this time (Stagl 48), channeled her learning.

In the contemporary age, homeward orientation still exists in many travel texts. Take, for example, Pico Iyer's *The Lady and the Monk,* a memoir of his 1980s stay in Kyoto. Sponsored by *Time,* Iyer sets his foot in Japan to interpret the country for a western audience. Because to Iyer "Japanese public life [is] empty ritual and pageantry," knowing the real Japan must be done through a private relationship, as Traise Yamamoto critiques (333). Hence Iyer turns his Japanese lover Sachiko into a representative case study. Iyer hints to "us" (Iyer 261), those who are accustomed to a cultural ideal of individuality even in a married couple, that Japanese women like Sachiko are incomprehensible exactly because they efface their individual preference to please their men. When dining out, Sachiko will order the same dishes Iyer does, although it bothers her stomach (Iyer 260–61). What underlines Iyer's narrative is his identification with western cultural values as opposed to non-western values, represented by Sachiko (Yamamoto 329–30).

Another recent example is Peter Hessler's memoir *River Town: Two Years on the Yangtze,* based on his experience as a Peace Corps English teacher at a college in Fuling City, Sichuan Province, 1996–98. As Hessler says himself, he also collects material for his book (60). Often he writes or takes notes while taking a trip. However, when his fellow Chinese travelers inquire about his writing, Hessler hedges, "'I am writing my foreign language.' That was enough to satisfy nearly everyone—If you know a foreign language, it was obvious that you would spend a great deal of time writing it. Nobody seemed to realize that in fact I was writing about them and everything else around me" (204–5). Episode after episode, Hessler shares with his western readers "the Chinese way" of doing things (390). This is the bond between a travel writer and the home-cultural readers Steve Clark refers to. It is a bond determining a writer's choice of material, the angle from which to render the material, and the ways in which it is rendered.

Why Address a Local Audience?

It is fair to say that although journal writing is a way for students to express themselves and reflect on their experiences, we have not examined the point of view in students' writing. Writing to an implicit homogenous audience poses a dichotomist relationship between students and local people. Students like Bill tend to see his cultural values as superior and opposite to local values: hence their venting at the expense of local people. Is it possible for an outsider—a traveler, a study-abroad student—to write with a local audience in mind? What will be the purpose of doing so? In what ways is writing to a local audience a more effective way of learning than writing to a homogenous audience? The rest of this article will discuss the purpose, feasibility, and preparation for students to share their writing with a local audience.

Asking students to write with an awareness of a local audience and making arrangements for them to discuss their writing with local people supports the ultimate purpose of study abroad. We have study abroad programs because we would like our students to understand via direct experience that people in different parts of the world do not have the same habits, customs, expressions and ways of thinking, and to develop sensitivity towards differences (Laubscher 88). Writing to a local audience will help students realize how our fundamental communication system, language itself, is culturally based. In an explication of the cultural theory of reading, Peter Smagorinsky argues that meaning is determined by its cultural context (135). Even people who speak the same language do not necessarily understand each other's message. John Platt cites the example of a Chinese "routine" greeting translated into English as "Have you eaten yet?" which a speaker of English, who does not know about the routine, may assume is a prelude to a meal invitation (19). The example represents a large pattern of "speakers who share, at least to some degree, the same language system but not, or at least not to the same degree, the same cultural system" (Platt 13).

Writing for a local audience will help students learn from cultural shocks without disrespect for the local culture. If local people can be arranged to discuss the writing with students, the writing will be instrumental in promoting focused and ongoing cultural dialogues. Instead of just being the subject of outsiders' learning, locals and our students will become learners about each other. As our students share their thoughts and feelings with local people, the latter will be likely to learn about the students as individual Americans. In these ways, students and local people engage in relationships, rather than perceiving each other as opposites. Only in these ways can students learn how to communicate differences with others.

Sikkema and Niyekawa define cultural shock as "the state of disorientation experienced by a person entering a new culture…as he [or she] discovers for the first time that many of the things to which he [or she] is accustomed are unique to his [or her] own culture" (6). I would like to add that culture shock does not occur just in the beginning stage of students' cross-cultural experience, as if there would not be anything unexpected after a while. As they keep exploring the local culture, students are likely to come across unfamiliar situations. Furthermore, the fact that some students can overcome certain culture shocks does not mean that these shocks will not recur, as Wagner and Magistrale point out (85). Therefore, culture shock can occur at any point of students' overseas experience.

Sikkema and Niyekawa argue that culture shock itself is an important component of learning, because it functions as a wake-up call to cultural differences (43; also Whalen 2). However, culture shocks do not necessarily lead to increased cultural tolerance and sensitivity (Talburt and Stewart 1). In fact, some students returned home earlier than expected because they were too homesick (Whalen 4). The cited journals speak to the degree of students' frustration. An important fact to keep in mind is that if students do not look at cultural differences from a cross-cultural point of view, they are not going to learn. Once they do, however, they are likely to keep an emotional distance from the cultural differences they experience, and learn what these differences mean to local people. My own experience in teaching study-abroad writing courses speaks to this fact. One winter, while teaching Travel to Learn at Yavapai College, I took a class of 28 students, from 16 to 80 years of age, to the People's University in Beijing. The first night students arrived at the hotel of the University after a delayed trip of 25 hours, they found out that there was no hot water to take a shower. The hotel had hot water only a few hours a day. Instead of complaining about this inconvenience, Robert Widen wrote from the point of view of local people. Among a few other observations of an energy shortage, Widen comments,

> When we arrived at the hotel and discovered the 'hot water hours,' I knew China has a serious energy shortage. This immediately gave rise to an understanding of the importance, to China, of the Three Gorges Dam project on the Yangtze River, currently under construction.... I admire how the hotel saves energy. The key to the room turns on and shuts off electricity as one enters and leaves.

Lisa Willson's writing shows her perspective and explores that of natives:

> One day, we went to a different part of the Great Wall called Gu Bei Kou Great Wall. I was in charge of the group. While I was trying to enjoy my climb a hustler caught up with me, telling me that he had told our shuttle driver to pick us up at a different location. But if I gave him 20 Chinese yuan, he would make sure that the shuttle picked us up right at the foot of the Wall. I argued with him and said that I would pay him 20 yuan if and when he made sure that the shuttle picked us up on schedule and right where it should be. Finally the hustler went away. I was extremely mad. But writing this episode from the point of view of local people has made me less angry, and I understand the whole situation better. I am thinking that China's privatization of the economy and its tourist industry have brought drastic changes to the villagers near the Great Wall. Prices are at least 10 times as high as they were a decade ago, while earnings have not matched up. How can a local peasant keep up with inflation? The appearance of foreign tourists certainly magnifies the gap between the rich and poor. We do have a lot of money comparatively speaking, and we are easy targets. Twenty yuan is less than $3 for us.

Let us return to Bill's journal entries about Sweden that were discussed previously and found in *Writing Across Culture*. Were students asked to address a local audience, common sense would have told them that saying: "You do not have normal salads, produce, breakfast, water, telephone system and toilets" is culturally insensitive. What is normal to an audience from home may not be normal to a local audience. Therefore, to communicate with local people, students must write about their cultural shocks in ways that make sense to the locals. For example, rather than becoming angrier and angrier with his host brother, Bill could have written: "I am used to a culture where it is a common courtesy for family members to introduce guests of the family to the family's friends. I have realized that in Sweden guests are expected to introduce themselves or the guest will not be included in conversations. I am still struggling to get used to this custom." When students write with a local audience in mind, they will reflect on their own cultural standards instead of reflexively using them to charge the locals. Thus, a change of audience does not diminish the role of students' memory of home in making sense of their new cultural experience.

As Whalen argues, memory helps turn experience into learning if it functions as an effective comparison between the home culture and the new culture (9). When addressing a local audience, students can use their memory to explain why they feel in certain ways and learn how to express their own feelings without hurting those of others. If Bill shared the hypothetical journal entry with his host family, they might have explained to him Swedish customs and encouraged him to try them out. Such sharing does not have to be done in writing; verbal communication based on writing may be more congenial.

Addressing a local audience is also an efficient way of learning for short-term programs. Wagner and Magistrale's design of the analytical journal—in which, for the beginning period, the prominent period of cultural shock, students more or less just describe how they feel and then move on to analysis—may work only in the context of the traditional semester or year-long programs. Since 1990, when the Institute of International Education issued a mandate to diversify study-abroad programs to accommodate students who cannot afford a semester abroad for economic, family or other reasons, short-term programs such as programs for one or two months in the summer and during the winter break have been on the rise. To make the most efficient use of the short period of time, addressing a local audience will get students to analyze cultural differences from the beginning, as Lisa does.

Even though "extended, meaningful interactions" with host nationals enable students to gain significant insights into the host culture (Talburt and Stewart 1), many study-abroad instructors concur that "all but the most confident and outgoing students spend most of their leisure time moving in packs with other Americans" (Engle; O'Leary; Ward 232), not to mention that they are already "housed with other Americans and taught in courses set up just for them" (Engle). This manner of spending time resembles segregated tours, where "a community of language users in exile" stay in their safety net and observe the locals from a distance (Curtis and Pajaczkowska 207). They are "physically close but socially distanced from the native community" (Wang 148). American students are accustomed to studying with a syllabus. If we do not spell out policies to make sure they do their homework, many students probably will not do it or not do it well. Likewise, in study abroad, if we do not have an effective means of encouraging them to interact with host locals, many students probably will not make an effort to do so.

Involving host nationals in the writing process facilitates dialogic learn-ing between insiders and outsiders. In *Tourism and Modernity,* Ning Wang points out that "locals view their place of residence in a utilitarian and realis-tic manner" (161). They may not see the whole system because they are "act-ing within it" (Leed 62). However, to travelers, what is to the locals "the ordinary, the usual, and paramount reality" can be "the extraordinary, the unusual, and paradise" (Wang 161). Because both outsiders' and insiders' perceptions are influenced by their respective historical and cultural condi-tions, exchanges of observation and interpretation of culture between outsid-ers and insiders prompted by writing to local people can open up horizons that are not possible with writing to a relatively homogenous audience. A cross-cultural dialogue can offer "a chance…to interrogate and negotiate, if not eliminate, both the traveler's cultural prejudices and those of the peoples he or she encounters" (Holland and Huggan 201).

My proposal for using writing to a local audience as a means of dialogic learning in study abroad is also supported by current literature on cross-cultural studies such as ethnography. In conventional ethnography, an out-sider anthropologist presents the results of his or her participant observation and interpretation of a culture to a home audience just as travel writers do. In recent decades, however, many ethnographers have realized the limitations as well as the power imbalance implied in conventional ethnography. Some have started to co-author with native experts (Clifford, *Predicament* 50–51). In *Cross-Cultural Encounters: Face-to-Face Interaction,* Richard Brislin discusses the value of locals' "commentary" on ethnographic works, includ-ing reasons why some locals may be "upset with some writings," how some ethnographic generalizations are based on "limited experiences" and "pre-conceived points of view," as well as discussing what ways ethnographic works "could be of help" to the locals (312–13).

James Clifford believes that "with expanded communication and inter-cultural influence" (*Predicament* 22), a culture should be defined discur-sively, as "an open-ended, creative dialogue of subcultures, of insiders and outsiders, of diverse factions" (46). All these studies, from that of Ning Wang to James Clifford's, suggest that the soil is ripe for us to plant the seed of dialogic learning in study abroad via writing to host audiences.

Can Participation of Local People in Study-Abroad Writing Be Arranged?

Significant as it is, having a local audience join the discussion of students' writing in study abroad may not be an easy task that leads to instant, across-the-board success. Differences in language, culture, institutional policies, communication styles, classroom cultures, teaching methodology, and political alliances all pose challenges. However, despite challenges, online writing to cross-cultural partners already has been a success. I also have had successful experiences arranging for local students to discuss issues with my students. Innovation and a flexible attitude is the key to success. It has been proven that writing to a cross-cultural audience can be done even when writers and readers are of different levels of English, different years of school, different class sizes and ages. More important, we do not have to wait for all conditions to be ready to ask students to address a cross-cultural audience. Just to imagine speaking to an audience outside of one's home culture is likely to make students empathize with a plethora of cultural behaviors and standards.

Helsinki University of Technology in Finland, Czech Technical University of Prague, and Indiana University in the United States experimented with a collaborative writing course via e-mail among students of the three universities in 1993. Students first got to know each other by discussing personal and academic topics. Then, in collaborative groups, they decided on paper topics according to common interests, conducted research on the topics, and eventually produced a paper (Kasikova 126). Instructors at all three universities guided and monitored the e-mail communication to ensure clarity of expression and academic quality (127).

Although there was an uneven level of English proficiency among the students, the course produced benefits that a usual writing course on a U.S. campus will not. Students enriched their knowledge of other countries (133) by asking, in their own words, "real people about their opinions, ideas, feelings, customs" (129). In addition, cross-cultural partnership kept students excited, and they wrote far more than they would have in a regular writing course.

In 1989, 26 sophomores, ranging from 19 to 41 years of age, in an English class at Indiana University, Purdue University, and five comparative literature majors, ranging from 21 to 31 years of age, in a master-level literature class at the University of Tampere in Finland shared an online drama-reading course. Students in each country had different writing assignments but had a common reading list (Schwartz 5). The American students wrote their interpretations in a regular journal and communicated them to their Finnish learning partners. All students commented that real cross-cultural partners helped them "understand what to include" in their writing and thus enhanced their communication skills in a global context (7). Students saw the relevance of their daily experiences in their interpretation and used them to explain to their cross-cultural peers why they interpret texts in their own ways (6–8). Sometimes, though, cultural stereotypes surface in students' generalizations of their experiences. Even so, most readers can detect these stereotypes and respond to them in a light-hearted manner (8). A survey at the end of the course indicates that the American students valued most the journal entries, which provided their online exchange of interpretations.

In 1988, Manderley Grove Community School in London and Costa Mesa High School in California grouped students from both sides of the Atlantic into pairs to write on topics from personal names to Shakespeare's plays. There were risks and misunderstandings, but over the course of a year, students felt comfortable and confident in revealing themselves to their cross-cultural peers (Freedman 187). Teachers from both schools played a major role in ensuring the success of this writing project. They were sensitive and knowledgeable enough of the different classroom cultures and educational methods to explain to their respective students, for instance, why they received the kinds of peer responses they did (118–19). All three projects indicate that cross-cultural audience awareness motivates students to take their writing more seriously than they would have in regular courses (Kasikova 129), and to sort out "culturally bound" perspectives (Freedman 1).

If these online cross-cultural collaborative courses can be successful, we also can make successful collaboration in writing to host nationals in study abroad. At the present time, most study-abroad programs are in "English-speaking countries" (Goodman), but the trend is turning to non- Anglo-European countries (Desruisseaux). Writing to a local audience certainly is not limited to native English speakers. As we have seen, students of English as a second language in Finland and the Czech Republic could communicate very well with U.S. students. English is also spoken as a second language in many Asian and African countries. In China, for example, a foreign language is often a required subject starting in grade school (Cheng 162). However, these countries often face the challenge of limited resources for learning a second language. Therefore, many college teachers in these counties value the opportunity for their students of English to interact with native speakers;

this was the incentive for Czech Technical University of Prague to have been involved in the online cross-cultural writing course (Kasikova 125).

In 1999, I managed to experiment with a joint discussion of cross-cultural views between my students from Yavapai College and a group of 20 students from the Chinese Literature Department of the People's University in Beijing. For most of the meeting, students chatted about their backgrounds, motives for being university students, career goals, dating opportunities, and leisure activities in a relaxed and friendly atmosphere. The year 1999 was also a time when the issue of freeing Tibet comprised much of the talk in the U.S. media. Not surprisingly, one of my students asked why China did not free Tibet. Immediately, many people in the room felt tense. A few Chinese students explained their views and one raised the question of why now and then the United States sends troops to other countries to engage in war, and whether the U.S. people can stop the government from sending out the troops if they do not like the participation in war. The answers from my students led to a Chinese student's further inquiry on how democracy works in the United States. My students were firing their different answers across the room. I made a comment at this point to this cross-cultural student body: "See, this is democracy in action," and everyone laughed. Despite tension and disagreement, our meeting ended with students breaking into smaller groups trying to get to know each other and exchanging good wishes. In their journals and essays, my students valued this meeting the most. Not only did they learn some Chinese perspectives, but also they respected the Chinese students for openly discussing even sensitive issues with them.

In March 2001, from Embry-Riddle Aeronautical University (ERAU), I organized an optional field trip for my travel literature class to Beijing University of Aeronautics and Astronautics (BUAA). Because of schedule conflicts and time constraints, we were not able to hold classroom meetings with students from both universities. However, a mutual determination of both universities to facilitate quality interaction between students led to our experiment of using our shuttle bus as a mobile classroom. On a daily basis, four BUAA students of English would hop on the shuttle with 12 students of mine to places of interest. My students would discuss issues in their journals such as pollution, the legacy of Mao, and dating in college with BUAA students, who appreciated so much this rare opportunity of practicing and learning English, if not American culture.

When students from both universities visited the same sites, such as the Tomb of Mao Ze Dong, they would discuss what the visit meant to them and had an on-the-spot experience of cross-cultural interpretations. Such close and extended interaction resulted in the budding of lasting friendships, despite, not surprisingly, disagreements on certain issues. Even so, our departure day was hard for students from both universities. Based on the enthusiastic responses from students and faculty of both universities, our two institutions have planned an intensive collaborative class over six weeks on the campus of BUAA in the summer of 2002, pending sufficient enrollment. The course is called Contemporary China. My students will be reading a textbook on the changes in Chinese society since it opened its door in the late 1970s; going on organized excursions to companies, schools, factories, and individual homes, as well as to places students themselves decide helpful to their understanding of China; and writing journals and essays about their out-of-classroom experience with an intended audience of BUAA peers. Three times a week, BUAA students of English will take turns to join the class, offer peer response to my students' writing, answer their questions, and help my students decide where to go and/or whom to interview in order to develop their understanding.

Because of different institutional policies as well as linguistic and cultural differences, collaborative classes may not always be feasible. Even in such situations, we can consider involving "a representative of [the local] audience in the writing process," as Lisa Ede and Andrea Lunsford suggest (89), through inviting him or her to class discussion or giving students' journals by turns to the representative. This representative reading is similar in a way to how "we ask a colleague to read an article intended for scholarly publication" (89).

Preparation for Collaboration in Writing to Host Nationals

To ensure the success of writing to a local audience as a structure of collaborative learning in study abroad, partners at home and abroad need to be well prepared, as Annette Scheunpflug recommends for all types of cross-cultural learning (113). In addition to foreign language and cultural knowledge, the most important element of preparation is that both partners understand how writing to a local audience works in collaboration, and the role each partner plays in the learning process. The purpose of such preparation is to make students take charge of the learning process, and become self-motivated learners. For many institutions, this process-oriented preparation has resulted in semester-long pre-departure courses, as reflected in Sikkema and Niyekawa's work and Brian Whalen's emphasis on the importance of teaching students the learning process (10–13).

Part of the cultural knowledge should consist of communication styles of each culture. Communication experts argue that countries such as China and Spain are "associative cultures," in which meaning is largely derived from associations rather than cause and effect as in "abstractive cultures," like the United States and France (Korac-Kakabadse 8–9). In associative cultures, communication tends to be "indirect and implicit," whereas in abstractive cultures, communication tends to be the opposite (9). Understanding this general pattern of communication styles will help cross-cultural learning partners decide how to explain themselves and when to ask questions.

To avoid hasty generalizations, both learning partners need to know how people tend to perceive each other in cross-cultural situations. Dennison Nash states that in cross-cultural contact, visitors and locals tend to conceive each other not "as individuals, but as strangers of a particular type" (44–45), as representatives of each other's culture (37). In a study of "Participants' Perspectives," Wilkinson also notes that American students tend to distinguish themselves as individuals on home campuses. Abroad, however, they group themselves as Americans (32). This is so, Eric Leed explains, because one finds one's affiliation with one's own type as one identifies strangers as their own type, a "defense against the strange and unusual" (68). Regular discussions and interactions between people of different cultures should reduce this tendency of generalization, as they get to know each other more and more as individuals. Since to predict and adapt to the audience are "two of the basic principles of human communication" (Samovar 67), we should have cross-cultural learning partners get to know each other and discover common interests via e-mail prior to departure, as in the case of the successful first stage of writing in the tri-institutional, tri-national online writing course in Kasikova's article (126). In the case of my summer collaborative learning course, our partners at BUAA will read and discuss sample journals and essays of my students before our arrival.

At Embry-Riddle Aeronautical University, I created and have been teaching a study-abroad preparation course titled "Observation in Asian Cultures." The purpose of the course is to help students understand the history and complexities of learning abroad, how to use writing to structure learning overseas, how writing to host nationals can significantly enhance the learning, and the general methodologies of ethnography. There are four parts to this course. The first part is an overarching study of cross-cultural contact and research. James Clifford's "Introduction to Writing Culture"(1–26) and Mary Louis Pratt's "Field Work and Travel Writing" (27–50) are the primary texts. Although students in the class are neither anthropology majors nor professional travel writers, they can see that study abroad involves the same ethnological method of participant observation, the same need of collaborative interpretation of culture, the dialectical relationship between the observer and the observed, and, very importantly, the observation of changes in oneself as one gains knowledge about other cultures.

Part Two is a survey of Anglo-European travel writing about Asia, including excerpts from such texts as Egeria's *Travels* (122–23), Marco Polo's *Travels* (163–65), Anathasius Kircher's *China Illustrata* (192–94), and Lady Mary Montagu's *Turkish Letters* (90–92). Through the reading and discussion of these excerpts, my students have learned how travelers' writing is influenced by the milieu in which the travelers live, as well as such factors as gender, occupation, and the purpose of their travel and writing. Students also learn to see how modern anthropology evolves from travel writing. Knowledge from this survey lays a foundation for students to critique their perspectives in study-abroad writing.

Following this survey is the third and central part of the course, using two contemporary travel texts: Peter Hessler's *River Town* and Pico Iyer's *The Lady and the Monk*. These two texts are chosen because our university's Asian Studies program centers on East Asia and our study abroad program is in China. Students are asked to analyze an individual traveler's process of learning, how a traveler deals with daily challenges, how a traveler observes and makes sense of his or her encounters in another culture, the degree and manner of interaction between the traveler and the locals, cultural and gender stereotypes, and implied audience. This analysis takes students through vicarious processes of learning abroad.

The last part of the course is the practice of writing to host nationals. The class members discuss sample writing from previous study-abroad students; they also practice writing to different audiences, including exploring the degree to which one needs to explain oneself, effective wording, and alternative ways of organizing a piece of writing, as recommended by Ede and Lunsford (91) and Icy Lee (353). As a result of such a preparatory course, students will be able to understand studying abroad from a historical, methodological aspect, in-depth case studies, and hands-on practice. They will have cultivated serious and realistic attitudes toward study abroad, self-reflective habits, and a readiness as well as a willingness to use writing as a means of communication with their host peers with whom they already will have established a relationship.

Good preparation provides the foundation on which to start the process of writing to host nationals on site. In the process, we need to continue to guide students to specify the local audience as they come to know the hosts more and more. Cultural sensitivity can never be overstressed; this includes making efforts at legible handwriting when computers and typewriters are not available, slower pace of speech, and listening with patience and intensity (Samovar 117). As expected, exchanging views in a cross-cultural environment is likely to bring about disagreement and conflicts (Freedman 118–19). Although my students did not take disagreements personally, there is always the possibility that they may. To help keep up students' self-esteem, we need to make sure that collaborative discussion is done supportively and constructively.

John Marcum, director of the University of California Education Abroad Program, believes that the future of U.S. study-abroad programs should be "characterized essentially by collaborative engagement with other countries," rather than by a more imperial projection of American interest" (B8). Through our efforts of creating cross-cultural collaborative learning via students' writing to a local audience, future U.S. students abroad can become participants in ongoing, mutual-learning dialogues. They will form a new generation of global citizens.

Works Cited

Altschuler, Glenn. "La Dolce Semester: Studying Abroad Is Most Students' Favorite College Experience. But Not Necessarily for the Right Reasons." *The New York Times* 8 April 2001, sec. 4A: 17.

Brislin, Richard. *Cross-Cultural Encounters: Face-to-Face Interaction.* New York: Pergamon, 1981.

Campell, Mary. *The Witness and the Other World: Exotic European Travel Writing, 400–1600.* Ithaca: Cornell UP, 1988.

Cheng, Chin-Chuan. "Chinese Varieties of English." *In the Other Tongue: English across Cultures.* Ed. Braj Kachru. 2nd ed. Urbana: U of Illinois P, 1992. 162–77.

Clark, Steve. "Introduction." *Travel Writing and Empire: Postcolonial Theory in Transit.* Ed. Steve Clark. London: Zed Books, 1999. 1–28.

Clifford, James. "Introduction." *Writing Culture: The Poetics and Politics of Ethnography.* Eds. James Clifford and George Marcus. Berkeley: U of California P, 1986. 1–26.

———. *The Predicament of Culture: Twentieth-Century Literature, Ethnography and Art.* Cambridge: Harvard UP, 1988.

Curtis, Barry, and Claire Pajaczkowska. "'Getting There': Travel, Time and Narrative." *Travelers' Tales: Narratives of Home and Displacement.* Eds. George Robertson, et al. New York: Routledge, 1994. 199–215.

Desruisseaux, Paul. "Fifteen Percent Rise in American Students Abroad Shows Popularity of Non-European Destinations." *Chronicle of Higher Education* 10 Dec. 1999: A60.

Ede, Lisa, and Andrea Lunsford. "Audience Addressed/Audience Invoked: The Role of Audience in Composition Theory and Pedagogy." *Cross-Talk in Comp Theory: A Reader.* Ed. Victor Villanueva. Urbana: National Council of Teachers of English, 1997. 77–95.

Engle, John. "Creating More Rigorous and More Appropriate Study-Abroad Programs." *Chronicle of Higher Education* 17 Mar. 1995: A56.

Freedman, Sarah Warshauer. *Exchanging Writing, Exchanging Cultures: Lessons in School Reform from the United States and Great Britain.* Cambridge: Harvard UP, 1994.

Geloin, Ghislaine. "Avoiding a U.S. Curriculum Transplant Abroad: The Ethnographic Project." *Innovative Approaches to Curriculum Design in the Study Abroad Program.* Ed. Deborah Hill. Columbus: Renaissance, 1987. 23–34.

Goodman, Allan. "America Is Devaluing International Exchanges for Students and Scholars." *Chronicle of Higher Education* 12 Mar. 1999: A56.

Hessler, Peter. *River Town: Two Years on the Yangtze.* New York: HarperCollins, 2001.

Holland, Patrick, and Graham Huggan. *Tourists with Typewriters: Critical Reflections on Contemporary Travel Writing.* Ann Arbor: U of Michigan P, 2000.

Iyer, Pico. *The Lady and the Monk: Four Seasons in Kyoto.* New York: Vintage Books, 1992.

Kasikova, Stanislava. "Creating an International Classroom through E-mail." *Effective Teaching and Learning of Writing: Current Trends in Research.* Eds. Gert Rijilaarsdam, Huub van den Bergh, and Michel Couzijn. Amsterdam: Amsterdam UP, 1996. 124–35.

Kircher, Athanasius. *China Illustrata.* Trans. from the 1677 Latin edition by Charles Van Tuyl. Bloomington: Indiana UP, 1987.

Kline, Michael. "Study Abroad and the Liberal Arts: The Canon in Disarray." *Innovative Approaches to Curriculum Design in the Study Abroad Program.* 1–14.

Korac-Kakabadse, Nada, et al. "Low-and High-Context Communication Patterns: Towards Mapping Cross-Cultural Encounters." *Cross Cultural Management* 8 (2001): 3–24.

Laubscher, Michael. *Encounters with Difference: Student Perceptions of the Role of Out-of-Class Experience.* Westport, CT: Greenwood, 1994.

Lee, Icy. "Exploring Reading-Writing Connections through a Pedagogical Focus on 'Coherence.' " *Canadian Modern Language Review* 57 (2000): 352–56.

Leed, Eric. *The Mind of the Traveler: From Gilgamesh to Global Tourism.* New York: Basic Books, 1991.

Marcum, John. "Eliminate the Roadblocks." *Chronicle of Higher Education* 18 May 2001: B7–9.

Montagu, Lady Mary Wortley. *Selected Letters.* Ed. Robert Halsband. Penguin Books, 1986.

Nash, Dennison. "Tourism as a Form of Imperialism." *Hosts and Guests.* Ed. Valene Smith. Philadelphia: U of Pennsylvania P, 1989. 37–54.

O'Leary, Michael. Letter. *Chronicle of Higher Education* 12 May 1995: B4.

Park, Douglas. "The Meaning of Audience." *The Writing Teacher's Sourcebook.* Eds. Gary Tate, Edward Corbett, and Nancy Myers. 3rd ed. Oxford: Oxford UP, 1994. 233–42.

Platt, John. "Some Types of Communicative Strategies across Cultures: Sense and Sensitivity." *English across Cultures.* 13–29.

Polo, Marco. *The Travels.* Trans. and intro. by Ronald Latham. Hammondsworth, Middlesex, Penguin Classics, 1972.

Pratt, Mary Louise. "Fieldwork in Common Places*." Writing Culture: The Poetics and Politics of Ethnography.* Eds. James Clifford and George Marcus. Berkeley: U of CA P, 1986. 27–50.

Samovar, Larry. *Oral Communication: Speaking Across Cultures.* 11th ed. Los Angeles: Roxbury, 2000.

Scheunpflug, Annette. "Cross-Cultural Encounters As a Way of Overcoming Xenophobia." *International Review of Education* 43.1 (1997): 109–16.

Schwartz, Helen. "Cross-Cultural Team Teaching: E-mail for Literary Analysis." Fiche: ED 319 060.

Sikkema, Mildred, and Agnes Niyekawa. *Design for Cross-Cultural Learning.* Yarmouth: International, 1987.

Smagorinsky, Peter. "If Meaning Is Constructed, What Is It Made From? Toward a Cultural Theory of Reading." *Review of Educational Research* 71 (2001): 133–39.

Stagl, Justin. *A History of Curiosity: The Theory of Travel 1550–1800. Australia*: Harwood, 1995.

Talburt, Susan, and Melissa Stewart. "What's the Subject of Study Abroad? Race, Gender, and 'Living Culture.'" *The Modern Language Journal* 83 (1999): 163–75.

Vanouse, Donald. "American Readers and Writers in England." *Innovative Approaches to Curriculum Design in the Study Abroad Program.* 74–82.

Wagner, Kenneth, and Tony Magistrale. *Writing Across Culture: An Introduction to Study Abroad and the Writing Process.* New York: Peter Lang, 1995.

Wang, Ning. *Tourism and Modernity: A Sociological Analysis.* Amsterdam: Pergamon, 2000.

Ward, Martha. "Managing Student Cultural Shock: A Case from European Tirol." *Anthropology and Education Quarterly* 30.2 (1999): 228–37.

Whalen, Brian. "Learning Outside the Home Culture: An Anatomy and Ecology of Memory." *Frontiers: The Interdisciplinary Journal of Study Abroad* 2 (1996). <http://www.frontiersjournal.com /back/two/l.html.> 1–22.

Widen, Robert. "A Travel Experience in China." Course Paper. Yavapai College, 2000.

Wilkinson, John, ed. and trans. *Egeria's Travels.* 3rd ed. Warminster: Aris and Phillips, 1999.

Yamamoto, Traise. " 'As Natural as the Partnership of Sun and Moon': The Logic of Sexualized Metonymy in Pictures from *The Water Trade* and *The Lady and the Monk*." *Positions: East Asia Cultures Critique* 4.2 (1996): 321–41.

Chapter 10

Sweet Enchantment: Writing the Journey, Perceiving the Human Condition

Twila Yates Papay

Of stones and savage places. In the Coleridge sense, enchanted. In seeking out wildness, open space, privacy of time and place in nature, we seek our deeper selves. In
sociologist Eamon Slater's terms, we seek past time, a solution to post-modern dilemmas. Perhaps it is reassuring to find the neolithic peoples, so alien to us, engaged
in the same deep searching, creating their patterns, making meaning in the face of
the inscrutable.

Whatever those alignments represent, their presence through time is a charmed
miracle, a reminder of spirit and a will to beauty. But perhaps I love them best as an
expression of the love of wildness, the recognition of the power of nature-hewn
stone to voice the silent passions of our lives.

—Papay, *Journal of a Sabbatical* (138)

This journal reflection on Brittany's stunning megaliths, the Alignments of
Carnac, illustrates what happened to me during some sabbatical explorations
of travel writing. My research revealed the sheer size and diversity of the
genre. More importantly, though, I became the traveler with a quest, seeking
the self in the context of the other. I set out as a teacher, studying the genre to
teach it. My logic was simple: Our students go off on journeys unprepared,
returning with little more than a suitcase of souvenirs and some pictures they
cannot identify. I wanted travel to touch their lives; I knew writing to be the
vehicle of transformation.

What I did not expect was to be myself enthralled. How could I know that
my sabbatical metamorphosis would entail an encounter with the ancient stones,
a sense of connection to Neolithic peoples, enhancing through them my contact
with the earth? Like so many journeys, mine began in text and conversation,
talking with Dublin colleagues, examining passage grave theories, discovering a
symbology emphasizing union with earth, sky, and community. By the time I
reached the passage graves of Newgrange, I was possessed. The language of my
journal veered through narrative expressive analysis and transactional feminist
contemplation to philosophical speculation to an eventual halting attempt at the
poetic:

I touch the stone, I follow the majestic passageway, I hear the wind and feel the rain
and contemplate a slanting ray of sunshine. Most of all, I conclude these mysteries
must surely be a form of celebration. As is all beauty, all art, all giving voice to the

spirit each must follow. A passage through stone is a doorway, a metaphor, a way of seeing the universe, a way of reaching inside…and beyond…the self. (54)

So I pursued the ancient stones: Across Ireland and Scotland, along the Brittany coast, until at last I stumbled upon the people who introduced this prehistoric temple structure to Europe, leaving those most ancient of temples in Malta nearly 7,000 years ago to honor a great Mother Goddess. After a complex analysis of the Tarxien Temples, my journal tone shifted:

> Yet this isn't what I thought when I saw them. Strolling through light drizzle, I'd murmur to my husband Joe, "Look at that!" Or, "Ah, have you seen this?" The temples were an amazement beyond my powers of coherence. Like the passage graves, like the alignments, like the stone circles, they reach up out of an alien past to speak mutely of another way of seeing, another kind of knowing. Of all the works these people could have attempted, they chose the temples. To find the megaliths, to smooth the stones, to shape and lift and arrange them. Without so much as a wheel. And why? Well, because of their connection to the earth, perceived as the great Mother. Their creations of massive loveliness grip my heart and soul. And so we wandered twice through the lovely maze of smooth standing and twisted fallen rock, stunned to silence by the elegant cut of stone. (293–94)

To my growing obsession with those early peoples and their stones I credit a new finding of myself, connections to a wider knowing, a contextualization that helped me become the teacher I had often tried to be—learner among learners, she who journeys with questions unanswered and accepts the small obscurities to which our hopes are sometimes consigned.

Here is the problem. I began this investigation for my students. To my great joy, they too are fascinated by travel writing, while the genre offers much I wish to teach. So this article is itself a sort of journey, my effort to figure out what travel writing teaches—and how—and why it is so compelling.

The students themselves are sufficiently intriguing. My research began as I was preparing students going abroad to keep meaningful journals. Then there have been Independent Studies, like that of Rob, who built a two-week winter climb of Mount Rainier with a professional expedition into a writing project. "What I'm afraid of," he wrote me the day before he left, "isn't the physical stuff. But I think of writing where the personal is integrated with a wider comprehension of the place. I'm afraid I can't learn to do that, and that's what traveling and writing together are all about."

More typical of travel writing classes was Angus, who in seeking to comprehend his trip to Alaska working on salmon boats became an independent thinker. Cary, who used the class to prepare for a term's study at Oxford, was fearful that going to England without understanding place and expectations would render her time there as empty as her memories of a high school visit to France. At the advanced level, in a course entitled "The Traveler's Mind," I met Lee, who had lost her family and wanted to explore in writing the persistent tug of Colorado, a place she frequently visited but dreaded actually moving there. There too was Abdul, writing the conflict between his childhood in Casablanca and the southern Morocco of his grandparents, a place of happy dreams but harsh realities where his own children might become sexist, racist, religious bigots. Then there was Todd, exploring the wasted opportunities of army years in Germany, contrasting the traveler he would now like to be with his youthful tendency to follow his buddies and behave like an American tourist.

However, travel writing is compelling to less deliberate students, too, accommodating varied content. For a first-year seminar, I fashioned "Fabulous Journeys: Connecting with the Earth and Each Other." Also an orientation to college life and to Central Florida, it envisioned students as travelers in the alien culture of Rollins. Thus, we journeyed to such exotic sites as the writing center, library, art museum, the president's office, a campus lecture, a play, before taking on the wider culture of the area: Big Tree Park, Birds of Prey Sanctuary, Zora Neal Hurston Museum. Groups reported orally on further visits. To learn to live within the culture, my two peer mentors introduced students to local cultural problems: the social scene, substance abuse, gender issues. Papers ranged from Emily's discovering her spiritual side in Ireland and Alan's identifying his failures as a bored adolescent traveler in need of his newly discovered "commandments of travel," to Melissa's seeing her lifelong journey through music as a means of building connections to the outside world. Justin wrote compellingly of the Great Smokey Mountains, illustrating nature entwined with the growth of the human spirit.

Teaching this mélange of students invites an equally diverse array of materials. Photographs and conversations on previous journeys are good starters, drawing everyone into the course's questions. Indeed, a discussion of the photographer's decisions offers a fine lesson in travel versus tourism. What makes for an interesting picture? Unusual textures, colors, contrasts, lightings, or points of view, students might propose. However, what describes the character of the country? If photos are bits and pieces of the world, whose pieces are we representing? Thus, Japanese postcards of a Shinto temple might focus on some mossy stones, while an American student photograph is more likely to center the temple against a blue sky. Such a conversation might lead naturally into reading Davidson's *Thirty-Six Views of Mount Fuji* (1993), which posits that views of Japanese life are just as diverse as Katsushika Hokusai's woodblock prints. Readings, though, seem to go out of print as soon as ordered, but a quick stroll through any major bookstore's travel section offers replacements. In fact, an entire class trip to a bookstore offers rich discussion on the impossibility of categorizing or narrowing the genre. Short trips on and off campus to familiar or seldom visited sites also provide collaborative experiences, though most students bring their own materials in their heads. What is essential to teaching the genre is eloquently stated in a comment adapted from Proust, a writing prompt I give my students early on: "The real voyage of discovery consists not in seeking new landscapes but in having new eyes" (559). Prompts written at the beginnings of class periods enable us to redefine the journey, coming to an understanding that most travel writing is focused on either people or places. ("What surprised me most about the people of _____ was..." begins a favorite prompt.) The definition of a good traveler takes much longer and occupies bits of conversation throughout the course. ("To be a real traveler requires that I..." is a good opening prompt.) However, as students come to see travel as a state of mind, not location, they evolve as observers, analyzers, and critical thinkers, all of which is evinced in the final projects they produce. In my classes this assignment is defined as "a substantial piece of travel writing for a designated audience and purpose, situating the reader and illustrating the mind of the traveler touched by the alien." Crossing borders is recommended.

Much of the practice, though, for shaping writing to experiment with topics, styles, and ways of thinking comes initially in focused journal entries. "Journal Journeys," for example, are trips into the past, efforts to retrieve fading memories, raise new questions, practice detail and dialogue. Here is Alicia, introducing a very local journey, her efforts to better understand a connection between her college environment and a childhood memory:

> One year later I discovered another mysterious feature of Rollins: its bird population. Everywhere I went, birds' feathers followed me. I could not escape them. So I began to listen to them instead. I watched them. I became familiar with them. And the feathers, another form of bizarre magic, persisted. I saw in the occurrences a sign, though I did not know how to interpret it. So I left it as a connection I had with birds. And thinking about it this way, I uncovered a truth about myself. (Stevens 15)

What follows is a complex consideration of her childhood preoccupation with birds, while the next entry on a term in London uses birds metaphorically to represent her own conflicting moods. A very different sort of knowing resulted from Vanessa's entry for "Imaginary Journeys," in which students record stories, playing with fantasies or exploring inner spaces. Vanessa wrote of birds in her native Mexico, a weird and recurring series of images from her dreams, until at length she realized this repeated scenario actually recalled a childhood incident on a beach her family frequented.

These entries offer practice for more complex thinking to come. In "Ethical Reflections" writers are invited to raise questions and assess their own values in relation to other cultures. As this is difficult for student writers, I offer some advice for reflection. Travel, after all, is an exercise in values, a state of mind and spirit that keeps us exploring our ethical stances, seeking options, making comparisons. Students return from third-world countries to face the culture shock of wasted water and the abundance of food. They have heard local students celebrating terrorism in a bar in Prague or children fighting over schoolbooks in San Juan. What could this mean? Thus, the class is asked to examine a host of complicated questions in the context of travel. "Am I tourist or traveler? Am I making or taking impressions? How were my expectations altered? How do I embrace the alien or face cultural alternatives? Are there places I might choose not to visit? What about traveling with a group versus traveling alone? How does the guidebook differ from the travel journal or a book about place? What do guidebooks fail to tell us? What are my obligations as traveler (perceptions, behaviors, comparisons, alternatives)? What are the ethical obligations of the travel writer?"

In this vein Bill described his initial distaste for Mexicans amassed along a border en route to Tijuana, where "scores of young men loitered, watching and waiting for a sign or opportunity to cross into America." However, as he returns from his journey into "this land of plenty," still fearing those who are "willing to stand alongside a wire fence day after day, risking everything for a chance to melt into the fabric of this wonderful nation," his attitude shifts. He notices the children. "I can appreciate," he concludes, "how hard I too would work to come where my children could grow up free from want, where opportunity is real.... I too would stand along the fence, peering into the abyss of freedom, waiting for just the right moment to stake my claim for a piece of the American dream" (Harle 17–18).

Beyond "Ethical Reflections" lie "Decisions Revisited," opportunities to reconsider how a travel experience might have been salvaged with better understanding of values. Travel, after all, is fraught with decisions, alternatives, comparisons, each choice being a reflection of values. Revisiting problems they have faced as travelers, students assess their decisions, analyzing and considering other choices. How does the troublesome process of decision-making, I ask them, shape our values and illuminate our mistakes? Hence, they write about the drug scene in Budapest, the drinking in Sydney, the lost opportunities and moments missed. "Home," Nancy concludes, having walked out on her family in Caracas and her relatives in Montpellier, "is where you can eat in bed and set the teacup anywhere. It is the place where you experience enormous desire to go back every night. Home is where I wanted to be at that precise moment of my life when I knew I had no home remaining. And home is what I was looking for as I got off the train in Dijon with three medium-sized boxes on the platform and a suitcase in my hand" (Alvarez 1).

Although these journals sometimes represent very rough writing, they are compelling in the search for meaning. For advanced classes new options suggest themselves, like "Quests and Explorations" or "Dialogues, Descriptions, Re-creations," both being opportunities for students to create scenes that pull the reader into the moment or reconstruct the meanings they sought versus those they found in their journeys. For "Character Commentaries" students recreate unexpected people found in their travels: Irish pub musicians, Maori dancers, train compartment companions, and, everywhere, children. Some students capture in writing busloads of tourists, bicycling business people, early morning Tae Kwon Do practitioners. Amber found her study at a crowded party in Madrid, where drinking games passed for amusement and an estranged couple pretended to be casual acquaintances:

> Everywhere stand girls in tiny pants, pursuing cocky guys for a moment of fake intimacy. The guys move from girl to girl, offering drinks, sneering at drunkenness. In a group stand Stephanie and Will, talking, pretending there was never anything between them, while all around people vie for even a façade of what they two have just lost. Why is Stephanie so unconcerned with the mad scramble all around her? Why are they so desperate to find a one-night stand filled with empty words and false closeness? Why doesn't she grab Will and escape? (Riley 2–3)

Perhaps this passage parodies the romance novel because of Amber's reading, though she never mentioned it. "Reader Response" is another journal option, encouraging students to read of the places they have traveled, to respond to novels of place or reflect upon the images they carried from books to their journeys. Kevin did this as he approached Indonesia:

> Once on the plane I spied drifting diesel barges steaming up from the South China Sea and through the Strait of Malacoa; we crossed the dark, humid, indistinct line around the middle of the earth, flying over and sometimes beside the heart of an intra-African-like treetop jungle, fully forested, with dark green steep-sided valleys. The tenebrous jungle reminded me of Conrad's eerie tale of death's mystery. Why, I wondered, had I carried this white man's bleak vision of Africa into the depths of West Sumatra? Approaching the landing strip of Padang, a coastal trading town, I found myself pondering the images we carry and cannot escape. (Miller 15)

In a later draft Kevin went back to Conrad, contrasting the author's metaphor with his own cheery and—in retrospect—simplistic vision of a water-skiing resort in West Sumatra where he might vacation with his family. "Such an easy thing to picture, paradise is," he concludes. "Conveniently, I never dreamed of the problems. I never dreamed of cultural differences or the snake pit I might have created." All such practice with alternative contexts leads to richer, more complex texts.

However, the intriguing question remains: What is so compelling, so encompassing about travel writing? To help students get at this issue, I offer a writing prompt drawn from Ursula K. Le Guin: "It is good to have an end to journey towards; but it is the journey that matters, in the end" (220). What actually enthralls us, students often conclude, is probably the concept of the journey as metaphor. The class, the teaching, the research, the discovery within the writing: All are perceived as journey. Here in a single course lies the human condition, a connection to the whole person. Travel, after all, is what we do—as people and through time. Somehow the travel writing we produce captures our position within the larger context of the human situation, as when I set myself in relation to the neolithic rocks, or in the following passage where I try to capture the very human sense of wonder in contrast to the vast wild panorama of Iguassu Falls[1]:

> And there we stood, spray-drenched, in the midst of the mist, a thousand thousand droplets rising upward out of the drowning roar before and to our sides and dropping off below into fogmist. And we stood in the mist of the Great Waters, skin-soaked, shirts clinging, globules and beads of the Iguazu River shivering like snowflakes in our tresses, then trickling down our giggling, laugh-stained faces. For we had climbed the Brazilian panorama of the Iguaçu Falls (all 275 of them), then crossed back for the drenching baptismal Iguazu close-up to be reached across a nearly mile-long wooden bridge in Argentina. (382)

If what holds the course curriculum together, then, is not the artificial boundaries of an assignment, but rather the excitement of travel as human condition, the repeated discovery of interconnectedness, we must think of writing in a new way. Categories we have created become too circumscribed, although travel writing incorporates and demands the same concepts, but they emerge almost incidentally. Alan's Travel Commandments project is a clear example, a transactional document for an audience of student travelers. However, it arose from his own expressive reflections upon himself as traveler, his reading and research evolving from the project. Consider Justin's poetic description of dawn in the Great Smokies, just before his encounter with a bear:

> Clear and cool. A layer of rippling mist blanketed the ground. The sound of a nearby creek echoed like laughter through the great stand of hemlock trees. Barely lighting the treetops, the sun slid upwards. Mist floating above the ground parted as I walked through it, and a wake of swirling moisture followed me. Almost creation day. (Bowles 9)

Similarly, Lee's project on Colorado elicited argumentative and descriptive, research and reflective writing, while Cary's report-writing on Oxford was dappled with poetic expectations and frank analyses of values and choices. Thus, each document of travel writing offers its own universe of problems to solve and strategies to embrace.

For me the happiest resolution it offers is a way out of the dilemmas of expressive writing. Long a proponent of the personal, I am well versed in the human and intellectual growth such writing spawns. However, I struggle with the "Me-focus," which can disintegrate into whining narcissism. The travel mode is a way out of this, because it both enlarges the canvas and deepens the perspective.

In short, travel writing demands that we contextualize. Students enjoy moving between the internal and the external in travel writing, fitting themselves naturally into the world they are exploring, yet allowing themselves to be touched by it. Thus, however expressive the writing, it still forces a global context. To be a traveler, one must think beyond the self. Values are compared as well as examined. Jane, for example, wrote her term project on a train wreck in Kenya, the harrowing tale of some carefree college students huddled (as instructed) in the back car through a night of uncertainty, annoyed at the delay in their journey. At dawn they finally stepped out to discover that only their own car had been spared, that victims dead and alive lay scattered across the plain, some having been ravished in the night by lions. How these students mustered their courage and their minimal first-aid supplies, comforted the dying, and bandaged the injured until help came much later in the day is an exploration of values in context. In exploring and explicating such emerging texts in peer groups, students expand and deepen critical thinking skills as well.

This same advantage emerges in discussions of the traveler. In some lights, travel may seem quite selfish, imperialist even. Certainly it may damage the environment. Visitors have been known to steal local treasures or display condescension toward local people. We have all encountered tourists more interested in snapping photos and criticizing the toilet paper than understanding the culture. As the whole problem of traveler versus tourist emerges, the writer cannot ignore the underlying question of values in a more global context. Figuring out who we are and who we want to be, what values are reasonable in a needy world, leads to worthy arguments. Making sense of what's out there is how students contextualize themselves in relation to the other.

When we do it right, then, travel has to affect us. The effects emerge in the traveler's writing. So it becomes very hard to stick with old beliefs—one's own or those of one's parents. Even the pleasures we cherish most in our travels come to be questioned and cross-questioned, as in this confession of mine:

> Another title for this entry might be "Life Before Humans," reflecting amusement at my frequent disdain for all things human, my preferring the pristine beauty of the countryside we travel through (albeit on a road made by and for people in a vehicle designed and fueled only because we live in a technological society). How often I consider how a given land must have looked to its first visitors, or how explorers must have felt in encountering, say, that magnificent Sydney Harbour or the Falls of Iguassu. How the land must have looked before we did that which we have done upon it!
>
> And yet, even were it possible for my comfort to remain and I to find a world of "life before humans," I would not choose such a place. This would be inconsistent with my great joy in the works of humans that stun and touch and lift me out of myself and bring me to a serenity beyond the me. Like the alignments of Carnac. Beethoven's *Ninth Symphony*. And now as well the Temple of Borobudur. (519)

This habit of questioning becomes infectious, as in this very article, which feels like a series of questions. Here is another: If I have become traveler and writer as well as teacher, then what is my role in the classroom? Not the tape-recorder tour guide who has all the information in advance and spits it out in sequence no matter what the tourists are doing on the bus. Nor the tour escort getting passengers to hotels. Oh, I am the agent who planned the trip and wrote up the syllabus, but it had better be more than a triptik! And as teacher I'd better go along as simply a more experienced traveler, one still willing to be changed. Since I've traveled, I have to model the receptive character of the traveler willing to be touched by people and place, willing to laugh at herself. I have to be open to students having seen things differently. As a teacher I can set some guidelines, but I must not define the journey in advance.

Perhaps I model this best when I share my own writing, show that I too can be touched or overwhelmed. Near Yogyakarta (Java) I climbed the 1200-year-old Buddhist temple, Borobudur, struggling with a knee disability to mount 150 rough stone steps, many higher than my knees, rounding tiers to follow 1500 relief sculptures of the life of Siddhartha, but headed for 72 latticed stupas and the enormous stupa on the very top. Then I wrote:

> I only know I loved this beautiful temple, felt a harmony with the gracious scenery of its setting, rejoiced in my heart that I had managed to climb it, to touch the latticed stupas of the Buddha, to feel the great serenity of this place.

> And then the painful descent. But I didn't mind; I only thought of how much joy I felt, that I am so rich as to come to Borobudur still able to climb, to descend with Joe's gracious help, his tender presence a reassurance in much that is alien. Serenity. I felt it there today. (518)

Part of the wholeness travel brings is that I usually feel that serenity in the classroom as well. However, another question evolves: Can you teach this if you're not a traveler/writer yourself? Odd question to pose to literature and writing teachers, travelers all, who know the vicarious journeys of their books. Odd question, too, when the journeys lie all around us, and Thoreau is said to have remarked that he had traveled widely in Concord. Here is a more serious question: can a teacher not be a traveler? Are not the best classes always journeys? Can we not incorporate the metaphors and materials of travel writing into many of our classes? Recognizing any writing, any literature course I teach as a journey of intellect and spirit, through uncharted space with a group of fellow travelers whose special talents will only emerge at need, I can see that what so intrigues my students is the blank slate, the sense of potential, the eager anticipation of something wholly unexpected, yet somehow strangely familiar. They are looking for connection in a world that worries them. So am I.

The final question: Have I found what I went looking for, for my students, for myself? For both, I suspect, the secret lies in that Proust passage, seeing with new eyes, thinking in new ways, accepting while challenging. Did I find it? You be the judge. Written off the coast of Chile, this journal entry is entitled "Sweet Enchantment."

> Last night I saw three moons of Jupiter, floating clearly, pale luminous reflecting spheres of mystery all in a row off to the right of the shining planet. The fourth was still a ghost, invisible. At my request our ship's astronomer turned his powerful binoculars toward the brilliance of Alpha Centauri, up to Beta, then off to the left, to the second visible patch of light, focusing upon Omega Centauri, the first globular cluster I've ever seen, gorgeous, a luminous fuzzy pin-dotted glow of 100,000 stars rotating around a common core, all in turn a rotating part of our Milky Way. Long and longingly I gazed into the white radiant brilliance of the Milky Way, tracing the Southern Cross and Carina the Ship, past Canopus and Sirius, all the way to Orion and Aldebaron, and down where the Pleiades had already sunk for the night. And then I had another look at the moons of Jupiter, three shining orbs I'd never dreamed to see. And if this is not exploration, yet surely it is enchantment, to see and comprehend, to hold in one's hand, as it were, a bit of the eloquence that binds this universe in which we sail so many separate journeys in search of our private stars. (Papay 391)

Note

1   In a previous journal entry I wrote of preparing to visit Iguassu Falls, here spelled out in English. In the draft passage quoted, I wrote of seeing the Falls from both Brazil (hence, the Portuguese spelling *Iguaçu*) and Argentina (noted in the Spanish spelling *Iguazu*).

Works Cited

Alvarez, Nancy. *English 360 Journal*. Unpublished Class Project, 2002.

Bowles, Justin. *RCC100 Journal*. Unpublished Class Project, 1994.

Conrad, Joseph. *Three Short Novels: Heart of Darkness; Youth; Typhoon*. New York: Bantam Books, 1960.

Davidson, Cathy N. *Thirty-Six Views of Mount Fuji*. New York: Plume/Penguin, 1993.

Harle, William. *English 360 Journal*. Unpublished Class Project, 2002.

Le Guin, Ursula K. *The Left Hand of Darkness*. New York: Ace Books, 21st Printing, 1981.

Miller, Kevin. *English 360 Journal*. Unpublished Class Project, 2000.

Papay, Twila Yates. *Journal of a Sabbatical*. Unpublished Travel Journal, 1991–92.

Proust, Marcel. *Remembrance of Things Past*. Translated by C. K. Scott-Moncrieff. New York: Random House, 1934.

Riley, Amber. *English 360 Journal*. Unpublished Class Project, 2002.

Stevens, Alicia. *English 360 Journal*. Unpublished Class Project, 2002.

Chapter 11

Writing Ireland: Travel Writing as Study and Practice for Students Going Abroad

Christine S. Cozzens

This Ireland exists: but whoever goes there and fails to find it has no claim on the author.
—Heinrich Böll, dedication page, *Irish Journal* (quoted in Powers 3)

One of the oldest and most cross-cultural of literary genres, travel writing springs from a human need to understand places, exotic or familiar, and to find in them some connection to group or individual identity. Like many travelers, I knew I wanted to write about places before I knew there was a literary genre to encompass my efforts. Even travelers with no aspirations to write or to publish will keep journals of their trips to remember but also to work out an understanding of the new place, thus claiming it and making it their own. I had a great-grandfather who left no other writings except a travel journal he kept when he crossed the United States in the 1880s. Notebooks and journals travel with us; essays and books emerge later on, as we continue to ponder the meaning of place. Travel writing is the final stage of a trip, the moment when the writer gathers the fragments of experience and memory into something like a whole. As Heinrich Böll suggests in the disclaimer to his account of a sojourn in Ireland, a personal story of a place ultimately transcends the physical location, becoming an entity unto itself, a place-story that lives in the imagination long after the writer has moved on and long after the place has been discovered by others and, perhaps, transformed into something else.

Ever since traveling in Ireland as an undergraduate and studying Irish literature in graduate school, I knew I wanted to lead a student trip that would try to put these great works of imagination in context. Although I had studied Ireland formally, my most developed connection comes from many subsequent visits to the country and from travel writing I have done for the *New York Times* and other publications. I wanted to find a way to turn that interest into a course that would appeal to undergraduates and prepare them for their own travel experiences.

The practical realities of launching such a venture within the existing international education program at Agnes Scott College, where I teach, helped shape the original design of the course. Viewed as the culmination of a semester's study, college-sponsored trips follow the fall or spring term, taking place during three weeks in either January or May. Before the trip, students study a topic related to the country or countries they'll visit, enrolling in one or two designated courses. After the trip, they produce an essay, a presentation, a performance, or some other kind of work based on their travel experience. Having done most of my traveling in The Republic of Ireland and Northern Ireland in the winter months, I knew that contrary to popular wisdom, the so-called off-season would be the best time for a trip, with few other tourists on hand to crowd the many sites and monuments we would visit and the weather not as bleak as most people (including the Irish) imagine. Fall courses followed by a January trip would be the most desirable format.

According to the college formula, two courses, usually from different departments, are designated as prerequisites for the study trip, and the two instructors are the trip leaders. A colleague in the English department, Linda Hubert, shared my interest in Irish literature and travel. Because the two trip courses would be in the same department, we made an effort to define our topics as differently as possible to appeal to the widest range of students. Linda's course would introduce students to twentieth-century Irish literature—especially plays and poetry—in the context of Ireland's political struggles. Drawing on my interest in the reading and writing of travel literature, I proposed a creative writing course that would teach travel writing as study and practice. The course would focus on the history and development of travel writing about Ireland, and the students would learn to write travel essays. Because of this dual focus, I named the course using the purposefully ambiguous title "Writing Ireland."

A topic that is interesting and worthy of study does not always translate naturally into a feasible undergraduate course. Once I had defined the topic, I had to confront the special circumstances inherent in teaching this genre. With some experience teaching travel writing in nonfiction courses, I had an idea of what to expect. Travel writing seems like an intriguing concept to undergraduates, full of promise and potential adventure, but few have read widely or at all in the genre, and many have a limited concept of what it can encompass. Such limitations can be disheartening when these would-be travel writers—who may have traveled very little—face their first assignments. Each time I taught the course, for example, students voiced fears that their only travel experiences to date—family trips to Disney World, Washington, DC, or grandparents' homes—lacked the exoticism and sense of derring-do that they thought all travel narratives required. Student writers don't necessarily see that unpleasant places can be the basis for a great travel narrative, or that a sense of place and a sense of the traveler's identity and character—what Paul Fussell calls "the autobiographical narrative at the heart" of travel writing—is far more important to travel writing than a sense of adventure (14).

In choosing works of travel writing for the students to read and emulate, I had to consider their value as representations of Ireland and as inspiration for writers. Many readers find contemporary travel writing compelling, but few of them trouble to wade through the dense and difficult early texts. I quickly realized I would have to begin our study of Ireland with contemporary examples of travel writing that could excite the students about the genre; essays such as those collected in *A Woman's World, The Best of Granta Travel,* or *The Best American Travel Writing* series could show where travel writing is today, though they contained no works about Ireland. How would I inspire my students to be interested in the early works that reveal so much about the genre's origins and about the history and culture of the country we were planning to visit?

As a remote island attracting the interest of adventurous European explorers and as England's first colony, Ireland played a significant role in the development of travel writing. The earliest narratives about Ireland were almost all written by Englishmen who traveled throughout the neighboring island often on government business, but sometimes for personal reasons. My vision of introducing students to Ireland using the writings of visitors through the centuries had sprung from a remarkable collection published in 1991 called *The English Traveller in Ireland: Accounts of Ireland and the Irish Through Five Centuries,* edited by John P. Harrington. The fascinating accounts Harrington collected begin as early as 1571 with excerpts from Edmund Campion's *A History of Ireland* and include works by famous statesmen, authors, and thinkers such as Edmund Spenser, William Makepeace Thackeray, Thomas Carlyle, and Harriet Martineau. These early English visitors to Ireland consistently see Ireland as "a problem," a problem for the English to solve (9):

> Another feature common to all these works is persistent confusion: these writers perceive Ireland as a spectacle essentially different from England, and they hazard explanations for it…in the form of generalizations about national character. These writers also confront Ireland with their own vested interests, whether they are political appointees seeking preferment, adventurers seeking fortune, travel writers seeking picturesque material. (9–10)

As the phrase "a spectacle essentially different from England" suggests, the essays and excerpts in the book show how travel writing arose from awkward, often uninformed and contentious, always speculative attempts to explain difference—the strange appearance and ways of people and landscapes far from home.

Much of the early travel writing about Ireland and about other places in the world uses cultural encounters to define the writer's own national identity rather than to understand or explain the place visited. These early works show little or no consciousness of the traveler's inevitable bias or of the individual experience of travel. Until the nineteenth century, when European romanticism raised the possibility of finding personal meaning in encounters with landscapes and cultures, most travel writing about Ireland presents a fairly negative view of the country. The accounts in Harrington's collection raise complex issues about the growth of empire, English-Irish relations, and the meaning of national identity, but they are frequently critical, often dismissive of the culture and people of Ireland. For students encountering the history and literature of Ireland for the first time, it might be difficult to come to a complex understanding of the country if seen only through such portraits, especially in the context of a creative writing course where the nuances of historical documents were not the central focus. Would the students be able to see in these works any semblance of the early forms and strategies of the genre they were learning to write? Would they be able to place such alien views of the Irish culture and landscape in their historical context? These currents inevitably accompany the teaching of travel literature, fostering tension and argument but ultimately a more profound understanding of the genre.

The creative writing component of the course had to complement the reading, exploring at least to some extent the modes, voices, and tropes others had employed in the telling of their stories about Ireland. While studying Irish history and the evolution of travel writing, students would learn to write about places in a variety of formats, preparing to write a piece about some aspect of their trip to Ireland during the January intersession. The first travel writing assignments would have to focus on Atlanta or on places the students knew well enough to write about or were planning to visit during the term. Given the variety—or in most cases the limits—of travel experience in the class, I would have to make sure the students understood that "travel" included walking to a far corner of the campus and sitting in a grove of trees or riding a MARTA train from Decatur to downtown Atlanta, as well as the journey from their homes to college.

The process of planning and writing a travel essay—familiar to me from the perspective of my own writing—had to be turned inside out and broken down into steps that students, most of them with little or no experience of creative writing, could follow. To determine how to fashion and teach the writing assignments, I began to look for theoretical essays about the genre—mostly found in prefaces to anthologies—and to dissect my favorite pieces of travel writing. Paul Fussell defines successful travel writing as mediating "between two poles: the individual physical things it describes, on the one hand, and the larger theme it is 'about,' on the other, that is, the particular and the universal" (16). Readers tend to think that travel writing requires mainly description. Certainly travel writers must learn how to describe what their senses take in and the thoughts that accompany experience, but good travel writing depends even more on the portrayal of scenes and anecdotes that bring a place to life. Mere description can seem dry, whereas a lively scene that incorporates dialogue, action, and description is usually more successful at recreating a place and excavating its meaning. The sequence of scenes and anecdotes tells its own story, with contrasts, parallels, and pacing all contributing to a three-dimensional account that is not just remembered but relived.

In addition to setting the scene and conveying what happens, a travel writer must create for the reader an autographical narrative running through the work, a sense that the writer is on location surrounded by the sights and scenes of the unfolding drama of place. Some nonfiction writers like to think of this narrative as "the movie playing in the writer's head," and analysts of travel writing often use cinematic terms (long shot, wide shot, lead frame) to describe the writer's moves in constructing a travel narrative (see the table of contents in Travel Writing by L. Peat O'Neil). Readers want to know about the place the travel writer is describing—the landscape, the history, the culture, the daily life—but more than anything else, they want to know who the writer was in that place.

A travel essay tied to a place or a group of places with a strong personal narrative interwoven throughout—that would be the culminating assignment, the work the students would write based on their trip to Ireland. Shorter assignments during the previous semester would exercise the skills necessary to write the final piece, ease the students into the longer project, and create links through topic or type of writing to the readings, both contemporary and historical. The first time I taught Writing Ireland, I divided the early assignments into two categories according to the two general modes: informational and reflective. While this division suggested orderly assignments (Informational: devise a walking tour for the campus. Reflective: compare sitting on the front porch of your dormitory to sitting on the front porch at home), the students found it almost impossible to disentangle reflective writing from writing that yields information. They soon realized that the latter is hardly palatable without at least some of the former. I had to agree with their resistance to what turned out to be, in the actual writing process, an artificial distinction.

In the two subsequent versions of the course, I abandoned that approach, moving instead to a more flexible series of assignments that I came to call the "travel writing project" that would teach the two modes more realistically as interdependent. Over the course of five weeks, students wrote five short (500 words) drafts or "starter essays." The topics were designed to push their writing in some of the directions that travel writing moves and to negotiate between the poles of information and autobiography:

1. Take a journal entry from the weekend and work on it, adding more description (avoid adjectives!) and perhaps a little bit of story.
2. Tell the story of a significant place that you remember from your childhood. Recreate the place for us in words, helping us to understand why the place stays in your mind even today.
3. Write a "how to go there" and "how to experience" piece about a place or site within thirty minutes of Agnes Scott. You'll need to provide factual details, but you also need to communicate the experience and make us want to go there, too.
4. Write about your hometown as a place that others might want to visit. Tell us what the place is like, what we should see and do when we are there, and what we'll learn about you as we come to know the place where you grew up.
5. Choose from these possibilities for today's starter essay:
    a) Write about something that you learned while traveling;
    b) Document the experience of someone who is new to the U.S. (an international student, for example);
    c) Write about a place created in literature (Hardy's Wessex, "Sweet Home" in Toni Morrison's *Beloved*);
    d) Write about a place that represents a person (the Margaret Mitchell House, Graceland, the Martin Luther King Jr. Birthplace, and so on);
    e) Write about a place that you go back to after being away from it for a long time. (Writing Ireland Syllabus, 2002)

After discussing these drafts with the class and in small groups and receiving comments from me, the students would choose three of the five pieces for final revising and editing for a grade. This series of assignments gave both the students and me more flexibility regarding topics and connections to the readings. The use of a portfolio allowed the students to determine what kind of writing about places they found most comfortable, while still pushing them to explore a range of approaches. In this new version of the course, the second half of the semester was devoted to writing a longer, more sustained travel essay, a real precursor of the essay they would write about Ireland.

In 1998 these realizations were still in the future. With the two courses defined, an initial approach to the writing assignments outlined, and a list of writers and literary sites beginning to emerge, my colleague and I planned the itinerary for the trip to Ireland. In addition to literary sites and landscapes connected to our readings, we included a list of places of natural beauty and historical interest that would give our students a sense of Ireland's past and present identity. Our trip would encompass the rural and the urban Ireland with a clockwise tour of the country and multiple night stays in Dublin, Waterford, Killarney, Galway, Sligo, and Belfast.

Writing Ireland now had three goals: to introduce the history, culture, and landscape of Ireland in preparation for the trip abroad; to study the evolution of travel writing as a literary genre with Ireland as the main example; and to teach writing about travel and about places in the context of the larger genre of creative nonfiction. The key to making this ambitious plan succeed would be to find ways to overlap and integrate these themes and to create a unified, coherent course. I taught this course three times over six years, leading three groups of students on variations of the itinerary described above. Each version of the course and the trip yielded a deeper understanding of what travel writing is and of how central this genre has been to the story of human encounters with landscapes and cultures.

The Travel Writer's Voice

The challenge for that first semester in 1998 was to make my three ungainly goals or subjects work well together. Providing an overview of Irish history and culture was the easiest of the subjects to manage. To introduce the class to Ireland's history, particularly the relationship with Britain, which has haunted Irish literature and travel writing, I had a textbook and several documentary films. Over the three versions of the course, I added more interactive activities for this unit: small group study questions or miniature research projects that asked students to research an influential myth, a historical figure or event, or key term and present their findings. Moving the five-week history unit from the first part of the semester to the middle segment allowed our early discussions of contemporary travel writing about Ireland to pique students' interest in the historical background, encouraging them to develop questions that would drive their study more effectively than my insistence on its importance. The history readings paralleled the travel literature readings. For example, we would read about the initial colonization of Ireland during the reign of Elizabeth I and study travel accounts by her emissaries such as Edmund Spenser and Richard Stanihurst. In a different scenario, we would consider the rediscovery of the Gaelic language culture in the late nineteenth century and follow J. M. Synge's tour of the Gaelic-speaking communities on the Blasket and Aran Islands.

The main problem the students encountered during the first version of the course was finding a voice and a structure or a variety of structures for their stories about places. As Joan Didion notes about writing nonfiction, "In many ways writing is the act of saying I, of imposing oneself upon other people, of saying *listen to me, see it my way, change your mind*" ("Why I Write" qtd. in Smart 179, original emphasis). Nonfiction—travel writing included—requires a daring "I," not the pronoun itself but the unmistakable presence of a self that sees, feels, thinks, and writes in every moment of the work. Travel writing is especially demanding in this sense as it asks readers to accept—at least while reading the work—one person's way of connecting the miscellanies of experience, one person's cultural perceptions, one person's inevitably flawed but always potentially insightful vision of the world.

Newcomers to the genre struggle with this problem, asking themselves "Who am I when I am writing this piece? Where should I be in it?" All of this is conveyed not only by what happens in the piece but by the writer's voice, "the sum effect of all the stylistic choices a writer makes to communicate not only information about a subject but also information about himself or herself to a particular audience" (Hickey 1). The aspiring travel writers of Writing Ireland faced doubts and questions about their role and their voice, even when the assignments seemed fairly easy. What kind of authority did they have to write about any place, even when they knew it well, such as a hometown, an often visited neighborhood, or their college campus? In addition, well-trained in the genre of the research paper with all its proper deference to other thinkers and other texts, these undergraduate students found it difficult to liberate themselves from the research paper voice and to find a personal voice with which to tell their own stories of place.

Neither the culturally embattled tone of most of the essays in *The English Traveller in Ireland* nor the breezy man-or-woman-against-the-elements style of the contemporary travel writing selections assigned offered a voice for the students to model, though these works were useful in demonstrating the dramatic arc of a travel essay. Some of the selections in *Ireland in Mind* came closest to providing helpful examples of voice, but as in so many travel writing anthologies, most of the works in this volume are excerpted, and there were few complete examples to suggest how the writer's voice developed or how a whole piece of travel writing might be structured. When I first gave an assignment to write a travel article, I offered samples from the *New York Times* travel section, some of my own included, as models for blending autobiographical narrative with thoughtful analysis and useful information. The resulting student essays tended to succeed at covering the content of a travel feature but failed entirely at developing an appropriate voice and tone, falling back on sales pitches to "sell" the place they were writing about or failing completely to find a role for "I" in the research paper-like essays they produced.

In an effort to teach students to be at ease with their writing voice, I had assigned regular journal writing throughout the semester with an emphasis on writing about places as a component of the course. The writer could sit under a tree on campus, eat dinner at a local Mexican restaurant, ride the public transportation system, or visit the Margaret Mitchell house downtown as long as she wrote about what it was like to be there and about the associations the place stirred in her own mind—what I call the outer and inner life of the place, the two always entwined and interdependent in travel writing. The journals in this first course were only partly successful. The entries about places would cover what happened there without capturing the look, the feel, the mood, the associations stirred in the writer's mind. The student writers needed to learn how to relive the experience on the page; I needed to find an active way to teach them to do this.

Working with journal writing seemed to be the best way to establish a sense of identity and purpose as a writer. I announced that we would begin to take walking field trips to nearby areas—the campus art museum, the courthouse square in downtown Decatur—so that the students could write as they went, honing their powers of observation and learning that what may seem unimportant at the time of a visit or trip sometimes plays a large part when writing about the place later. I took as our inspiration the "Day in the Life of" books, in which photographers attempt to capture the essence of a country by working in the same twenty-four hours, spreading out across the assigned region and finding images of ordinary life that tell the story of that day (*A Day in the Life of Ireland, A Day in the Life of Africa, A Day in the Life of Hawaii*). The class had about ninety minutes to spend doing very much the same thing in writing for a few square city blocks that encompassed stores, restaurants, a park, several public buildings including the county courthouse, and abundant street life. When we arrived at the courthouse in the center of town, I told the students to fan out, write about whatever they saw or experienced, but not to talk to anyone from the class during the allotted time. At the next class meeting, we read snippets of our informal writings and were surprised to hear a remarkably vivid portrayal of an hour in the life of downtown Decatur emerging from what had begun as casual observations.

The next week, I repeated the assignment with more focus. This time each student was given five minutes to claim a region of Agnes Scott's small residential campus where she would spend an hour writing about life on the campus. One student observed a dance class; another followed a couple of gardeners as they went about their work; another invited herself to a history lecture; still another sat down in the snack bar and wrote about the patrons' comings and goings. With writing skills honed by the first "hour in the life" experiment and benefiting from being assigned to a more readily knowable subject (their own college), the student writers were able to write especially compelling observations. We were so pleased with the compiled texts that we edited and "published" them in the sense of making them available electronically on campus as *A Day in the Life of Agnes Scott College.*

The interest this work generated on campus inspired confidence in the class. The next assignment asked students to write a short informational travel essay about a place within an hour's drive of the campus by car or public transportation. Our first publishing experience emboldened us to use these essays to compile a guidebook for new students. Groups of students in the class shared responsibility for arranging, editing, formatting, and illustrating this book, all of which engendered a cooperative spirit that would serve us well on the trip to Ireland. Publishing the works of the student travel writers became a regular and important part of the course, including the trip.

These writing activities bolstered the group's and individuals' confidence in their authority to write about places because the students found that their classmates and others were interested in what they had to say about places— even well-known places such as the local bar or pizza restaurant—when the accounts were descriptive, personal, and full of lively scenes and examples. Seeing the results of their journal note-taking turned into published writing that others would read made the journals seem worth doing. After our class jaunts with journals and pens in hand, the students also found themselves increasingly comfortable with writing in public places. One of my happiest moments on the Ireland trip with this group was on our last night during a farewell dinner and sing-along at the Abbey Tavern in Howth. During a lull in the show, five students at my table suddenly whisked out their journals and, as if moved by the same spirit, began scribbling away. The group may have attracted some stares, but I knew that that moment would become, for each of them, a small part of a travel narrative to be.

Broadening the Definition of Travel Writing

The first course and trip, while quite successful in our minds and according to the evaluations, opened my mind to a new way of looking at travel writing, which led to a revamping of the readings for the course during the fall semester of 2000. The travel writing about Ireland that I had assigned, while revealing in its commentary on the history and culture of past centuries, did not provide an adequate orientation to contemporary Ireland or to the landscapes and sites we had visited. As predicted, the older works—tinged as some of them were with English prejudices about the "mere Irish," their squalid settlements, and untamed land—tended to create a negative picture of the country that the students resented at times (Edmund Campion qtd. in Harrington 31). To counterbalance this colonial representation of Ireland, I needed to offer a more complete view of the land and its people, one that was recounted through history by insiders, by the Irish.

Travel writing always depends on the articulation of a sense of place, an element shared by literature. Following the lead of Paul Fussell's *The Norton Book of Travel* and several recent anthologies that attempted to portray Ireland in a variety of literary modes (*Ireland in Mind, The Ireland Anthology),* I decided to define travel writing broadly to include both accounts by visitors that scrutinized the land, the culture, and the people, and other literary works by visitors and natives. Poetry, fiction, drama, essays, and other nonfiction works were now within the scope of the course. From the late nineteenth century forward, as Ireland moved toward greater resistance to British rule and eventual partition and independence for what is today the Republic of Ireland, the Irish generated an outpouring of works of literature and analysis describing and claiming their culture. Writing about Ireland had come to be increasingly the province of Irish writers, in both the English and Irish languages. Including a broader range of works by Irish writers to the course would bring the voices of the colonized into the chorus of views in Writing Ireland.

For Writing Ireland, poetry would play an especially important part in exploring the deepest meanings of place in Irish culture. Even though instruction in the course centered on prose, I wanted these creative writing students to understand the special intensity of poetic language. Poetry was part of both Ireland's history and, according to the broader definition, part of its repertoire of travel literature. Irish poetry of the sixth through tenth centuries is "full of the life of the people" and the way they lived on the land, according to contemporary poet and translator Thomas Kinsella (xxiv). Poetry records the clash of cultures that occurred when the Anglo-Normans turned their attention to colonizing the land to the west, marking it with their distinctive castles, market towns, and fortresses. In the centuries during which British politics and culture dominated Ireland, poetry and song were the chief literary repositories of the indigenous culture.

Another incentive for adding poetry to the readings came from an unexpected source. On that first trip our tour company CIE (Córas Iompair Éireann) assigned us a driver-guide named Michael O'Brien, a largely self-educated expert not only on Irish history and culture but on poetry as well. As we drove along Irish roads, Michael recited verses and verses of poetry, often from the works of his favorite, Patrick Kavanagh, but also from the monastic poets, the Gaelic bards, the balladeer Thomas Moore, William Butler Yeats, Seamus Heaney, and many others. The connections among these poems and the places we visited powerfully illustrated how writing brings landscape and culture to life.

Though I had to be careful not to overwhelm the students with reading in this writing course, the inclusion of some poetry, a novel (*Reading in the Dark* by Seamus Deane), an autobiography (*The Islandman* by Tomás O'Crohan) and other short works of literature added Irish voices to the portrayal of Ireland. These works also widened the range of strategies these novice travel writers would have at their disposal as they began to tell their stories of places and their meanings.

Travel Writing and the Spoken Word

By the third time I taught Writing Ireland in the fall of 2002, I had found relevant, suggestive combinations of historical readings, travel writing, and literary works to convey the stories that were part of the course and part of the trip around Ireland. Still, I thought we could do more to make the travel writing we were reading back home come alive for the students. On the second trip one day during our visit to Sligo, a student had taken the bus microphone to read aloud some of the poems Yeats had written about the places we had just visited: Lissadell House, "that old Georgian mansion" where the speaker recalls "the talk of youth, / Two girls in silk kimono, both / Beautiful, one a gazelle"; and Glencar Waterfall, "Where the wandering water gushes / From the hills above Glen-Car, / In pools among the rushes / That scarce could bathe a star" (Yeats 230, 19). Hearing Yeats's words, read by a student in the places that had inspired them, brought us a new sense of the importance and beauty of what he had said, of how he put his ideas and his feelings about these places into words.

Why not add students' voices to Michael's as we made our way around literary Ireland? For the third trip "bus readings" became a formal and surprisingly popular part of the trip. Before leaving home, I asked students in the class to choose readable selections from the works we studied so we could compile an anthology. Through formal assignments but often spontaneously from their own interest and enthusiasm, students soon began to share the airwaves of the bus's public address system. Works studied in the classroom took on new meaning on the road. After visiting the monastery at Glendalough where St. Kevin lived as a recluse, a student read us "The Hermit's Song" extolling the simple beauty of the "little hut in the wilderness" with its "clear pool to wash away sins" in a "choice land with many gracious gifts" (Hoaglund 28–29). As we approached Dingle Bay on the peninsula of the same name, another student read Blasket Islander Tomás O'Crohan's description of his first visit there as a child in the 1860s:

> We reached the quay, and my eyes were as big as two mugs with wonder. I saw gentlefolk standing there with chains across their bellies, poor people half-clad, cripples here and there on every side, and a blind man with his guide. Three great ships lay alongside the quay, laden with goods from overseas—yellow grain in one of them, timber in another, and coal in the third. (43)

Our understanding of the abandoned buildings staggered across Ireland's western landscape was deepened by hearing Heinrich Böll's description of a deserted village on Achill Island as "all those gray triangles and squares on a green-gray slope of the hill...the white sheep huddling like lice among the ruins" *(Irish Journal* qtd. in Powers 11). The words of these authors spoke to us when we read them in the classroom, but their eloquence was magnified as we engaged in our own experiences of the places that inspired them.

As Heinrich Böll suggests, there are as many Irelands as there are writers to tell about it. Over the years, the students of Writing Ireland and I were fortunate to have the special opportunity of reading travel writing about Ireland as we traveled around the country, stopping at many of the places we'd read about but discovering them anew through experience and through writing of our own. If the students had struggled with some of the older works when we studied them at home, traveling in those writers' footsteps helped establish a more readable context. The preparatory activities that had shed some light on how travel writers work made carrying out research and preliminary writing in Ireland both natural and necessary, but the most important change from the first version of the course to the third was the positioning of travel writing firmly within a written and spoken literary canon. Once the student writers understood that this unfamiliar genre comprises all the familiar strategies and moves of any imaginative work, they were more able to discern how it differs and how they might find a voice for the story of their travels.

Works Cited

The Best of Granta Travel. London: Granta Books, 1991.

Böll, Heinrich. *Irish Journal.* 1957. Evanston, IL: The Marlboro Press, 1998.

Bond, Marybeth, ed. *A Woman's World: True Stories of Life on the Road.* San Francisco: Traveler's Tales, Inc., 1997.

Cohen, David Elliot, and Lee Liberman, eds. *A Day in the Life of Africa.* Publishers Group West, 2002.

Cozzens, Christine S. "The Art of the Travel Journal." *Abroad View Magazine* http://www.abroadviewmagazine.com/resources/preparing_abroad/keeping_journal.html; from spring 2003.

———. "A Cabin, a Lake, a Memory." *New York Times* 8 September 1996: 33.

———. "Capturing a Moment: Travel Writing Inside Out." *Abroad View Magazine* Spring 2003: 49.

———. "Hooked on a Single Place." *New York Times* 18 May 2003: 23.

———. "Tracing Tragedy in Ireland." *New York Times* 1 June 1997: 13ff.

Crotty, Patrick, ed. *Modern Irish Poetry.* Belfast: The Blackstaff Press, 1995.

Deane, Seamus. *Reading in the Dark.* London: Vintage, 1997.

Didion, Joan. "Why I Write." *The New York Times Magazine.* 5 December 1976: 50.

Dunne, Seán, ed. *The Ireland Anthology.* New York. St. Martin's Press, 1997.

Erwitt, Jennifer, and Tom Lawlor, eds. *A Day in the Life of Ireland.* Chino Hills, CA: Collins Publications, 1991.

Fussell, Paul, ed. *The Norton Book of Travel.* New York: W. W. Norton & Company, 1987.

Harrington, John P. *The English Traveller in Ireland.* Dublin: Wolfhound Press, 1991.

Hickey, Dona J. *Developing a Written Voice.* Mountain View, CA: Mayfield Publishing Company, 1993.

Hoaglund, Kathleen, ed. *1000 Years of Irish Poetry: The Gaelic and Anglo Irish Poets from Pagan Times to the Present.* New York: Welcome Rain Publishers, 2000.

Kinsella, Thomas, ed. *The New Oxford Book of Irish Verse.* Oxford: Oxford UP, 1986.

O'Brien, Maire, and Conor Cruise O'Brien. *A Concise History of Ireland.* London: Thames and Hudson, 1985.

O'Crohan, Tomás. *The Islandman.* 1937. Oxford: Oxford UP, 2000.

O'Neil, L. Peat. *Travel Writing.* Cincinnati: Writer's Digest Books, 1996.

O'Sullivan, Maurice. *Twenty Years A-Growin'.* Dublin: J. S. Sanders & Co.

Powers, Alice Leccese, ed. *Ireland in Mind.* New York: Vintage, 2000.

Smolan, Rick, and David Elliot Cohen, eds. *A Day in the Life of Hawaii.* Workman Publishing Company, 1990.

Synge, J. M. *Collected Works II: Prose.* Washington, DC: Catholic University of America, 1982.

Theroux, Paul, ed. *The Best American Travel Writing 2001.* Boston: Houghton Mifflin, 2001.

Yeats, William Butler. *The Collected Poems of W. B. Yeats.* New York: The Macmillan Company, 1956.

Part IV
Teaching Resources

Although the following list is not exhaustive, it does include many of the works discussed by the contributors, and it may help teachers integrate travel literature into their classrooms.

Primary Works

Battuta, Ibn. *The Travels of Ibn Battuta A.D. 1324–54*. 3 vols. Ed. H. A. R. Gibb. Cambridge: Hakluyt Society, 1958–71.

The Best of Granta Travel. London: Granta Books, 1991.

Bird, Isabella L. *A Lady's Life in the Rocky Mountains*. Norman: U of Oklahoma P, 1988.

Bond, Marybeth. *A Woman's World: True Stories of Life on the Road*. San Francisco: Traveler's Tales, Inc., 1997.

Brenan, Gerald. *South from Granada*. London: H. Hamilton, 1957.

Brophy, Brigid. *In Transit: An Heroi-Cyclic Novel*. New York: Putnam, 1969.

Byron, Robert. *The Road to Oxiana*. London: J. Lehmann, 1950.

Cahill, Tim. *Hold the Enlightenment*. New York: Villard, 2002.

———. *Road Fever*. New York: Vintage Books, 1991.

Chatwin, Bruce. *The Songlines*. New York: Penguin Books, 1988.

Clark, Eleanor. *Rome and a Villa*. New York: Pantheon, 1975.

Cohen, David Elliot, and Lee Liberman, eds. *A Day in the Life of Africa*. Publishers' Group West, 2002.

Cozzens, Christine S. "The Art of the Travel Journal." *Abroad View Magazine*. http://www.abroadviewmagazine.com/resources/preparing_abroad/ • keeping_journal.html; from spring 2003.

———. "A Cabin, A Lake, A Memory." *New York Times* 8 September 1996: 33.

———. " Capturing a Moment: Travel Writing Inside Out." *Abroad View Magazine* Spring 2003: 49.

———. "Hooked on a Single Place." *New York Times* 18 May 2003: 23.

———. "Tracing Tragedy in Ireland." *New York Times* 1 June 1997: 13ff.

Crichton, Michael. *Travels*. New York: Ballantine Books, 1988.

Darwin, Charles. *The Voyage of the Beagle*. New York: Bantam Books, 1972.

Daugherty, William J. *In the Shadow of the Ayatollah. A CIA Hostage in Iran*. Annapolis: Naval Institute P, 2001.

Dinesen, Isak. *Out of Africa and Shadows on the Grass.* New York: Vintage Books, 1985.

Erwitt, Jennifer, and Tom Lawlor, eds. *A Day in the Life of Ireland.* Chino Hills, CA: Collins Publications, 1991.

de Botton, Alain. *The Art of Travel.* New York: Pantheon, 2002.

Dillard, Annie. *Pilgrim at Tinker Creek.* 1974. New York: Bantam Books, 1982.

————. *The Writing Life.* New York: Harper and Row, 1989.

Fisher, M. F. K. *Two Towns in Provence.* New York: Vintage, 1964.

Fuller, Margaret. *Summer on the Lakes, in 1843.* Urbana: U of Illinois P, 1991.

Ghosh, Amitav. *In an Antique Land.* New York: Knopf, 1993.

Gopnik, Adam. *Paris to the Moon.* New York: Random House, 2000.

Harrington, John P. *The English Traveller in Ireland.* Dublin: Wolfhound Press, 1991.

Herr, Michael. *Dispatches.* New York: Knopf, 1978.

Hessler, Peter. *River Town: Two Years on the Yangtze.* New York: Harper-Collins, 2001.

Horowitz, Tony. *Baghdad without a Map, and Other Misadventures in Arabia.* New York: Dutton, 1991.

Iyer, Pico. *The Lady and the Monk: Four Seasons in Kyoto.* New York: Vintage Books, 1992.

————. *Video Night in Kathmandu. And Other Reports from the Not-So-Far East.* New York: Knopf, 1988.

Jacobs, Harriet. *Incidents in the Life of a Slave Girl.* New York: Modern Library, 2000.

James, Henry. "Americans Abroad." *The Nation* 3 October 1878: 208–9.

Kahn, Charlotte. "Emigration without Leaving Home." *Immigrant Experiences.* Ed. Paul H. Elovitz and Charlotte Kahn. Madison: Fairleigh Dickinson UP, 1997. 255–73.

Kane, Joe. *Savages.* New York: Vintage Departures, 1996.

Kingsley, Mary. *Travels in West Africa, Congo Francais, Corsico, and Cameroons.* London: Cass, 1965.

Kircher, Athanasius. *China Illustrata.* Trans. from the 1677 Latin edition by Charles Van Tuyl. Bloomington: Indiana UP, 1987.

Krakauer, Jon. *Into Thin Air.* New York: Doubleday, 1997.

Matthiessen, Peter. *The Snow Leopard.* New York: Viking, 1978.

Melville, Herman. *Moby-Dick.* New York: Houghton Mifflin Company, 1956.

Morris, Jan. *The World: Travels 1950–2000.* New York: W. W. Norton & Company, 2003.

Morris, Mary. *Nothing to Declare. Memoirs of a Woman Traveling Alone.* New York: Penguin, 1989.

Murphy, Dervla. *Eight Feet in the Andes.* Woodstock, NY: The Overlook Press, 1983.

Naipaul, V. S. *The Writer and the World.* New York: A.A. Knopf, 2002.

Nature's Pictures Drawn by Fancies Pencil to the Life. Book II: Feigned Stories in Prose. 2nd ed. London: A. Maxwell, 1671.

Newsham, Brad. *Take Me with You. A Round-the World Journey to Invite a Stranger Home.* New York: Ballantine, 2000.

O'Flaherty, Liam. *A Tourist's Guide to Ireland.* 1929: Dublin: Wolfhound Press, 1998.

Orwell, George. *Homage to Catalonia.* London: Secker & Warburg, 1997.

Paulsen, Gary. *Zero to Sixty. The Motorcycle Journey of a Lifetime.* San Diego: Harcourt Brace, 1997.

Percy, Walker. "The Loss of the Creature." *The Message in the Bottle.* New York: Farrar, Straus, and Giroux/Noonday Press, 1975, 1997. 46–63.

Pham, Andrew X. *Catfish and Mandala.* New York: Picador, 1999.

Polo, Marco. *The Travels.* Trans. and intro. by Ronald Latham. Hammondsworth, Middlesex: Penguin Classics, 1972.

Raban, Jonathan. *A Passage to Juneau: A Sea and Its Meanings.* New York: Random House, 1999.

————. *Hunting Mister Heartbreak. A Discovery of America.* New York: Vintage Departures, 1998.

Robb, Peter. *Midnight in Sicily: On Art, Food, History, Travel & Cosa Nostra.* Boston: Faber and Faber, 1998.

Roethke, Theodore. *Selected Poems.* London: Faber and Faber, 1969.

Rowlandson, Mary. *The Narrative of the Captivity and Restoration of Mrs. Mary Rowlandson.* 1682. Boston: Houghton Mifflin, 1930.

Salzman, Mark. *Iron and Silk.* New York: Vintage Books, 1990.

Smith, Zadie. *White Teeth. A Novel.* New York: Random House, 2000.

Smolan, Rick, and David Elliot Cohen, eds. *A Day in the Life of Hawaii.* Workman Publishing Company, 1990.

Smollett, Tobias George. *Travels through France and Italy.* New York: Oxford UP, 1979.

Snyder, Gary. *A Place in Space.* Washington, DC: Counterpoint, 1995.

Steinbeck, John. *Travels with Charley: in Search of America.* New York: Penguin Books, 2002.

Stevenson, Robert Louis. *Travels on a Donkey in the Cevennes. And Selected Travel Writings.* New York: Oxford UP, 1992.

Sullivan, Zohreh T. *Exiled Memories. Stories of Iranian Diaspora.* Philadelphia: Temple UP, 2001.

Theroux, Paul. *Fresh Air Fiend. Travel Writings 1985–2000.* Boston: Houghton Mifflin Co., 2000.

———. *The Happy Isles of Oceania. Paddling the Pacific.* New York: Ballantine, 2002.

———. *The Pillars of Hercules: A Grand Tour of the Mediterranean.* New York: G. P. Putnam's Sons, 1995.

• Thoreau, Henry David. *Walden.* 1854. New York: Alfred A. Knopf, 1922.

Thubron, Colin. *In Siberia.* New York: HarperCollins, 1999.

Twain, Mark. *The Innocents Abroad.* Hartford: American Publishing Company, 1869.

Vaughan, Alden T., and Edward W. Clark, eds. *Puritans among the Indians: Accounts of Captivity and Redemption 1676–1724.* Cambridge: The Belknap Press of Harvard UP, 1981.

Wilkinson, John, ed. and trans. *Egeria's Travels.* 3rd ed. Warminster (UK): Aris and Phillips, 1999.

Wollstonecraft, Mary. *Letters Written during a Short Residence in Sweden, Norway, and Denmark.* 1796. Ed. Carol H. Poston. Lincoln: U of Nebraska P, 1976.

Zwinger, Ann. *Run, River, Run: A Naturalist's Journey Down One of the Great Rivers of the American West.* Tucson: U of Arizona P, 1975.

Theory

Aciman, André, ed. *Letters of Transit. Reflections on Exile, Identity, Language, and Loss.* New York: New York Public Library, 1990.

Adams, Percy G. *Travel Literature and the Evolution of the Novel.* Lexington: UP of Kentucky, 1983.

Blanton, Casey. *Travel Writing. The Self and the World.* New York: Twayne, 1997.

Bloom, Lynn Z. "American Autobiography and the Politics of Genre." *Genre and Writing: Issues, Arguments, Alternatives.* Eds. Wendy Bishop and Hans Ostrom. Portsmouth, NH: Boynton/Cook, 1997. 151–59.

Bloom, Lynn Z. *Fact and Artifact. Writing Nonfiction.* 2nd ed. Englewood Cliffs: Prentice Hall, 1994.

Brislin, Richard. *Cross-Cultural Encounters: Face-to-Face Interaction.* New York: Pergamon, 1981.

Bruner, Jerome. "The Autobiographical Process." *The Culture of Autobiography:Constructions of Self-Representation.* Ed. Robert Folkenflik. Stanford, CA: Stanford UP, 1993. 38–56.

Caesar, Terry. *Forgiving the Boundaries: Home as Abroad in American Travel Writing.* Athens: U of Georgia P, 1995.

Campell, Mary. *The Witness and the Other World: Exotic European Travel Writing, 400–1600.* Ithaca: Cornell UP, 1988.

Clark, Steve. Ed. *Travel Writing and Empire: Postcolonial Theory in Transit.* Intro. New York: Zed Books, 1999.

Clifford, James. "Introduction." *Writing Culture: The Poetics and Politics of Ethnography.* Eds. Clifford and George Marcus. Berkeley: U of California P, 1986. 1–26.

———. *The Predicament of Culture: Twentieth-Century Literature, Ethnography and Art.* Cambridge: Harvard UP, 1988.

Cohen, E[rik]. "A Phenomenology of Tourist Experiences." *Sociology* 13.2 (1979): 179–201.

Cristóvão, Fernando. "Le Voyage dans la littérature de voyage." Maria Alziro Seixo, ed. *Travel Writing and Cultural Memory. Écriture du voyage et mémoire culturelle.* Proceedings of the 15th Congress of the International Comparative Literature Association "Literature as Cultural Memory." Leiden August 1997. Amsterdam: Rodopi, 2000.

Culler, Jonathan. "Semiotics of Tourism." *American Journal of Semiotics* 1 (1981): 127–40.

Desmond, Jane. *Staging Tourism: Bodies on Display from Waikiki to Sea World.* Chicago: U of Chicago P, 1999.

Dodd, Philip, ed. *The Art of Travel: Essays on Travel Writing.* Totowa, NJ: Frank Cass, 1982.

Duncan, James, and Derek Gregory, eds. *Writes of Passage: Reading Travel Writing.* New York: Routledge, 1999.

Edwards, Jane. *Travel Writing in Fiction & Fact.* Portland, OR: Blue Heron, 1999.

Feifer, Maxine. *Tourism in History: From Imperial Rome to the Present.* Briarcliff Manor, NY: Stein and Day, 1985.

Frederick, Bonnie, and Susan McLeod, eds. *Women and the Journey. The Female Travel Experience.* Pullman: Washington State UP, 1993. *Frontiers, 1630–1860.* Chapel Hill: U of North Carolina P, 1984.

Fussell, Paul. *Abroad: British Literary Traveling between the Wars.* New York: Oxford UP, 1980.

Geertz, Clifford. *The Interpretation of Cultures.* New York: Basic, 1973.

Gilbert, Helen, and Anna Johnston, eds. *In Transit: Travel, Text, Empire.*

New York: Peter Lang, 2002. Vol. 4 of *Travel Writing Across the Disciplines*.

Gilroy, Paul. *The Black Atlantic. Modernity and Double Consciousness.* Cambridge, Harvard UP, 1999.

Glaser, Elton. "Hydra and Hybrid: Travel Writing as a Genre." *North Dakota Quarterly* 59.3 (1991): 348–53.

Helleiner, Jane. *Irish Travellers. Racism and the Politics of Culture.* Toronto: U of Toronto P, 2000.

Holland, Patrick, and Graham Huggan. *Tourists with Typewriters: Critical Reflections on Contemporary Travel Writing.* Ann Arbor: U Michigan P, 1998.

Kaplan, Caren. *Questions of Travel. Postmodern Discourses of Displacement.* Durham: Duke UP, 1996.

Khazanov, Anatoly M., and André Wink, eds. *Nomads in the Sedentary World.* Richmond, Surrey: Curzon, 2001.

Kolodny, Annette. *The Land before Her: Fantasy and Experience of the American Frontiers, 1630–1860.* Chapel Hill: U of North Carolina P, 1984.

Kowalewski, Michael, ed. *Temperamental Journeys: Essays on the Modern Literature of Travel.* Athens: U of Georgia P, 1992.

Krist, Gary. "Ironic Journeys: Travel Writing in the Age of Tourism." *The Hudson Review* 45 (winter 1993): 593–601.

Leed, Eric. *The Mind of the Traveler: From Gilgamesh to Global Tourism.* New York: Basic Books, 1991.

MacCannell, Dean. *The Tourist. A New Theory of the Leisure Class.* Berkeley: U of California P, 1999.

"Modern Tourism." *Blackwood's Magazine* 64.394 (August 1848): 185–89.

Nash, Dennison. "Tourism as a Form of Imperialism." *Hosts and Guests: The Anthropology of Tourism.* Ed. Valene L. Smith. Philadelphia: U of Pennsylvania P, 1977. 33–47.

———. "Tourism as a Form of Imperialism." *Hosts and Guests.* Ed. Valene Smith. Philadelphia: U of Pennsylvania P, 1989. 37–54.

Nicholson-Lord, David. "The Politics of Travel: Is Tourism Just Colonialism in Another Guise?" *The Nation* 6 Oct. 1997: 11–18.

Philip, Jim. "Reading Travel Writing." *Recasting the World: Writing after Colonialism.* Ed. Jonathan White. Baltimore: Johns Hopkins UP, 1993. 241–55.

Porter, Dennis. *Haunted Journeys.* Princeton: Princeton UP, 1991.

Pratt, Mary Louise. "Fieldwork in Common Places." *Writing Culture: The Poetics and Politics of Ethnography*. Eds. James Clifford and George Marcus. Berkeley: U of CA P, 1986. 27–50.

———. *Imperial Eyes: Travel Writing and Transculturation*. London and New York: Routledge, 1992.

Russell, Alison. *Crossing Boundaries: Postmodern Travel Literature*. New York: Palgrave/St. Martin's Press, 2000.

Said, Edward. "Reflections on Exile." *Reflections on Exile and Other Essays*. Cambridge: Harvard UP, 2000. 73–186.

Salgado, Sebastião. *Migrations: Humanity in Transition*. New York: Aperture, 2000.

Secrest, Joseph. "Hospitality & Tourism." Internet. 19 Jan 2003. Available http://coursesites.blackboard.com/bin/common/search.pl.

Siegel, Kristi, ed. *Gender, Genre, and Identity in Women's Travel Writing*. New York: Peter Lang Publishing, 2004.

———. *Issues in Travel Writing: Empire, Spectacle, and Displacement*. New York: Peter Lang, 2003.

Spurr, David. *The Rhetoric of Empire. Colonial Discourse in Journalism, Travel Writing, and Imperial Administration*. Durham: Duke UP, 1993.

Stagl, Justin. *A History of Curiosity: The Theory of Travel 1550–1800*. Australia: Harwood, 1995.

Urry, John. *The Tourist Gaze: Leisure and Travel in Contemporary Societies*. London: Sage, 1990.

Von Martels, Zweder, ed. *Travel Fact and Travel Fiction: Studies on Fiction, Literary Tradition, Scholarly Discovery, and Observation in Travel Writing*. New York: E.J. Brill, 1994.

Wang, Ning. *Tourism and Modernity: A Sociological Analysis*. Amsterdam: Pergamon, 2000.

Wesley, Marilyn C. *Secret Journeys: The Trope of Women's Travel in American Literature*. Albany: State U of New York P, 1999.

Wülfing, Wulf. "On Travel Literature by Women in the Nineteenth Century: Malwida von Meysenburg." *German Women in the Eighteenth and Nineteenth Centuries. A Social and Literary History*. Eds. Ruth-Ellen B. Joeres and Mary Jo Maynes. Bloomington: Indiana UP, 1996. 289–304.

Articles in Travel or Outdoors Magazines
Buford, Bill. Editorial. *Granta* 10 (Winter 1981): 5–7.

Greenfield, Karl Taro. "Under the Billboard Sky." *Outside* 24.2 (December 1999): 105–10, 158–59.

Kluge, P. F. "Return to Paradise." *National Geographic Traveler.* October 2002: 40–52.

Stone, George W. "Around the World in 80+ Books." *National Geographic Traveler.* April 2002: 63–69.

Encyclopedias

Netzley, Patricia. *The Encyclopedia of Women's Travel and Exploration.* Westport, CT: Oryx Press, 2001.

Speake, Jennifer. *The Literature of Travel and Exploration: An Encyclopedia.* New York: Fitzroy Dearborn Publishers, 2003.

Anthologies and Collections

Birkett, Dea, and Sara Wheeler, eds. *Amazonian: Penguin Book of Women's New Travel Writing.* New York: Penguin Books, 1998.

Bryson Bill, ed. *The Best American Travel Writing 2000.* Boston: Houghton Mifflin, 2000.

Curtis, Barry, and Claire Pajaczkowska. "'Getting There': Travel, Time and Narrative." *Travelers' Tales: Narratives of Home and Displacement.* Eds. George Robertson, et al. New York: Routledge, 1994. 199–215.

Dark, Larry, ed. *The Literary Traveler: An Anthology of Contemporary Short Fiction.* New York: Viking, 1994.

Fussell, Paul, ed. *The Norton Book of Travel.* New York: W. W. Norton, 1987.

Gates, Henry Lewis, Jr. General Editor. *Collected Black Women's Narratives.* New York: Oxford UP, 1988.

Gilbert, Sandra M., and Susan Gubar. *The Norton Anthology of Literature by Women.* New York: W. W. Norton, 1985.

Mayes, Frances, ed. *The Best American Travel Writing.* Boston: Houghton Mifflin, 2002.

O'Reilly, Sean, and James O'Reilly, eds. *Travelers' Tales. American Southwest.* San Francisco: Travelers' Tales, Inc., 2001.

Theroux, Paul, ed. *The Best American Travel Writing.* Boston: Houghton Mifflin, 2001.

Focus on Teaching

Altschuler, Glenn. "La Dolce Semester: Studying Abroad Is Most Students' Favorite College Experience. But Not Necessarily for the Right Reasons." *New York Times* 8 April 2001, sec. 4A: 17.

Brandt, Anthony. "The Adventure Craze." *American Heritage.* December/January 2001: 41–49.

Cubelli, Rose. "Early American Explorers." Internet. 19 Jan 2003. Available http://coursesites.blackboard.com/bin/common/search.pl.

Eickstedt, Ingrid. "Travel Orientation for the Yellowstone Region." Internet. 19 Jan 2003.
Available http://coursesites.blackboard.com/bin/common/search.pl.

Ezzo, Joseph. "History of Immigration and Ethnicity in America." Internet. 19 Jan 2003. Available http://coursesites.blackboard.com/bin/common/Content.pl?action=LIST&course_id=_4906.

Freedman, Sarah Warshauer. *Exchanging Writing, Exchanging Cultures: Lessons in School Reform from the United States and Great Britain.* Cambridge: Harvard UP, 1994.

Geloin, Chislaine. "Avoiding a U.S. Curriculum Transplant Abroad: The Ethnographic Project." *Innovative Approaches to Curriculum Design in the Study Abroad Program.* Ed. Deborah Hill. Columbus: Renaissance, 1987. 23–34.

Ghosh, Bishnupriya. "ENL 264 Literatures of Migration." Internet. 19 Jan 2003. Available http://wwwenglish.ucdavis.edu/English/graduate/spring2003.htm.

Grossman, Lev. "Road Scholars." *Time* 26 August 2002: 60–61.

Hesse, Douglas, ed. "Special Issue: Creative Nonfiction." *College English* 65.3 (January 2003).

Hickey, Dona J. *Developing a Written Voice.* Mountain View, CA: Mayfield Publishing Company, 1993.

Hulme, Peter. "LT351: Contemporary Travel Writing." Internet. 19 Jan 2003. Available http://www.essex.ac.uk/literature/Current/Teaching/Undergraduate/UndergraduateIt351.htm.

Jennings, Jennifer. "e-travel." Internet. 1 Jan 2003. Available http://coursesites.blackboard.com/bin/common/content.pl?action=LIST&course_id=_7098.

Kasikova, Stanislava. "Creating an International Classroom through E-mail." *Effective Teaching and Learning of Writing: Current Trends in Research.* Eds. Gert Rijilaarsdam, Huub van den Bergh, and Michel Couzijn. Amsterdam: Amsterdam UP, 1996. 124–35.

Keefe, Carolyn Jewett. "On the Road: Exploring Travel and Travel Writing in Composition Studies." Diss. Bowling Green State U, 1997.

Kiteley, Brian. "Travel Writing. English 4017: Advanced Creative Writing: Travel Writing." Internet. 19 Jan. 2003. Available http://ww.du.edu/~bkiteley/3017.html.

Lanser, Susan S. "The T Word: Theory as Trial and Transformation of the

Undergraduate Classroom." *Teaching Contemporary Theory to Undergraduates.* Eds. Dianne F. Sadoff and William E. Cain. New York: MLA, 1994.

Laubscher, Michael. *Encounters with Difference: Student Perceptions of the Role of Out-of-Class Experience.* Westport, CT: Greenwood, 1994.

Martin, Biddy. "Teaching Literature, Changing Cultures." Introduction. *PMLA* 112.1 (1997): 7–25.

Mercer, Trudy, and Meg Roland. Contributing Editors. *Margaret Fuller.* Website: http://courses.washington.edu/hum523/fuller/NoFrames.html.

Miner, Horace. "Body Ritual among the Nacerima." *American Anthropologist* 58 (1956): 50–37.

Moody, Ellen. "English 302: Advanced Writing in the Humanities." Internet. 19 Jan 2003. Available http//mason.gmu.edu/~emoody/travel.htm.

O'Neil, L. Peat. *Travel Writing.* Cincinnati: Writer's Digest Books, 1996.

Platt, John. "Some Types of Communicative Strategies across Cultures: Sense and Sensitivity." *English across Cultures.* 13–29.

Rhoades, Carol. Introduction to Literature: Women's Journey Literature. Syllabus. The University of Texas, Austin.

———. Teaching Women's Travel Literature. Unpublished notes. MLA 1998.

Rosenblatt, Louise M. *Literature as Exploration.* 3rd ed. New York: Rosenblatt, Noble and Noble Publishers: 1976.

Scheunpflug, Annette. "Cross-Cultural Encounters As a Way of Overcoming Xenophobia." *International Review of Education* 43.1 (1997): 109–16.

Schindler, Roslyn, et al. "The Classroom Abroad: Interdisciplinary Cross-Cultural Perspectives for the Adult Learner." *Innovative Approaches to Curriculum Design in the Study Abroad Program.* 104–12.

Scholes, Robert. *Textual Power.* New Haven: Yale UP, 1985. http://www.essex.ac.uk/literature/Current/Teaching/Undergraduate/Undergraduate/lt351.htm *Islands.* November 2002.

Schramer, James J., and Donald Ross. Introduction. *The Dictionary of Literary Biography 183: American Travel Writers, 1776-1864.* Detroit, MI: Gale Research, 1997. xv–xxv.

Schwartz, Helen. "Cross-Cultural Team Teaching: E-mail for Literary Analysis." Fiche: ED 319 060.

Sikkema, Mildred, and Agnes Niyekawa. *Design for Cross-Cultural Learning.* Yarmouth: International, 1987.

Smethurst, Paul. "ENGL2045 Travel Writing." Internet. 19 Jan 2003. Available http://www.hku.hk/english/courses 2000/2045.htm.

Talburt, Susan, and Melissa Stewart. "What's the Subject of Study Abroad?: Race, Gender, and 'Living Culture.'" *The Modern Language Journal* 83 (1999): 163–75.

Uruburu, Paula, Contributing Editor. *Mary White Rowlandson (1637–1711)*. Website:
http://college.hmco.com/english/heath/syllabuild/guide/rowlands.html.

Vanouse, Donald. "American Readers and Writers in England." *Innovative Approaches to Curriculum Design in the Study Abroad Program*. 74–82.

Wagner, Kenneth, and Tony Magistrale. *Writing across Culture: An Introduction to Study Abroad and the Writing Process*. New York: Peter Lang, 1995.

Zinsser, William. *They Went: The Art and Craft of Travel Writing*. Boston: Houghton Mifflin, 1991.

Contributors

John Bennion writes short fiction and novels about the western Utah desert and the people who inhabit that forbidding country. Publications include *Breeding Leah and Other Stories* (Signature Books, 1991) and *Falling Toward Heaven* (Signature Books, 2000). An associate professor at Brigham Young University, Bennion teaches creative writing and the British novel.

Ulrike Brisson teaches in the Department of Germanic Languages and Literatures at the University of Massachusetts, Amherst. She received her Ph.D. and M.A. in Comparative Literature at Pennsylvania State University. Travel writings, especially nineteenth-century women's travel narratives, have captured her research interest.

Denise Comer is a lecturing fellow at Duke University, where she teaches for the university writing program and the English department. Her academic interests include nineteenth-century British literature, travel writing, composition, and women's studies. Her current research focuses on Romantic-era British women's travel writing in India.

Christine S. Cozzens, after receiving her B.A. and M.A. from Stanford University and her Ph.D. in English from the University of California at Berkeley, taught writing at Harvard University and Emory University before coming to Agnes Scott College, where she directs the Center for Writing and Speaking and is associate professor of English. A travel writer whose works have appeared in the *New York Times, Abroad/View, Cara,* and many other publications, she teaches travel writing, nonfiction, and British and Irish literature and film.

Leeann Chen, born and educated in China and then at the University of Illinois in Urbana-Champagne, has presented various papers on travel writing and study abroad at domestic and international conferences, in addition to writing publications on the Chinese language. She currently teaches Asian Studies in both on-campus and off-shore courses at Embry-Riddle Aeronautical University (Prescott, Arizona).

Eileen Groom, a professor at Embry-Riddle Aeronautical University (Prescott, Arizona) since 1986, has taught a variety of writing and literature courses and both presented and published on a variety of topics, including using formal letters to teach writing and the incorporation of nature writing and travel literature into the classroom. She also edited a collection of nonfiction narratives about flying as passenger or pilot entitled *In the Air, Your Stories: A Talisman.*

Jeffrey Alan Melton (Ph.D. University of South Carolina, 1993) is an associate professor of English at Auburn University Montgomery in Alabama, where he began as an assistant professor in 1994. He is the author of *Mark Twain, Travel Books, and Tourism: The Tide of a Great Popular Movement* (U of Alabama P, 2002). He has published articles on travel literature and Mark Twain in *South Atlantic Review*, *Papers on Language and Literature*, *Studies in American Humor*, *Popular Culture Review*, *Studies in American Culture*, and *Thalia: Studies in Literary Humor.* He also has contributed to *American Travel Writers, 1850–1915, A Companion to Southern Literature*, and *The Literature of Travel and Exploration.*

Burton Olsen has been involved in outdoor education and recreation at Brigham Young University for more than 35 years. His special interests have revolved around hiking, camping, kayaking, canoeing, fly fishing, and initiative games. He works with all ages and has conducted workshops in these areas throughout the United States.

Twila Yates Papay is a professor of English and Writing at Rollins College. Having administered writing programs since 1973 and served as Rollins' Director of Writing Programs (including the Writing Center) for 14 years, she is currently Coordinator of First-Year Writing. She has published and spoken on topics as diverse as travel writing, autobiography, science fiction, composition pedagogy, collaboration, and writing for technology. While a 1992 sabbatical year found her exploring Europe, South America, and Asia, her 1999 sabbatical took her around much of Africa, where she also participated in Writing Center development at the University of the Western Cape and other institutions.

Valerie M. Smith is an assistant professor of English at Quinnipiac University. She received her B.A. from Wesleyan University and her M.A. and Ph.D. from the University of Connecticut. She teaches composition and creative nonfiction, including the travel essay. She currently is working on a book on cultural autobiography and imperial discourse.

Jacqueline S. Thursby, associate professor of folklore and English pedagogy in the English Department at Brigham Young University, earned a B.A. at Idaho State University in Secondary Education with a humanities emphasis in English, history, and art. Her M.S. in American Studies is from Utah State University, where her focus was folklore and ethnic studies. Her Ph.D., from Bowling Green State University, is in American Culture Studies with emphasis areas of folklore, anthropology, sociology, ethnic studies, and American literature and history. An interdisciplinary scholar, Thursby has written two books (*Mother's Table, Father's Chair: Cultural Narratives of Basque American Women* and *Begin Where You Are),* many articles and book reviews, and is a frequent lecturer.

Index

THEORY AND PEDAGOGY
Kristi Siegel, General Editor

The recent critical attention devoted to travel writing enacts a logical transition from the ongoing focus on autobiography, subjectivity, and multiculturalism. Travel extends the inward direction of autobiography to consider the journey outward and intersects provocatively with studies of multiculturalism, gender, and subjectivity. Whatever the journey's motive—tourism, study, flight, emigration, or domination—journey changes both the country visited and the self that travels. *Travel Writing Across the Disciplines* welcomes studies from all periods of literature on the theory and/or pedagogy of travel writing from various disciplines, such as social history, cultural theory, multicultural studies, anthropology, sociology, religious studies, literary analysis, and feminist criticism. The volumes in this series explore journey literature from critical and pedagogical perspectives and focus on travel as metaphor in cultural practice.

For additional information about this series or for the submission of manuscripts, please contact:

Peter Lang Publishing. Inc.
Acquisitions Department
P.O. Box 1246
Bel Air, MD 21014-1246

To order other books in this series, please contact our Customer Service Department:

(800) 770-LANG (within the U.S.)
(212) 647-7706 (outside the U.S.)
(212) 647-7707 FAX

Or browse online by series:

www.peterlangusa.com